Michael A. Weinstein

I0593031

This book is a major reassessment of Michael Weinstein's political philosophy. It situates his singular contribution, designated as "critical vitalism," in the context of both canonical American and contemporary continental theory. Weinstein is presented as a philosopher of life and as an American Nietzsche. Yet the contributors also persuasively argue for this form of thinking as a prescient prophecy addressing contemporary society's concern over the management of life as well as the technological changes that both threaten and sustain intimacy. This is the first full scale study of Weinstein's work which reveals surprising aspects of a philosophic journey that has encompassed most of the major American (pragmatic or vitalist) or Continental (phenomenological or existential) traditions. Weinstein is read as a comparative political theorist, a precursor to post-structuralism, and as a post-colonial border theorist. A different aspect of his *oeuvre* is highlighted in each of the book's three sections. The opening essays comprising the "Action" diptych contrasts meditative versus extrapolative approaches; "Contemplation" stages a series of encounters between Weinstein and his philosophic interlocutors; "Vitalism" presents Weinstein as a teacher, media analyst, musician, and performance artist. The book contains an epilogue written by Weinstein in response to the contributors.

Robert L. Oprisko is a research associate at Indiana University's Center for the Study of Global Change. His research focuses on contemporary political philosophy, international relations theory, and critical university studies.

Diane Rubenstein is Professor of Government and American Studies at Cornell University. Her teaching and research focuses on contemporary continental theory—semiotics, deconstruction, psychoanalysis, post-structuralism, Western Marxism—as well as the manifestations of theory in current Franco-American politics and ideology.

Routledge Innovations in Political Theory

For a full list of titles in this series, please visit www.routledge.com

Michael A. Weinstein

Action, Contemplation, Vitalism

**Edited by Robert L. Oprisko and
Diane Rubenstein**

Routledge
Taylor & Francis Group

NEW YORK AND LONDON

First published 2015
by Routledge
711 Third Avenue, New York, NY 10017, USA

and by Routledge
2 Park Square, Milton Park, Abingdon, Oxfordshire OX14 4RN

First issued in paperback 2016

Routledge is an imprint of the Taylor & Francis Group, an informa business

Library of Congress Cataloging-in-Publication Data
A catalog record for this book has been requested.

Typeset in Sabon
by Apex CoVantage, LLC

ISBN 13: 978-1-138-28733-4 (pbk)
ISBN 13: 978-1-138-01308-7 (hbk)

To our "beloved colleagues," Maureen and Philip.

Contents

Foreword

Deena Weinstein

I will not break the semipermeable membrane of privacy that surrounds our intimacy of more than a half century of shared life. Discussing Michael Weinstein's cooking, lovemaking, driving, companionship, and sweet temperament is beyond the scope of this book. Relevant and most importantly, we have shared an intellectual life from the beginning. Our coauthored books and articles are outcroppings of that intellectual life, which has been a major focus of our constant conversations. Michael often tells me that we are a "theory collective," among other things. In that regard, I want to highlight a couple of features of his philosophical practice.

Michael is a living philosopedia. There is no need for books or the Internet when he is around. How does he do it? The answer is by intensive work. I've seen him read 400-page books and be satisfied coming out with but one insight buried on one page. I've seen him copy in his illegible handwriting whole chapters of books. He spent one entire summer copying Whitehead's *Process and Reality* word for word and writing glosses on each paragraph, self-consciously imitating a medieval commentator—and he never turned that work into his own public writing. He is not satisfied until and unless he understands as fully as he possibly can the text he is addressing and makes it his own—part of what he calls his "home discourse." That is why he never forgets writers' names and their ideas and arguments. "Love Piracy" is very hard work, but Michael loves doing it. He is the most perceptive reader I have ever met; he has learned how to separate the textual gold from the dross.

Related to his distinctive hermeneutics, Michael is everybody's homie. I see supermarket clerks look thrilled when they see him; he always finds some way to have philosophical conversations with them. He does that with everyone, no matter what their background or station, from the underclass to the most educated intellectuals and everyone between. He takes their point of view and then works to engage them in dialogues of joy and fresh insight. He is the model of the aristo-democrat.

As a philosopher, Michael never writes or says anything he hasn't first lived. I have witnessed him form, live, and keep developing his philosophy—and that has been a most privileged experience.

Acknowledgments

It is entirely in keeping with the appreciative philosophy that is the subject of this book that we offer our acknowledgments to those people and institutions that have contributed to its realization. Michael Weinstein, the subject in so many senses of this book, has inspired and sustained this project with his philosophic friendship. Deena Weinstein cheerfully contributed whatever needed to be tracked down—whether photographically, bibliographically, or biographically—with her distinctive wit and insight.

This book was developed out of a short course, "Critical Vitalism: Inspirations and Innovations from Michael A. Weinstein," held at the 2013 annual meeting of the American Political Science Association in Chicago, Illinois. We thank APSA for facilitating the congenial meeting of the contributors. Some participants would like to acknowledge Iwan Ries for their conference hospitality and forbearance for philosophic banter.

Further thanks go to Routledge and our editor Natalja Mortensen, whose early enthusiasm for the project and continual support greatly contributed to its actualization. We also thank Deepti Agarwal.

Purdue University Press granted permission to use the cover art from *Meaning and Appreciation: Time and Modern Political Life* (1978). *Garowe Online* and *Theoria and Praxis* extended similar generosity in granting permission explicitly or via the Creative Commons attributions license to use excerpts from previously published material authored by Michael or by other commentators on his work.

This book would not have been possible were it not for Purdue University and its Department of Political Science. Several of the book's contributors comment on the paradoxical propinquity of radical thought in such a "hotbed of student rest." As all of the contributors have shared a collective history at Purdue, whether as undergraduates, graduates, or colleagues, we acknowledge teachers, mentors, and friends: Berenice Carroll, Rosalee Clawson, Robert Melson, Louis Rene Beres, Harry Targ, William McBride, and Traci Emerson and those transdisciplinary supports in the departments of American Studies and English and the program in Philosophy and Literature.

However, this book would not be *thinkable* were it not for the generations of Weinstein students whose creativity, generosity, and infinite kindness are the best commentary one could offer on the vitality of Michael's life philosophy.

The development of this book benefitted from institutional support from Butler University, with special thanks to Jay Howard, Pam Crea, Manish Gupta, Steve Prothero, Victoria Rose, and Kathy Mallon for their personal support and to Luke Perez, Michael DiGregorio, Murray Bessette, Alexander Wendt, and Sergei Prozorov for their inspiration. Thanks go as well to the Yale Club of New York City for providing spaces for quiet reflection and writing, and to Cary Howie and Marine Baudrillard for their scintillating conversation. We hope that this book will, in turn, provide a structure of intellectual and academic support for those who represent the next generation of Weinstein scholars, including Kirstie Dobbs, Kathryn Cleary, Robert Fenton, Emma Meyer, and Aviral Pathak.

We would not be honoring the embodied pleasures of finite existence if we did not thank our life companions: Maureen Yann and Philip and Rachel Protter.

1 Michael Weinstein's Posthumous Thought for Our Times

An Introduction

Robert L. Oprisko and Diane Rubenstein

> . . . there can be no encounter with Weinstein's political thought that is not at the same time a larger encounter with the historical trajectories of twentieth century experience, and by approximation, with the quickly enfolding futures of the twenty-first century.
>
> Arthur Kroker, "Nietzsche for Our Times"[1]

This book is a critical affirmation of the work of Michael Weinstein. It has multiple purposes: the proximate project of tracing a line through a philosophic itinerary, sharpening our sense of his distinctive contribution to American political thought. But we also seek to resituate him as a comparative political theorist, engaged with non-Western thought and nations such as Somalia, as a border theorist *avant la lettre*, and as a homegrown critic of governmentality. This would be the *rhizomatic* acknowledgment of his nomadic thought as it traverses geographic, temporal, and disciplinary boundaries. Weinstein's *oeuvre*, a term capacious enough to include his published writings in all their venues—books, print and electronic articles, weekly photography criticism for *New City*, art catalogues—as well as performance art, music, and teaching, enacted or, more accurately, *fleshed out* the philosophic personae: border savage, a "Latin in Saxon skin" or the "civil savage as monkey playing in the culture jungle." Weinstein is a political theorist of the body, first singing it as "electric," now rapping its digital modalities. These were all manners of reformulating finalist ontology capable of addressing the hatred of existence or *ressentiment*, all too often the default form of being under neoliberal rule.[2] The intellectual portraits drawn by the contributors to this volume, former students from the late sixties through to the present, who have not ceased drawing upon his teachings, argue for a reading or rereading of Weinstein as avowed avatar of posthuman/postcivilized thought, a postcursor to Nietzsche's adage that "We are fully posthumous beings." As all such posthumous beings, his time has only just arrived, quickened with renewed interest in vitalism/philosophies of life, anarchism, new materialisms calling for attentiveness and care to all aspects of the material world, speculative realisms, thing theory, trans-humanism, and the search for new political ontologies.

Weinstein's conceptual contribution can be designated as *critical vital-ism*. Critical vitalism is an evolution of classical vitalism, concurring in its partisanship for life and lived experience. However, he blends Sartrean and Bergsonian traditions, engaging with the structure of being from the body/self of the individual. The critical element of Weinstein's vitalist ontology is in his focus on proceptive drive(s) in lieu of propulsive *élan vital*, as Justin Mueller will detail in Chapter 4.

Critical vitalism embraces life as tragedy. Weinstein details the torment that individuals experience as unified beings often of two or more minds. Weinstein believes man to be trapped in agonic contradiction, seeking both the logical structure of the Cartesian *cogito* and the freedom brought by rejecting simple narratives and singular structures of Pascal. He writes,

> And who am I? I am a contingent being . . . I know who I am! I am a dependent being, independent of neither organizations nor other human beings . . . I am relative . . . My circumstances can only be saved by eliminating them . . . my own theory of history tells me that the person is more significant than any theory of history. . . . Agony is not a choice, but the element that defines personality.[3]

This philosophy emphasizes the contingent nature of the individual and the groups, societies, and relationships that are formed by collectives of individuals. For Weinstein, everything is situated and positioned in time and space. Nothing is meaningful without context, without seeing how it is experienced relationally. This is the vital element—the requirement that life cannot be understood as such but must be lived. As Camus asserts in *The Myth of Sisyphus*, life's meaning must be constructed through constant and continuous confrontation and revolt.[4] Critical vitalism embraces the passion for life, freedom from devotion to singular abstract narratives, and revolt against philosophical suicide while embracing the failure (as real lived experience) to achieve and maintain ideal situations. Its foundation in historical and temporal contingency reinforces the finitude of perfection.

The book is divided into three sections. The first, "Action," pairs two essays from students framing Weinstein's career at Purdue University: Arthur Kroker (from the Vietnam War era) and Robert Oprisko, a post-9/11 student of the most recent cohort. To remain within the Nietzschean parameters of Arthur Kroker's essay, there is only one sense in which Weinstein is a "last man." Weinstein is the last remaining political theorist in the political science department. Upon the graduation of his last student, Justin Mueller, there will be no more graduate program in that subfield. There is a disquieting if perverse irony that it is Weinstein's own ruthless examination of the *failed* project of American's founding logics of political subjectivication that best explains this trend in American political science departments. It will thus be in the spirit of Nietzsche that we designate the essays that follow the "Purdue School."[5]

These two essays that comprise this part are poised as a polarity representing two dissymmetrical ways of approaching the Weinstein corpus. The first is an inward meditation, effectively translating Arendtian "negative being," Nietzschean "suicidal nihilism," and Heideggerian "fully completed nihilism" into the quintessentially American philosopher (Weinstein) in his most American of books, *The Wilderness and the City*. As such, this chapter presents a narrative of the death of life philosophy in American modernity. Oprisko's chapter, while equally attentive to the nuances and theoretical challenges of Weinstein's work, is an example of what Fredric Jameson would call "cognitive mapping," detailing affinities as well as tensions with theorists working from a Bohrian epistemology such as Karen Barad, Slavoj Zizek, Alain Badiou, and Gilles Deleuze. What both introductory essays share is an appreciation of Weinstein's revolutionary approach to metaphysics and ontology.

The second section of the book, "Contemplation," stages a series of theoretical encounters between Weinstein and other theorists, American, European, and Mexican, who have proved critical interlocutors in the formulation of his life philosophy. These essays demonstrate Weinstein's methodology of "love piracy": extracting the precious bits that can be useful to his project without subjecting himself to the superegotic injunctive to take everything else that went along with it. This practice is congruent with what Barthes and other French theorists have referred to as "*bricolage*": it is what Guattari calls "being an ideas-thief" and what Deleuze, borrowing from Guattari, references as theory as a "tool kit."[6] What emerges from these engagements occasioned by writings such as *Wilderness and the City*, *The Polarity of Mexican Thought, Finite Perfection, Culture/Flesh*, or a dedication found at the beginning of the 2006 book on Oliver Wendell Holmes is a singular *American* philosopher who is also a thinker of the border.

The third section, "Vitalism," comprises essays that address pedagogy in the larger sense of institutional practices. This takes the form of an extended meditation on a concept, "defensive life," found in *Culture/Flesh* remotivated in relation to the political and classroom realities of the nineties. There is, in addition, a collective portrait and appreciation by one of Weinstein's earliest undergraduate students. Two essays further demonstrate Weinstein's pedagogic role as public intellectual as they take up different media (use of the Web, blog posts, his band performances and lyrics) in the context of non-Western societies (Somalia, Islam). A concluding essay reflects upon the Weinstein seminar experience as an instance of Guattarian transversality.

Arthur Kroker, in "Nietzsche for Our Times: Three Meditations," specifies the singularity of Weinstein's intellectual contribution: *at once*, a *political philosopher* charting modern individualism's ambivalent trajectory, an *existentialist* on questions of human autonomy and freedom, a *finalist ontologist* on matters of social justice, a *tragic thinker* attendant to melancholy, and finally, a *passionate dissident* advocating for the marginalized, invisible, and excluded. This would make Weinstein's deconstruction of the individual in its American philosophic vernacular a contribution to the history of ideas as well as metaphysics. But Kroker—and, by extension the authors in this volume—argues that its import is neither past nor present, but in a Nietzschean futural mode, it is a stunning truly American account of the death of the social, as American society swerves between anhedonia/cultural fatigue/*acedia* and war fever. Rather than the creative cultivation of either Jamesian "inner tolerance" or "unillusioned individualism" (which might be one of the modern gifts of Freudian psychoanalysis), American society is a site of unrelenting hostility, anger, appeals to injury, and forms of *ressentiment*. Kroker brilliantly heralds Weinstein as the interpreter of "backlash," whatever its ideological tendency, as reposing upon what is disavowed concerning the form of American life philosophy: the necessary tropological foundation of USA power. And he situates this "prophetic" thought beyond the two death drives of "transhumanism and anger politics."

Weinstein does not only stage and enact the philosophic eclipse of the modern individual; for he embodies his finalist ontology, as expressed by Kroker's testimony from 1967 antiwar politics that allow interlocutors to fully experience "the life of the mind, how that is, two thousand years of metaphysics—in depth, patient, critical, necessarily undermining, often synoptic, philosophic thought—could be summed up in the grain of a voice and in the political vision that that voice urged its intently listening audience to consider, and once considered, to begin to act on the fateful results of that consideration."[7] Other students from this time such as Kathy Ferguson will note that this activated passionate engagement ironically began at an engineering school more known for its instrumental use of reason.

Robert Oprisko dives into Weinstein's tragic finalist ontology in his essay "Strings: A Political Theory of Multidimensional Reality." Oprisko's "unfaithful interpretation"[8] of Weinstein's oeuvre from the late 1960s through the early 1990s peers into the void of finalist ontology and finds, within that nothing, everything. Using Weinstein's methodologies of love-piracy, agonic doubting from *Tragic Sense of Political Life*, and aspectival totalization from *(Post)modernized Simmel*, Oprisko argues that international relations theory, political philosophy, and ontology are intimately and irrevocably intertwined. Buried deep within all of them is the Heideggerian *mitsein*, the being with, which presupposes Nancy's being singular plural. In an effort to showcase critical vitalism, Oprisko weaves Weinstein's tragic interpretation of sociopolitical structure with Karen Barad's Bohrian epistemology, Alain Badiou's set theory, and Slavoj Zizek's philosophy of failure to produce a unified theory of politics that links the individual to the international, the finite with the infinite, and the particular to the universal. Oprisko's focus on processes and action provides a glimpse of Weinstein's dialectic between the ontological and the ontic, the agonic contradiction that provides the motivation for much of his work.

The next section of the book, "Contemplation," shifts from the synoptic evaluations of a life philosophy to microreadings of specific interlocutors. Justin Mueller's essay, "This Flesh Belongs to me: Michael Weinstein and Max Stirner," presents the existentialist-phenomenological underpinnings of Weinstein's "critical vitalism": a "process-oriented" theory for "concrete durational human beings." Drawing upon some well-known figures such as Henri Bergson, Miguel de Unamuno, and William James as well as some lesser-known ones such as Samuel Alexander and Josiah Royce, Weinstein also critically engages with a "minor" figure of nineteenth-century continental thought, Max Stirner, familiar to most through Karl Marx's line-by-line critique of his masterwork, *The Ego and Its Own*, in *The German Ideology*. Mueller honors Weinstein's deep theoretical debts to both Bergson (intuition) and Unamuno (agonic doubting) in the elaboration of a new methodology that could account for our polemical nature as desirous and finite beings. Max Stirner's concept of "radical self-possession" or "Ownness," which replaces most if not all of the transcendental signifieds—"God, Law, Morality, Rights, Mankind, Society, the State, Freedom"—is built upon a notion of the Unique, *der Einzige*, that has been misunderstood by twentieth-century theorists as either a new regulatory ideal or a negative liberty. Nor is it the self-possession of contract theory. "Ownness" concerns the attempt to free oneself from what is alien to it, ghosts or residues or "spooks." Mueller demonstrates how Weinstein has translated Stirner's ideas into a Nietzschean idiom that can at times be read as a critique of Stirner. However, by reading Weinstein against Weinstein, using his work on Justis Buchler's "proception" (as the "composite, directed activity of the individual") and on love ("sacrifice in the service of love"), Mueller aligns Stirner's with Weinstein's larger project.[9]

Stirner frames the "post-ontological role for pleasure"[10] in Jonathan McKenzie's "Weinstein's American Philosophy: Intimacy and the Construction of the Self." "Ownness" is that which the philosophic self must hold on to in erotic life. McKenzie offers a rereading of Weinstein centered on the concept of intimacy as "a privatist philosophical concept."[11] This is in part a rescue operation from the standpoint of the American philosophic tradition that opposes freedom and commitment (Thoreau), presupposes a burden of "choice" (James), or overgeneralizes eros (Whitman). Weinstein's 2006 book on Oliver Wendell Holmes—its dedication to "his beloved colleague"—as the initial incitement—provides an alternative concept of "disordered volition" that targets individualism's double bind: "in order to strategize one's own inwardness, one has to make demands upon love that intimacy can not supply or keep. In order to sustain one's intimacy, one must sacrifice intimacy."[12] It also addresses the aporetic relation between the condition for public philosophizing/philosophy ("the fact that my life is open to that which differs from myself makes communicable . . . that act of free valuation . . . ") and its private counterpart ("whereas the closure of my life, its intimacy, makes that act personal and unique"[13]). The "positive" virtue of intimacy here is always deconstructively linked to the possibility of its failure. McKenzie finds within two of Weinstein's most openly Nietzschean books, *Finite Perfection* and *Culture/Flesh* (in which the former text attempts to "rescue the self's capacity for love while maintaining one's integrity" and the latter "transforms the intimacy of availability into the war for pleasure"[14]), the care for the self/self-construction and self-relating that are at the heart of American traditions of thought in ways not imagined by either transcendentalists or early pragmatists.

If McKenzie demonstrates how Weinstein's affirmation of finite life is performed in a spirit of "optimistic pessimism," Melba Hoffer's "Irreducible Ends: Michael Weinstein and the Value of Agony and Happy Pessimism" furthers the discussion of *"pesimismo* alegre" by shifting to other grounds (i.e., ethics) and thinkers—Søren Kierkegaard, Miguel de Unamuno, Jose Vasconcelos, and Antonio Caso—that pose a different American problem of dissent. Weinstein and Kierkegaard share the following affinities: the tension between *eros* and *agape*; the positive valuation of anxiety; and the centrality of agonistic doubting to authentic existence, a "vital self-contradiction." This implies a virtue approach to ethics as opposed to a consequentialist or deontological one. A combination of agonistic doubting from Unamuno and an ethical grounding in virtue finds its logical expression in a "fringe" area of thought, the Mexican "finalists" Vasconcelos and Caso. Finalism is closely related to vitalism, replacing vitalism's *élan vital* (a creative life force) with specific ends that promote "charitable actions, appreciation of others and aesthetic concerns."[15] It is an antipositivist worldview combatting the positivist one that was prevalent in the early twentieth century in Latin America. Hoffer tracks its historical instantiations in Mexico, Brazil, and Cuba, its intellectual trajectory from Bergsonism to Kierkegaard to Vasconcelos (and the Mexican finalists). They share Weinstein's desire to remain "open to others while pursuing one's projects."[16] This is not done by "consensus" but by "coordination," which works on a principle of comparison or analogy: "Once the analogies have been comprehended, the appreciator would inspect his experience of social relations and determine whether the world-view made it more coherent. Did it make him more aware of new dimensions to his relations, such as subtle forms of exploitation? Did it disclose new values to him, or present new projects?"[17] Weinstein found in finalism concepts such as *"zozobra"* that describe the endless vacillation of anxious and discordant life, both an invitation to welcome in but also uncertainty as to who to trust.

Ramón Soto-Crespo's "Unpacking My Weinstein: Border Thinking and Classical American Philosophy" also examines Mexican finalist philosophy through a close reading of Weinstein's *The Polarity of Mexican Thought*. If Hoffer reads the antipositivist project against Western cultural imperialism, Soto-Crespo situates it *at* and *as* "border thinking": "At the border, finalist thought affirmed vital life and critiqued positivism as an instrumentalization of living experience . . . Border thinking uses finalist insights in its politico-philosophical stance against the biopolitical management of life in modern societies."[18] Weinstein is shown to be a border thinker of "biopower from below,"[19] a critic of positivism whose texts, read from *Polarity* on through to *Data Trash*, meticulously detail the growing instrumentalization of life, what Deleuze referred to as despotic forms of power. Soto-Crespo covers some of the same historical ground in the account of finalism as Hoffer, but he focuses on the importance of Latin American philosophy as a method for thinking, which also left its trace on now-canonical authors of postcolonial thought: Octavio Paz, Gloria Anzaldúa, and Walter Mignolo. As we have seen with Mueller and McKenzie's expositions of American philosophy, Weinstein's embrace of life without reconciling or sacrificing one of its contraries did not find a counterpart. However, in finalist philosophy and in border thinking, Weinstein could find concepts adequate to "a critical examination and defense of our being as it is lived from within."[20] One of these was *zozobra*: "an attempt to 'burn the candle at both ends,' to coordinate heterogeneous elements in their totalities."[21] Soto-Crespo likens Weinstein's understanding of this concept to a kind of Deleuzian nomadic thought that dances or plays between "high and low intensities" as a kind of rhizome. Inspired by Vasconcelos and proleptically channeling Deleuze, Weinstein wanders into the persona of the "border savage," realizing/living contradictory desires simultaneously within a racial masquerade, "a 'Latin' in spirit masked by a Saxon skin."[22] It is from the position of border savage that Soto-Crespo performs a genealogy of Weinstein's work on American political thought starting with George Santayana through Jamesian and later Rorty's pragmatism. The civil savage of *Culture/Flesh* takes off from the necessary absence within finalist thought of a philosophy of conduct. What happens to one of finalism's central tenets—the cultivation of inwardness—in postcivilization? Happy pessimism is one way to apprehend the futurity of postcivilization.

The third section of the book, "Vitalism," contains essays that concur with Simon Critchley's adage that "teaching" is "the institutional form of thinking" in the university: "It is teaching people to have an orientation toward truth."[23] Julie Webber, in "I Am the Radical Reality: Weinstein's 'Defensive Life' as a Political Response in Postcivilization," presents a finalist life philosopher's practice of teaching that is, in Kroker's words, one of "critical appreciation, self-restraint and intellectual generosity."[24] It is one that she characterizes as "well knit." Webber's point of departure is the man she encountered as an undergraduate at University Hall in 1992, who was later to cochair her dissertation. Her chapter navigates between the Purdue University lecture rooms and seminars from 1992 to 1996 and the key text of that period, *Culture/Flesh* and its avatar, the civil savage. She offers a smartly condensed reading of that book's central insight concerning life's adversity and its force in constituting our disposition towards others, enlivened by reference to actual class notes (!), classroom vignettes, and contemporaneous political examples.

In several senses, the reading presented here of *Culture/Flesh* arcs back to that of Kroker's revisiting of *Wilderness and the City*. One might see it as a nineties time travel version; it serves a diagnostic function, offering a snapshot of a period in the nineties when the modernist project of the individual was relinquished. She similarly adumbrates Weinstein's peculiarly (and perhaps oxymoronic) "Yankee" or specifically American form of existentialism and offers a critique of pragmatism as a failed response to the challenges of postcivilized American life. If Kroker had demonstrated the difficulty of extricating Weinstein's thought from the historical mo(ve)ments that generate it, Webber supplements these genealogical insights with what she learned in Weinstein's classroom concerning periodization. Webber focuses specifically on the many forms defensive life can take, from anhedonia to war to romantic or religious idealizations. Yet by concentrating upon strategies of self-defense, her essay reads less as a future projection than as a Foucauldian history of the present, both of the present state of theory as well as the turn to ideologies of "care" and "health" as forms of neoliberal power. Weinstein is aligned here with Arendt and Foucault as overwritten by Agamben. Webber provocatively queries, might the "*homo sacer*" be the "uncivil savage?" The attention to self-defense also extends the austerity of Weinstein's presentation of *ressentiment* into a more feminist, sardonic idiom. "The civil savage" may be a masculine persona, as Weinstein states, but his women students are picking up some survivalist tips.

The opening chapter of *Culture/Flesh*, "Civilization," begins with a world tour, not only of the familiar Western Christian or Athenian antecedents to modernity but also of East Asian, Indian, and Islamic ones. It demonstrates Weinstein's engagement as a *comparative* political theorist. In "Weinstein's Methodology for Political Analysis," Robert Oprisko examines Weinstein's decade-long project on Somalia, implicitly underlining previous theoretical issues raised by Soto-Crespo concerning border theory and Webber on Agamben's *homo sacer*. Somalia can be read as a condensation of several Weinsteinian *topoi*. Among the most salient points of Weinstein's selection criteria is the fact that it is a *failed* state, again indicating the centrality of failure for his epistemological project. As a *homo sacer* or abject remainder existing on the fringe of the international relations, Somalia/the Somalian highlights the ethical dimension of his thought. When we turn to the rhetorical unconscious generated by the Somalia-sign and spectacularized in film, we find the figure of the *pirate*, the methodological self-image cultivated by Weinstein. Oprisko explicitly presents Weinstein's method for political analysis, in all its rigorous simplicity, as a model for future scholarship and covertly as an academic defense for seeing normative political theory as rigorous in method. But he is also attentive to the alternative media that Weinstein uses to disseminate his research. The electronic article in this reading becomes a defense of the fringe in academic writing, providing a "concrete durational being" of intellectual production for others to emulate and appreciate. The chapter's emphasis on the interior reduplication of content on the level of form beautifully concretizes Weinstein's pedagogy.

Joseph Kaminiski's chapter, " 'I Am the God of My Own Tribe': Weinstein and Islam," reveals Weinstein's pedagogy in another critical dimension: as lead vocalist and as lyricist for Vortis, a Chicago-based punk group. This chapter is an aspectual assemblage of biography—Weinstein's secular Jewish post–World War II childhood in New York, differing visual modalities (Arabic script and photographs of Weinstein performing in his band) that punctuate the narrative investigation of an enigmatic religious identification. Why would a self-declared "atheist Jew" such as Weinstein declare the deepest affinity for Islam among all the monotheisms? Kaminski argues that Weinstein is attracted to Islam because it mirrors his own personal agonic contradiction in its dialectical foundation that balances communal brotherhood and individual mystic contemplation. He finds further support in their shared ethos: a militant inclination to fight for truth and justice as well as an inclusivity and acceptance of diversity of background. Further, Kaminski suggests that it is Islam as a religion that has not yet been coopted by the dominant Anglo-European thought that attracts Weinstein; the perpetual underdog and defender of other underdogs, Weinstein celebrates his affinity for a religion that stands up against a bullying West. This has been a theme in some continental theorists such as Jean Baudrillard and Slavoj Zizek. Kaminski concludes that Weinstein's attraction to Islam does not convert him so much as it reflects his personal goal of self-control and provides the civility to his savage nature.

While pedagogy is not the central animating thread of Kaminski's chapter, it nonetheless discloses many aspects of the professor that is the subject of Kathy Ferguson's "A Remarkable Teacher." Like others in this book such as Hoffer, Webber, and Kaminski, she lauds his "creative improvisation" and demonstrates how a hatred of bullies is translated into mundane practices. She interrogates a seeming inconsistency within Weinstein's teaching tactics—a split between absolute flexibility (not having a pregiven syllabus, student-generated reading and discussion) and absolute inflexibility (not accepting late work, giving little to no direction on assignments). Ferguson argues that in comparison with the current discursive trend heralding student-centric learning, Weinstein's classroom of forty years ago was exemplary. She is able to convey how that experience—the responsibility or ownership one takes on for one's knowledge and pleasure—was both overwhelming and seductive for an undergraduate student. Weinstein is recalled as an "iconoclastic, intense, opinionated professor [who] effortlessly thought about politics and life, and simultaneously thought about his thinking on politics and life."[25] His self-reflexivity illuminates his humanity within the classroom and reinforces personal philosophy to be a process of continual renegotiation and amendment.

Ferguson recalls that Weinstein's classroom is one that was "where outsiders could flourish." Individuals, texts, and ideas that did not conform to established hierarchy and order were given a time and space to shine and challenge the status quo. This educational experience was transformative for Weinstein's students, who find themselves with depth of knowledge outside the established canon of political theory. His pedagogical method combines "comprehensive vitalism" with "ontological wonder," seeking to strengthen a philosophical position to the best ability before systematically critiquing it. Praxis and dialectical synthesis lay at the core of Weinstein in his professional role as professor and led him to undermine institutional authority, providing "a counter-mentoring that cherishes intellectual independence and honesty over everything else." It prefigured her future engagements with Foucault's political theory concerning truth and power. But Ferguson recounts the ambivalent legacy of this teaching; she arrived in graduate school with little knowledge of canonical authors but familiarity with figures that few of her peers had encountered. Yet it opened her to nonfoundationalist thought and poststructuralism, which felt like a "home discourse" to her.

Many of the facets of Kathy Ferguson's portrait of Weinsteinian pedagogy are echoed in Diane Rubenstein's "Michael Weinstein and Félix Guattari: A Militancy of 'Vivacious Despair.'" Rubenstein's framing of Weinstein's pedagogy by Guattari's institutional practice at the La Borde clinic elicits the free-form nature of each seminar—drawn up "from scratch," the empowerment of a previously subaltern population now included in tasks formerly relegated to the teacher/doctor and the invitation toward the "outsider" to come into sharper relief. Rubenstein extends Ferguson's analysis of transformative institutional practices by transposing the site of therapeutic or educational breakthrough (La Borde hospital, Purdue University) with the creative elaboration of concepts (transversality, civil savage) and practices (the grid or *grille*/the seminar). Both Guattari and Weinstein share a central focus on the subjectivication process, whether expressed as singularization or as individualization. They each affirm the necessity of what Weinstein calls "fundamental arts"—local, quotidian practices such as cooking, doing the laundry, and, in America, driving. The undoing of what is repressive within even militant subjectivity—what Weinstein might diagnose as backlash—is targeted by their institutional innovations. While Guattari's theoretical achievement—the concept of transversality (which is the rhizome's underpinning, if its underacknowledged precedent)—is an outgrowth of a prior reform, called the grid, it required a "mediating third object." Rubenstein exemplifies such an object with the Weinsteinian seminar, now read as a Barthesian space of love. The purpose of such a space and teaching relation is to displace conventional notions of transference and the dyadic Socratic (master–student) relation to one of the transversal production of differences, understood in the sense of making each relation "original." Rubenstein self-analyzes her experience of a Weinstein seminar in the mid-nineties while his colleague at Purdue. She witnesses the dispersive proliferation of home-grown Hoosier subjectivities—including her own—as the master teacher desupposes himself.

Weinstein's response that serves as epilogue is a performative enactment of a seminar among the contributors to this book. He introduces a new philosophic persona derived from NASCAR: G7, a simulation of G6. It is in part imagined colloquy, in part settling of accounts, at all times an outbidding of Alfred Jarry's surreal uphill bicycle race.[26] We leave the last words to him.

There are two appendices to the book: Appendix I is an intellectual (auto)biography of Michael by his "beloved colleague," Deena Weinstein. Appendix II is a condensed bibliography of Weinstein's writings and performances. The full bibliography will appear in an online version record at the Interuniversity Consortium for Political and Social Research.

NOTES

1. Arthur Kroker, "Nietzsche for Our Times: Three Meditations," in *Michael A. Weinstein: Action, Contemplation, Vitalism*, ed. Robert L. Oprisko and Diane Rubenstein, Routledge Innovations in Political Theory (New York, NY: Routledge, 2014), 21–2.
2. "Neoliberal rule, for Franco Berardi, designates the irreversible historical mutation formed by the intermingling of global capital with 'recombinant technologies.'" *After the Future, An Interview with Bifo*, ed. Gary Genosko and Nicholas Thoburn (Oakland, CA: AK Press, 2011), 177.
3. Michael A. Weinstein, *The Tragic Sense of Political Life* (Columbia: University of South Carolina Press, 1977), 175–6.
4. Albert Camus, "The Myth of Sisyphus, " in *The Plague, the Fall, Exile and the Kingdom, and Selected Essays* (New York, NY: Alfred A. Knopf, 2004).
5. This moniker tropes off of other constructions/fabrications of theoretical schools, however heteroclite such as the "Yale School theory," denoted by place, or "Chicago" for its economists and their ideological commitments. One could call the network comprising Weinstein a different "Chicago" school, drawing upon his art-critical and musical/performance practices there as well as the weekly shuttles between Lafayette and Lincoln Park. This would argue equally for the "I-65 school," affirming the "vicissitudes" of Weinstein's *drive* and his love of the car. Weinstein is also *the* theorist of NASCAR. We have chosen the Purdue School for its Nietzschean resonances and its asignifying semiotics.
6. Félix Guattari, "I Am an Idea-Thief," *Chaosophy* (New York, NY: Semiotext(e), 1995), 37–40; "A theory is exactly like a box of tools." Gilles Deleuze, "Intellectuals and Power," in *Language, Counter-Memory, Practice: Selected Essays and Interviews by Michel Foucault*, ed. Donald F. Bouchard (Ithaca, NY: Cornell University Press, 1977), 208.
7. Kroker, "Nietzsche for Our Times: Three Meditations," Oprisko and Rubenstein, *op cit.* 31.
8. Sergei Prozorov, *Foucault, Freedom, and Sovereignty* (Burlington, VT: Ashgate, 2007), 14.
9. Justin Mueller, in Oprisko and Rubenstein, *op. cit.*, 98.
10. See Jonathan McKenzie, in Oprisko and Rubenstein, *op. cit.*, 126.
11. *Ibid.*, 111.
12. *Ibid.*, 110.
13. Michael A. Weinstein, *Finite Perfection: Reflections on Virtue* (Amherst: University of Massachusetts Press, 1985), 13.

14. McKenzie, Oprisko and Rubenstein, *op. cit.*, 125.
15. Melba Hoffer, Oprisko and Rubenstein, *op. cit.*, 140.
16. *Ibid.*, 138.
17. *Ibid.*, 146–7.
18. Soto-Crespo, Oprisko and Rubenstein, *op cit*.155.
19. *Ibid.*
20. Michael A. Weinstein, *The Structure of Human Life: A Vitalist Ontology* (New York, NY: New York University Press, 1979), xi.
21. Michael A. Weinstein, *The Polarity of Mexican Thought: Instrumentalism and Finalism* (University Park: Pennsylvania State University Press, 1977), 109.
22. *Ibid.*, 10.
23. Simon Critchley, "What Is the Institutional Form of Thinking?" in *Derrida and the Future of the Liberal Arts: Professions of Faith*, ed. Mary Caputi and Vincent J. Del Casio, Jr. (London: Bloomsbury, 2013). Critchley's remarks are directed toward the humanities (that are under attack), and he gives philosophy pride of place. We believe that they would also be suitable for the type of social science Weinstein pursues as well as many of the sciences.
24. Kroker, Oprisko and Rubenstein, *op. cit.*, 29.
25. Ferguson, Oprisko and Rubenstein, *op. cit.*, 239.
26. Alfred Jarry, *The Ubu Plays: UbuRex, Ubu Cuckolded, Ubu Unchained* (London: Methuen, 2002).

Part I
Action

2 Nietzsche for Our Times
Three Meditations

Arthur Kroker

PHILOSOPHY FROM THE UNDERGROUND

In its inimitable fashion, the theoretical imagination typically follows its own rhythms from the underground, with the life of the mind often a strange tension between explicit intention and the silent passions of the heart. Definitely not teleological in its direction nor necessarily deterministic, the theoretical imagination has about it all the truly enigmatic qualities of intellectual singularity: unexpected detours of thought, strange bifurcations, fascination with inconvenient ideas, and always, importunate timing. I mention this as part of an examination of my own intellectual biography, which I have somewhat reluctantly undergone as part of my (re)encounter with the political theory of Michael A. Weinstein.

I set out with a clear project, namely to consider Weinstein's intellectual contribution from the standpoint of what I would describe as the contemporary (post)human condition—the *digital wilderness*. That is, to reflect upon his political thought or, what's more accurate, his "life philosophy" from the perspective of the fate of modern individualism in the context of the emergent posthuman culture of digitally networked society. Faithful to the written word, my reflections upon Weinstein's truly brilliant theorization of the perils and promise of modern individualism in the age of network society were to be guided, at first, by *The Wilderness and the City*,[1] his major philosophical encounter with the fate of the individual in American society viewed through the intellectual lens of its home-grown life-philosophers, whether the philosophical idealism of Josiah Royce and Charles S. Pierce, the philosophical naturalism of John Dewey and George Santayana, or the profoundly mediational pragmatism of William James. Paying close attention to Weinstein's assertion in the preface to *The Wilderness and the City* that he found the moral struggles and intellectual passions of William James closest to his own, my initial intention was to trace the fate of Weinstein's commitment to philosophical vitalism in the context of that radically new incarnation of the wilderness in the American imagination, namely the emergence of the digital wilderness as both the interior grounding of contemporary moral consciousness and the relentlessly aggressive framework for the construction of the posthuman future, with its entirely familiar program of cloaking not only Nietzsche's pronouncement of the death of god but also Weinstein's warnings concerning the death of the individual in the bright lights of that new conventicle of the city on the hill, what Talcott Parsons might have described, with some grim satisfaction, as the "adaptive enhancement" of those new pattern variables imposed by the digital social system. Following this trajectory of thought, my reflections on Weinstein's contributions would have elaborated arguments that we coauthored in a book titled *Data Trash: The Theory of the Virtual Class*, specifically that the much-celebrated digital universe was, in effect, only the most recent turn of a very ancient wheel—the reentry into history of the latest installment of the age of "fully completed nihilism," prophesied by Nietzsche, critically theorized by Heidegger, and, most definitely, engaged in its preparatory forms by Weinstein's thought.[2]

Now, while this bringing together of what Katherine Hayles would describe as the "tutor texts" of *The Wilderness and the City* and *Data Trash* was the overt intention of my contribution to this volume—an intention that was relatively straightforward, theoretically specific in scope, and, in my estimation, potentially significant in its aim of moving Weinstein's thesis on the death of modern individualism into the storm-center of digital reality—this statement of intention was upset by a relentless and certainly unstoppable drift in my own theoretical imagination. In short, while reflecting in depth on the arguments rehearsed in *The Wilderness and the City*, a theoretical text I have always viewed as the leading work of American political philosophy in the twentieth century, my intellectual attention drifted (historically) eastward, at first to that complex reading of revolutionary history provided by Leon Trotsky's *The History of the Russian Revolution* and then to those more mediated cultural analyses of human legacy of collectivism as one of the key historical processes of the twentieth century: Solzhenitsyn's *1914* and *1916*, Shopokin's trilogy on the fate of the Don Cossacks, and Arthur Koestler's *The Yogi and the Commissar* and *Darkness at Noon*. In the way of all intellectual life, my self-consciousness was, in the usual way of things, the very last witness to a theoretical meditation that might have begun with my daytime encounter with the fate of individualism in American life-philosophy and my nighttime meditations on the triumph of collectivism in Russian revolutionary philosophy. Why this sudden obsession with reading chronicles of socialist revolutionary history—its prolegomenon, its ambitions, and its truly ambivalent legacy—when engaged with such a profoundly original and, in that originality, truly disturbing account of modern individualism as the essence of American life-philosophy that is Weinstein's *The Wilderness and the City*? My sense is that my imagination was, in the face of Weinstein's account of the failed project of American life-philosophy, namely the unwillingness of American thought, whether evidenced by Dewey's commitment to the social community, James's much-celebrated "will to believe," or Royce's "ideal community," forcing my thought to a certain but creatively unsettling conclusion. And that is that there can be no encounter with Weinstein's political thought that is not at the same time a larger encounter with the historical trajectories of twentieth-century experience and, by approximation, with the quickly unfolding future of the twenty-first century. In this sense, my reawakened interest in the genealogy of Russian revolutionary history in the early years of the twenty-first century could be understood as an unconscious countergradient with and against Weinstein's exploration of the fate of the individual in American life-philosophy with its accompanying claim that a focus on the fate of modern individualism is the intellectual essence of the national philosophy of the United States. Here, the parallel emergence of modern collectivism in socialist revolutionary history would serve as the countergradient, bringing to the surface of visibility that which was gained but also lost in America's fateful gamble on the freedom of modern individualism: individuals fully free, that is, either to explore the wilderness of the interior abyss of subjectivity in a society that has not yet come to terms with the consequences of Nietzsche's understanding of the death of god or, in the more typical circumstance, equally free to jump over the void at the (disappearing) center of modern subjectivity by merging the fate of individual consciousness with that larger social and, recently, technological trajectory of the societal community. One thing was certain in this double play of my own fascination with the questions of individualism and collectivism, between, that is, parallel trajectories in the twentieth century between two great revolutionary movements—the individual and the collective, imperfect subjectivity and yet-to-be-perfected political destiny, freedom, and justice—and that was that there could be no consideration of Weinstein's political thought that did not simultaneously involve a consideration of the larger tapestry of social and political history. Weinstein is, in his ontological essence, that all-too-rare political theorist who draws into his intellectual meditations an insistent reflection upon the key laws of historical motion of the times in which he lives—certainly a *political philosopher* taking measure of the ambiguous legacy of modern individualism, particularly in the context of the gathering storm of posthuman collectivism, an *existentialist* on the question of human freedom, a *philosopher of finalist ontology* on the issue of social justice, a *tragic thinker* fully sensitive to key issues of melancholia in political thought and practice, and yet, for all that and perhaps because of all that, a passionate *dissident* of thought from the outside, a theorist who breaks the imposed silence of received frames of political interpretation time and again on behalf of the unrecognized, the prohibited, the excluded.

Strictly considered as a political metaphysician, Weinstein has fulfilled, as a result of a life-long commitment to the highest standards of intellectual probity and critical engagement, the indispensable but always elusive task of producing a series of major theoretical studies that promote an ethics of finalism with its demand for "inner tolerance" in the face of human imperfections and "restraint" as a way of resisting bursts of fanaticism, whether collectively orchestrated or individually authored. If the act of reading Michael Weinstein is always accompanied by the sounds of political struggle that is the modern century as well as by an understanding of the larger patterns of thought that frame society past, present, and future, that is because his thought not only runs parallel to the major events of contemporary political history but, in its sheer urgency, philosophical depth, and political acuity provides a critical analysis containing tangible hints about what's now necessary to prevent a terminal slide of society and individual subjectivity with it into the three deaths—the death of individualism, the death of the social, and the death of history—that are the sure and certain legacy of the powers and domination of twenty-first century experience. A Nietzsche for our times, Weinstein has elucidated the full consequences of a modern culture literally blasted apart by forms of technological acceleration that serve as simulacra of the divine in human affairs and the future of a posthuman culture that will most definitely be haunted by the remains of the human, whether by its terminal manifestations as cultural "acedia" or by episodic outbursts of the "war spirit."

THE ECLIPSE OF THE INDIVIDUAL

No society ever really escapes its metaphysical origins, particularly if its metaphysics are intricately related to its founding political subjectivity, thus raising the stakes of putatively metaphysical debates into a life-and-death wager on the fate of society itself. Consequently, in the same way that Martin Heidegger placed the fate of modern technological society into question with his austere deconstruction of the essence of technique—creative possibility or nihilistic death instinct—Michael Weinstein's *The Wilderness and the City* quickly moves beyond its original intention of exploring the metaphysical origins of American classical philosophy to rehearse some of the key hauntologies of American society itself, whether in its *past* formulation as a bitter struggle between scientific naturalism and religious idealism, its *present* formation as an increasingly atavistic contest between political fundamentalism and technological absolutism, or its *future* as the first of all the posthuman societies likely to make their appearance as the twenty-first century unfolds.

Thinking the future through the mirror of the past, Weinstein's key contribution is to have immediately grasped in his thinking the full dimensions of the metaphysical, which is to say the specifically social and political crisis, that is American society today. On its surface, *The Wilderness and the City* is a superbly rendered account of the trajectory of American classical philosophy, whether the philosophical idealism of Charles S. Pierce and Josiah Royce, the pragmatic naturalism of John Dewey, or the vitalism of William James. In its patient deconstruction of the passionate claims and failed ambitions of American classical philosophy, what is brought into the visibility of critical attention in this text is less a history of ideas than something else, something truly enigmatic, namely the founding logic of American political subjectivity.

A truly metaphysical thinker in the tradition of Nietzsche, Heidegger, and Karl Jaspers, Weinstein can so literally and so brilliantly follow a language of descent into the generative logic of American subjectivity because all of his thought is premised on a larger insight, namely that we are fully posthumous beings living in that twilight period long ago foreseen by Nietzsche, specifically that twilight of being lived in the shadows of the death of god. Always thinking at the height of his (American) times, carefully balancing in his thought both the full, creative force of the technological dynamo that is his national social habitat and the complex, existential dramas inherent to such an enigmatic fate and desperately seeking to discover a way of reconciling the irreconcilable, Weinstein is the one American political theorist who truly understands that the past *is* the future. Not in the teleological sense of American society as somehow culturally determined by its historical logic, but in the hauntological sense that the future of American society is fully implicated in its failure to resolve a continuing crisis of political subjectivity that, while first rehearsed in the tradition of American classical philosophy, finds now its denouement in the full-blown crisis of the subject or, what is the same, in the eclipse of the contemporary American mind under the double pressure of the relentless technological hollowing out of subjectivity from within and the reality of breached borders from without.

For Weinstein, individualism has always been the emblematic sign of American society, simultaneously its core article of political faith and its point of fatal crisis. For example, refusing not simply the juridical nomenclature of monarchy and the religious congregations of theocracy but also the energizing vision of the "masses" with its dictatorship of the proletariat and the will of the party that was the essence of the Russian revolution as well as the corporatist settlement that finally expressed itself in the contemporary political reality of the European Union, the American dream is at once simpler and more daring, namely to make of the existential sovereignty of the individual the bearer of American historical identity. Indeed, if Weinstein can read Nietzsche so closely, it is perhaps because he understands that the fate of the American prospect, with its Declaration of Independence of the individual, makes of American subjectivity the true inheritor of Nietzsche's dark prophecies. Consider Weinstein's following remark concerning the unbearable pressures placed upon modern individualism by the challenge of living in a world, as the philosopher Albert Camus once said, that was divested of its reason by the hard calculus of scientific rationality and technological instrumentalism.

> For Nietzsche, one of the aspects of world-sickness is self-loathing and self-hatred over the infirmities of the species which are revealed to human beings by their own science. The hatred of existence that may

arise from the vision of an empty wilderness, a desert of the soul, breeds the tendency toward nihilism. Such nihilism may take the form of severe acedia, leading to suicide, or to the war-spirit, which is revealed in its essence as the passion of the weak to trample the weak. Suicide and murder grow out of the same denial of life. The first one is a rebellion against life by withdrawal from it and the second is a rebellion by an attempted imperialism over it.[3]

Indeed, what is most noteworthy about the political thought of Michael Weinstein is his commitment to thinking through the moral consequences of the death of god. While Nietzsche may have anticipated in his writings the dark night of nihilism that would follow from a modern culture intentionally stripped of the protective veil of mythology as well as the sheltering horizon of religious belief, it was left to Weinstein to represent what might be called solitary thought after Nietzsche. In Weinstein's writings, we are present at the posthumous future that Nietzsche could only prophesy. Everything is there: "panic fear" over the dissolution of the boundaries of the self; self-awareness as a "vision of an empty wilderness;" "effective megalomania" as the triumphant political formula for increasingly fanatical imperial projects; alternating cycles of severe "acedia" and the "war spirit" as the flickering signifiers of American identity; and everywhere the death of the social.

If Weinstein's project could be confined to an elegant, although critically unrelenting, deconstruction of modern individualism in its American philosophical iteration, that would make of his contribution something purely historical, specifically an important contribution to the history of American life-philosophy. Against this, it is my thesis that what makes Weinstein's thought of decisive importance is that, like Nietzsche before him, he has already written out the history of the future. In the same way that Nietzsche could remark that he would only be understood posthumously by generations of thinkers yet to come, a full critical appreciation of Weinstein's thought will only really emerge with different generations—some to come, some in the present—of practitioners of the life of the mind who have dwelt as a matter of their own life experience within the dark night of nihilism that is everywhere present in his writings. In this sense, Weinstein's apocalyptic metaphysics bleeds through the written word to become a chilling, austere, and entirely accurate diagnosis of the death of the social. In this sense, Weinstein returns time and again from philosophical explorations of the origins of social violence, abuse ethics, panic fear, and the state of siege that is contemporary culture with a succession of profound insights. Here, *The Wilderness and the City* with its ominous conclusions concerning an American society veering between the extremes of cultural fatigue and militant blasts of the war spirit might be appropriately viewed as a brilliantly prescient vision of the fully posthuman future that is the essence of the emerging technological epoch. This is not intended to be a general observation but a textually specific response to Weinstein's thought. Indeed, in the way of all thought that seeks to filter political theory through the actual historical circumstance that it seeks to explain, I would argue that the concluding thesis on the fate of "modern individualism" in *The Wilderness and the City* rises beyond the realm of political theory proper to become something very different, namely a philosophical staging of the final eclipse of individualism, American style. Here, in a sustained philosophical reflection on the challenges of American individualism in thinkers as diverse as Josiah Royce, William James, George Santayana, Charles S. Pierce, and John Dewey, Weinstein concludes that the future of American individualism is likely to evolve in the direction of wild swings between *acedia* and the war-spirit.

> There has been in American culture during this decade abundant "romantic melancholy" and *acedia*, but there has been far more resentment and war-spirit, as compact groups have coalesced to push aside those who, in Sartre's words, are "in the way." There is a nearly universal sense of injury in America today, a will on the part of the many to "get even." The sense of a "declining life" has spurred, as Nietzsche's analysis predicts, a bitterness that is often overt but that even more frequently hides behind a brittle piety.[4]

While Weinstein's overall ethical project focuses on an "unillusioned individualism" that can "count only on an 'inner tolerance' and an 'inner check' to preserve civil society from the rule of a militant collectivism,"[5] his despairing sense that there is "little chance that the modern spirit will survive the twentieth century"[6] seems a more prophetic diagnosis of twenty-first–century experience. Here, instead of the development of an "unillusioned individualism" working its way through the spreading world-sickness of an almost primal "hatred for existence," American individualism has apparently moved in the reverse direction, transforming "world-sickness" with its alternating poles of acedia and the war-spirit into the animating metaphysics of that new form of technologically enabled individualism—the posthuman subject—making its appearance in the digital wilderness that is the essence of life in the twenty-first century. Consequently, what once could only be philosophically glimpsed in its germinal state by way of Weinstein's study of American classical philosophy has in the span of a single century broken beyond the framework of philosophical texts to become the center-point of that which it always was, namely a posthuman self feeding on the psychic residues within, while all the while accelerating at hypervelocity in networked society. If the future will bring increasingly strange journeys through the dark lights and bright (networked) spaces of the digital wilderness, that journey will be framed by a vision of the posthuman self first encountered in Weinstein's thought—with this twist: no longer a form of individualism restrained by an "inner check" or tempered by "inner tolerance" but just the opposite. Accelerated by information culture and seduced by the brilliant detritus of its own psychological implosion, post-human subjectivity absorbs the negative will of acedia and the murderous instincts of the war-spirit as its ontological homeland.

THE SLOW BURN RATE OF PSYCHIC RESIDUES

For any serious life-philosopher, as is the case with Michael Weinstein, the only real measure of his lasting contribution to the life of the mind is, in the end, whether his own practice of life-philosophy achieves *intellectual incommensurability*, that is, a personal practice of life actually lived with all the singular uniqueness of a thinker poised, at every moment, between a critical understanding of the larger historical situation and a form of social, indeed existential, practice in the daily life of the mind that expresses the necessary qualities of intellectual discipline, integrity, and probity. While I cannot document the vicissitudes of experience, with its coeval moments of happiness, tragedy, and forbearance, as they have been actually lived by Weinstein as a life-philosopher, what can be offered as philosophical evidence in this matter is the outstanding fact that on many occasions, his practice of a philosophy of life has been a brilliant expression of finalist ontology, with its simultaneous injunctions toward critical appreciation, self-restraint, and intellectual generosity. This is one philosopher who not only reflects upon the metaphysical history of American life-philosophy first and later life-philosophy in the geographically contiguous countries of Mexico and Canada but who also has demonstrated in his own practice of intellectual life that finalist ontology still exists as it properly should, in the complexities and complications of the intellectual pathway that is, most admirably, exhibited in his own fusion of thought and practice.

For myself, recognizing Weinstein's practice of finalist ontology with its sense of the finitude of human life is less an intellectual abstraction than a matter of direct historical experience. It was in the fall of 1967 and I was a new graduate student at Purdue University, just arrived from decolonization struggles in Canada and deeply concerned about the unfolding American military adventure in Vietnam. At that time, the social sciences were well meaning but uninspired—in my estimation, practical social eugenics for the production of regimes of intelligibility faithful to the requirements of power. Consequently, while I brought with me to this heart of the American heartland copies of Pierre Valliere's pamphlet *White Niggers of America*—a manifesto detailing the political vision of Quebec's then-nascent national-ist movement—my first collective graduate action was to help organize a student-sponsored war-crimes trial with the discipline of sociology as its first defendant. Like many members of my generation during that period, my consciousness may have been defined politically by the bitter clash of world cultures that was Vietnam, but it was framed culturally by a deepening real-ization of the poverty of official academic thought. That was, of course, until late one spring evening, when I attended a large antiwar protest in a darkened, outside amphitheater and heard, for myself, for the first defining time, Weinstein's passionate critique of America's involvement in Vietnam as well as his equally lucid analysis of the coming contradictions between the New Left and Old Left in American thought and, with that, the politics of backlash that was likely to be provoked by resistance politics. Before that moment, I had never really experienced, *existentially* experienced, as a matter of my own thought and practice, the meaning of the life of the mind, how, that is, two thousand years of metaphysics—in-depth, patient, critical, necessarily undermining, often synoptic, philosophical thought—could be summed up in the grain of a voice and in the political vision that that voice urged its intently listening audience to consider and, once considered, to actually begin to act on the fateful results of that consideration.

Now, I know that this is just one story about an antiwar protest at a Midwestern university, best known at that time and probably still for its commitment to all things engineering, but in the sometimes unexpected way of things, being in the actual presence of an inspiring intellectual imagination instantly and powerfully influenced my reflections on the life worth living. I might mention as well that at the height of Vietnam protest, my choice for a worthy object of study was the social theory of Talcott Parsons, a thinker I approached in the same spirit that early Christians thought of the Roman philosophy of Virgil, namely, in my case, an American social theorist who was important precisely because his thought provided an unrelieved depth analysis of the structures of power foundational to the American national enterprise of empire building abroad and subjective normalization at home. I mention this for the specific reason that, confronted with the general refusal of my sociology professors to approve my prolonged research on Parsons's thought, Michael Weinstein provided intellectual shelter for the solitary Parsons-focused thinker I was at that time. Demonstrating the sensitivity of a natural teacher, one for whom intellectual generosity and passionate curiosity were less exceptional than well-exercised habits of life, he understood that my interest in Parsons was in the way of a complex theoretical gateway to a full understanding of the underlying structural (cybernetic) dynamics of advanced capitalist societies. With amazing erudition, he not only provoked a wider consideration of the place of structural functionalism in the life of the (American) mind, but he also engaged my thought in those other expressions of American classical philosophy, from Royce and Santayana to James, Dewey, and Elijah Jordan. When many years later we coauthored our book on what we named the "virtual class"—the increasingly self-conscious ruling class of capitalist technocracy—I always thought that if Weinstein could be so deeply insightful about the politics, culture, and subjectivity of technological society, it was because he was capable of assembling discrete historical events—the rise of the disciplinary state, austerity economics, virtual mind management, social therapeutics of soft power—into a more comprehensive and compelling intellectual vision. In fact, not only synthesizing the often hidden forces mobilizing history but something else—specifically, to take careful measure of both what is permitted by the prevailing rhetoric of power and what is disavowed, prohibited, and excluded.

In the contemporary historical circumstance, Weinstein's intellectual and thus personal sensitivity to those forms of thought and, even more urgently, those singular individuals and, sometimes, whole collective identities marginalized by power has witnessed its own philosophical prohibition. For example, it is like scattering dust on a windy day to seek to raise into the proper rights of philosophical speech the fundamental concept of finalist ontology. Everywhere the fate of American life-philosophy has met its successful counterchallenge in the increasingly arid yet messianic language of technological liberalism and, as often as not, in the politics of anger that is the contemporary descendent of all the backlash native to the American spirit from its first Puritan beginnings. What, in the end, can finalist ontology say to forms of deindividuated subjectivity and modulated power that are the essence of transhumanism—the hegemonic ideology of the newly refreshed American empire with its active alliance of synthetic biology, Big Data, and the Quantified Self movement? In this case, when that restless spirit of the positivist side of American life-philosophy, exemplified first and foremost in William James's "will to believe," hits the California coastline of all the artificial intelligence (AI) labs, futurist Googles, and synthetic biologies of the American spirit, its overriding, predatory-like aim is to literally evacuate the self of its self. When the mind–machine merger happily envisioned by technocratic futurists in the eschatological form of "the Singularity" takes place, there will undoubtedly be as little space for finalism as there will be for understanding life's finitude. With Nietzsche, we could describe the contemporary epoch, and appropriately so, as one of suicidal nihilism; with Heidegger, we could speak of "fully completed nihilism" with its spasms of abuse value; and with Hannah Arendt, we could dwell on the meaning of "negative being." All these descriptions would be accurate to some extent, but not, I suspect, in the more ambiguous sense, the full ethical complexity entailed by a reflection on the death of life philosophy in the American mind. For that, we just need to follow the pathway established by Weinstein's thought to a critical reflection on the fuller meaning of the politics of anger that bursts right through the veneer of most contemporary American discourse.

Perhaps in this case, Weinstein's relentlessly austere account of the spirit of ressentiment resulting from the brilliant yet tragic failure that is American life-philosophy provides the best existent description of the "hatred for existence" that is the animating pulse of the politics of backlash, whether libertarian, conservative, or identity-based liberalism. When the "hatred of existence" begins to gnaw on the bone of subjectivity, the practical result is the triumph of death philosophy as the posthuman successor to the earlier hopefulness of "American classical philosophy as a moral quest." So then, while the contemporary situation of finalist ontology in the American mind

might be approached in terms of the eclipse of the individual, what is actually taking place is, I believe, something more epochal and, in the full sweep
of that epoch, metaphysically significant, namely that there are actually two
death drives—one the bitter politics of anger and the other the technocratic
will to finally escape the fate of bodily finitude—that mobilize what the
historian Chalmers Johnson has described as the "end of the Republic" and
the triumph of empire and, with that, the appearance anew of the howling
fates of hubris and nemesis. But, that said, if finalist ontology cannot practically realize itself in contemporary culture, perhaps that is because it is the
fatal remainder of American thought, the form of life-philosophy and life
practice that cannot be admitted precisely because its admission would definitely and quickly negate the necessarily tropological character of American
power—the fact, that is, that the stability of American political discourse
from the Republic to the Empire consists of forms of thought that join philosophical justifications and political strategies into the smooth symmetries
underlying acceptable regimes of intelligibility. The fact that Michael Weinstein's eloquent formulation of finalist ontology—its genealogy, expressions, and sometimes productive contradictions—is not acceptable in any
conventional measure to the current iteration of American tropology—the
twin death drives of transhumanism and anger politics—probably indicates
that, in this thought, is to be found something definitely and fully constitutive of the future, something that cannot be easily absorbed in the present
because, as in the way of all prophetic insight, his thought belongs to a
future of the finite self. Consequently, while finalist ontology awaits the rise
and decline of American death philosophy as its historical markers, it exists,
at this moment, in that most desirable of all intellectual situations—a form
of *thought from outside—(kynical) thought from below*—the memory of
which haunts and, indeed, panics the mindlessness of cultures of power.

The century to come promises to move at the speed of scavenger
time—not only the powerful scavenging for what remains of value in the
spreading ruins, sometimes bodily, at other times economic, of the weak and
the powerless but a more perverse form of scavenger hunt, with individuals literally evacuating, and thereupon vivisecting, their own subjectivities,
whether for pleasure or for duty. Heidegger once warned us about this. In his
thought, the approaching epoch would be typified by the overall sensibility
of boredom—not simply boredom with events or with others but a deeply
uncanny expression of terminal boredom in which an individual is bored
with its "self," certainly with its bodily self but increasingly with its own
cognition, desires, and affect. Breaking with millennia of tradition, modern individualism always was, in its essence, a radical experiment with the
possibility of creating a self, liberated from the theologies of tribalism and
piety. Consequently, when Heidegger discusses the more fundamental form
of boredom that is boredom with oneself, he is only reflecting in his thought
a greater sublimation, specifically a massive, pent-up anger accumulating
over the many centuries of modernism of having to maintain, sometimes

in the language of ethical renunciation, always in the rhetoric of inner violence, the boundaries of a stable self. This psycho-ontological experiment in crafting the reality of a solitary individual—invested by rights, burdened by duties, signified by ideologies, mobilized by dreams—out of the many expressions of collective consciousness that were premodern society could not endure and did not endure. This is perhaps why the evacuation of the modern self, from its inner subjectivity to its deepest affect, has so easily become the animating spirit of networked society. When modern individualism finally cracks, its very public burial is undertaken with immense enthusiasm and manic energy. Perhaps motivated by the belief that the "self" with its responsibilities toward inner tolerance and restraint was always something imposed on us from without, the new technocratic individual that emerges from the ruins has no illusions. For this, the first of all the many versions of the posthuman self to come, the drift of cultural acedia and the projection of power that is the war-spirit promise a way beyond the harsh solitude of modern consciousness. While technological futurists might like to declaim concerning the retribalization of humanity, Weinstein's overall prognosis is more convincing, that is, that finalist ontology has been blocked by a general cultural movement in favor of the will to technology, the reverse of which is a retreat into an increasingly atavistic self, mobilized by anger directed at phantasmatic objects of derision, contempt, and prohibition—the illegal alien, the always-foreign terrorist, Islamic extremists, the nomadic migrant. When the language of American individualism expresses itself in terms of good and evil—the sustaining rhetoric of America as a moral quest—what is left in the darkness that lies ahead are only two sounds: the sounds of the (human) being of finalist ontology being crushed into granular flows of data and the sound of those excluded, prohibited, and disavowed being pushed into the silence of nonrecognition as properly "moral" beings.[7] Weinstein's lasting contribution is to allow those dark sounds of the present and future to rise into political and, consequently, ethical visibility.

NOTES

1. Michael A. Weinstein, *The Wilderness and the City: American Classical Philosophy as a Moral Quest* (Amherst: University of Massachusetts Press, 1982).
2. Arthur Kroker and Michael A. Weinstein, *Data Trash: The Theory of the Virtual Class* (New York: St. Martin's Press, 1993).
3. Michael A. Weinstein, *The Wilderness and the City*, 130.
4. *Ibid.*, 155.
5. *Ibid.*
6. *Ibid.*
7. For a fuller account on the politics of recognition with its moral intelligibility concerning who is worthy of "grievability," see Judith Butler's essay on "Precarious Life, Grievable Life," in her book, *Frames of War: When is Life Grievable* (London: Verso, 2010), 1–32, as well as my own reflections on the place of Butler's vision of political melancholia in my text, *Body Drift: Butler, Hayles, Haraway* (Minneapolis: University of Minnesota Press, 2012).

3 Strings

A Political Theory of Multidimensional Reality

Robert L. Oprisko

> Existence can only be grasped in the paradoxical simultaneity of togetherness and disseminated singularity.
>
> (Nancy 2000, 7)

INTRODUCTION

Sergei Prozorov uncovered what is arguably the most important problematic in international political theory in his 2009 article "Generic Universalism in World Politics: Beyond International Anarchy and the World State," in which he links semiotics to the logic of consequences (Oprisko 2014a; Prozorov 2009). He concludes that altering the discipline's name from "international relations" to "world politics" is an agential act within the disciplinary literature that not only alters the nominal value of the discipline but also moves the discussion, and therefore how one conceives of the discipline itself, from one extreme, *identitarian pluralism*, to another, *generic universalism* (Prozorov 2009). Although Prozorov ends the article arguing that the world appears trapped within Schmitt's existential ontology of identitarian pluralism, he suggests, perhaps hopefully, that generic universalism does indeed exist:

> . . . the generic community actually exists in today's world as a finite fragment of its own infinite unfolding. Consigned to indiscernibility in the encyclopedia of contemporary global politics, the existence of the world community may be verified by concrete local practices that are able to force a momentary illumination of the truth of generic equality that the statist logic of the political obscures.
>
> (Prozorov 2009, 244)

Evidence of an occasionally awakened generic, human community within a political system dominated by identitarian states strongly suggests that neither identitarian pluralism nor generic universalism is representative of reality *en total*. A new political ontology is needed that will bind the universal to the particular without diminishing either, a unified theory of political reality.

The difficulty to construct such a unified theory lies in the seemingly irreconcilable position of the extremes available.[1] Badiou, perhaps, says it best: "Ontology has built the portico of its ruined temple out of the following experience: what presents itself is essentially multiple; what presents itself is essentially one" (Badiou 2005). Ontology must account for both the universal and the particular, much like theoretical physics is searching for a theory that connects the quantum to the cosmos.

Reality is an ever-changing unique presentation of active relational engagements in perpetual tension. Building a unified theory becomes possible through embracing agonic contradiction as the unifying reagent of ontology. I propose that reality is a complex not of opposites but of uniquely presented tensions that lie at the intersection of radical entanglement and radical separation. I suggest that praxis-as-tension between Barad and Weinstein is found in the failed act to achieve absolute separation or entanglement. I then argue for a multiplicity that combines Deleuze's focus on energy and Badiou's axiomatic sets to form social superstrings. I finish by developing social string M-theory as a universal system of phenomena that celebrates rather than diminishes particular existential agency.

METHODOLOGY

Weinstein's oeuvre speaks to me, resonates with me, and teaches me lessons on existence as it is and as it is perceived. Through home discourse, as I delve deeper into his mind, patterns emerge, but they are my patterns in his work, patterns that I perceive because I am proceptively directed to do so. As this is the case and because the nature of this argument is my reason brought to bear on the writings of a man rather than an attempt to definitively argue what he meant when he wrote it, this chapter is "not an exercise in exegesis" as Prozorov would say (Prozorov 2009, 14). My goal is to develop a theory for reality as a system of concurrent, overlapping abstractions based upon the textual corpus of his works and the lessons that they provide by employing Weinsteinian *love-piracy*.[2] This "unfaithful" interpretation of Weinstein is my homage; his oeuvre presents itself as the intellectual inspiration for my argument and should not be seen as either a defense for or validation of my unique understanding of him.[3]

In an effort to be true to the nature of the material under scrutiny, that of the oeuvre of work that self-reflectively posits itself as a postcursor of existential phenomenology, I feel compelled to follow suit (Weinstein 1977, 24). Weinstein's work presents itself as a progression with a goal to understand reality as it is in all of its agonic torment. This anguish focuses upon the individual, the self, the ego and its apprehension of the world around it. This reality is necessarily Other, alter, the mass from which the self is radically separated. Weinstein borrows Unamuno's method of agonized doubting, his "agonic dialectic between the will to immortality and the will to reason by proposing a tension between the will to historical meaning and the relativism that follows from careful examination of one's context through multiple perspectives" (Weinstein 1977, 24).

Agonized doubting is an active reflection, an embrace of the tensions within the person to consider oneself as an object to which one is subject. "It discloses a structure of existence that sustains each unique autobiography. This structure is the object of philosophy. Agonized doubting opens up the subjective insecurity and brings forth the person" (Weinstein 1979, 5). The methodological rigor of agonized doubting comes in the dual approaches that one must tread simultaneously in order to present an authentic examination of the self's autobiography as the basis for philosophical inquiry: sincerity and precision.[4]

Sincerity is rigorous because it is only too easy to slip from ontology into a positivism; to stop describing reality as it is and to start suggesting reality as the ego finds it ought to be. To be a "sincere examination of the heart" as José Vasconcelos calls it, requires that the ego of the author examine life *en total*, including the self's limited engagement with it. The author must describe totality, knowing that he has not the tools to do so. Man's limitations stem from his entrapment into a Stirnerian "bag of bones" that he cannot escape. Senses are finite. Intellect is finite. Power is finite. Will is finite. Being is finite. Man is finite. Yet the existentialist wrestles with the infinite in an effort to examine the finite well. An individual who experiences reality cannot be omniscient, omnipotent, or omnipresent. To be any of those things, a being would *be* reality, a universal truth, rather than operate within the limits set by reality as a radically separated being. The phenomenologist wrestles with the finite in order to tease out patterns within the infinite.

Precision is rigorous. Words are a medium through which the philosopher strives to be understood, knowing all too well that individual can never truly know one another. The act of discourse is one in which the infinite is tossed aside and placed into the processes of valuation and evaluation that shred the absolute into finite particles that can be described at the cost of all else in order to produce an intelligible meaning that will hopefully be received as it was intended by the writer (Foucault 1982; Luhman 2002; Oprisko 2012). Communication is always an activity of translation, even when all parties employ the same language. Meaning is negotiated, debated, and evaluated normatively as being either a good or bad effort, producing either a good or bad result. Philosophy is here shown to be an act of torment, an existential anguish that both frustrates the philosopher and provides the only outlet that may succor him. Precision, therefore, requires the use of terms that are precisely crafted, without falling into the jargon of philosophy so vehemently bashed by Theodore Adorno (2003).[5] Therefore, precision will be balanced with Simmelian aspectival totalization and aesthetic comprehension (Weinstein and Weinstein 2011, 12–13). Weinstein himself describes this method:

> Radical abstraction, detotalization, analogical elucidation, and the appreciation of forms of detotalized order are the prime elements of Simmel's method/style. Used together, they yield a cartography of the scene, a set of specialized maps tracing common elements that are not directly observable, like the patterns on a weather map. . . . Simmel's practice is a (playful) *discipline* of pattern recognition.
>
> (Weinstein and Weinstein 2011, 12)

Davis sees Simmel's method as being "aesthetic comprehension," which works by the procedure of "universalization through particularization" (Davis 1973, 153). Simmel has found a way to explore universal truth without compromise by exploring the patterns of human existence and describing them through particular instantiations as examples. Internal tension within the example, including the element of its own negation, is anticipated. The example itself is likely also in tension with an opposite or, at the very least, a competitor, such that the primary universal of social truth within Simmel's thought, and one that harmonizes with Weinstein's vitalism, is the agony of tension.

This present analysis and argument benefits, as Weinstein's oeuvre does, from being a postcursor to existential phenomenology with all of the benefits of philosophy that has come after its nadir. The critical response to existentialism by the critical philosophers of the Frankfort school, the poststructuralists, and the antipostmodernists help shape my thought processes and cannot be divorced from them. In a true Buchlerian sense, my proceptive direction drives me to engage with the truth as I know it in an effort to describe reality as it is rather than as I would like it to be, yet holding the belief that there are universally applicable patterns in the wake of a fully deconstructed state of positive truth. My method revels in agonic tension and presupposes the conclusion that reality *is* agonic tension and that living is how one balances said tension.

RADICAL ENTANGLEMENT: KAREN BARAD'S AGENTIAL REALISM

Karen Barad has taken issue with an essential failure of representationalism in science, noting that reliance on instrumentalism obscures the importance of the concepts that we use to inscribe value onto things. Meaning cannot be independent of the method of interaction. She initiates the ethico-onto-epistemology of Agential Realism:

> The universe is agential intra-activity in its becoming. The primary ontological units are not "things" but phenomena—dynamic topological

reconfigurings/entanglements/relationalities/(re)articulations. And the primary semantic units are not "words" but material-discursive practices through which boundaries are constituted. This dynamism is agency. Agency is not an attribute but the ongoing reconfigurings of the world.

(Barad 2003, 818)

Her binding of materialism to ideationism is predicated on the rejection of Cartesian epistemology and its "belief in the inherent distinction between subject and object, and knower and known" (Barad 2003, 813). In this rejection is a simultaneous acceptance of a Bohrian philosophy-physics that is agent-object rather than subject-object oriented. Bohr's model is premised on the problematic of measurement and his argument that theoretical concepts are defined by "specific physical arrangements" that "define relationships required for their measurement" (Barad 2007, 108). Observation, including experimental observation, involves "indeterminable discontinuous interaction," leading Bohr to determine, "there is no unambiguous way to determine between the 'object' and the 'agencies of observation' " (Barad 2007, 114). In order for an agent to recognize an object, there must be an agential cut that grants distinction of the object by separating said object from the world in which it is still interacting and interpenetrated. The separation and distinction is useful only to inscribe meaning onto the object of agency.

The beauty of Bohrian epistemology is that it presupposes a single system, the universe, and accepts that individuals cannot divorce themselves from being within the universe itself; it is impossible to be an external observer. Engaging the world is no longer by Cartesian observation, but by active engagement. For example, observing the stars from Earth requires that there be an agent who is actively looking at the stars at a particular moment in time and space. It also requires that there is something(s) that is directing the observer to observe. In the case of stars, they are engaged in nuclear reactions that generate energy, including light over vast distances. For Barad and Bohr, this is important; the observer-as-agent is located within the universal system with the stars. When observing their light, he sees into multiple pasts—each star is a specific distance away from Earth, thus each light photon must travel that distance, which is measured in time—the light-year(ly). The observer is witnessing the star's past, but from his agential cut, or parallax view, it is that star's relational present for that given situation and position in time and space. The revolutionary nature of Bohrian epistemology lies in the importance of perspective.

She employs a method of diffraction that rejects the sharp-edged distinction between the silos of study, most notably ethics, ontology, and epistemology; her position is that the social and scientific [material] relate through a process of "exteriority within" (Barad 2007, 93). Barad defends agential realism as a "legitimate interpretation of quantum mechanics" and champions its ability to successfully analyze interpenetrated phenomena/entangled practices, which "requires a non-additive approach that is attentive to the intra-action of multiple apparatuses of bodily production" (Barad 2007, 94). Agential realism is posthumanist, denying human exceptionalism, though necessarily inclusive of humanity and human phenomena within its material-discursive framework (Barad 2007, 140).

Agential realism argues for a reinterpretation of reality as one that is intimately unified through the aggregation of everything as a system within which all parts are in interpenetrative communion with all other things (directly or not), placing practice within theory. "There is no godlike approach possible to the physical world whereby we may know it as it is 'absolutely in itself'; rather we are able to know only as much of it as can be captured in those situations which we can handle conceptually" (Barad 2007, 125). Any meaning that may be communicated must operate as an apparatus that cuts the agent of observation from the object of observation in order to resolve semantic-ontic indeterminacy.

The ontological nature of Bohr's realism is premised upon not individuated existence independent of a measurement apparatus and that the measurement apparatus is dependent upon the phenomena in question that represents the intra-action from which the agents emerge. Barad rejects the linguistic turn in favor of a posthumanist performative understanding of discursive practices. "Performativity is properly understood as a contestation of the unexamined habits of mind that grant language and other forms of representation more power in determining our ontologies than they deserve" (Barad 2007, 133). Agential realism is, therefore, a relational ontology "between specific material (re)configurings of the world through which boundaries, properties, and meanings are differentially enacted" (Barad 2007, 139). Agents using apparatuses reconfigure the material world. "Apparatuses are not mere observing instruments but boundary-drawing practices—specific material (re)configurings of the world—which come to matter" (Barad 2007, 140). For Barad, "Phenomena are constitutive of reality. Reality is composed not of things-in-themselves or things-behind-phenomena but of things-in-phenomena" (Barad 2007, 140).

The premise of this ontology is that a part/portion of the universal reality initiates an active engagement with the rest/remainder of universal reality, which renders it momentarily distinct. Time and space emerge as important media through which the flowing processes of mattering matter. Mattering is the ongoing materialization of phenomena (Barad 2007, 151). Barad is also politicizing reality through her use of the apparatus as a boundary-drawing practice. What she desires is for her colleagues to recognize that a person is engaging (a particular part of) the universe in a particular way. Barad's agent affirms his sovereignty through a decisive act (Oprisko 2012). By deciding upon how to approach the universe and what parts of it to engage/give meaning, the observer is giving distinction to himself and to that which he engages, making both exceptional (Schmitt 1996, 2005).[6]

Barad's ethico-onto-epistemological theory of Agential Realism represents a fantastic advancement in arguing for radicalized entanglement/communion. The incompleteness of this framework, however, is evidenced when exploring the connection between matter as a materialist phenomenon and matter as an ethico-normative inscription of possessing value—to matter. The materialist reduction to matter and energy, yet inclusive of mental, social, and ethical phenomena has been the work of the eliminative materialism branch in neuroscience, with which Agential Realism appears to concur, especially state-space theory (Patricia Churchland 1986, 2002, 2011; Paul Churchland 1999, 2012).

Such a reduction, however, presents itself as problematic when rules are broken. We may all be nothing more than stardust that manifests in myriad ways, and personality may be nothing more than neural impulses that pattern themselves, inscribing a logic of habit onto a unique presentation of replicable DNA patterns; however, each unique presentation of consciousness is forced by the condition of vitality to direct its efforts in a singular, unified way. Individual agency transforms mere action into vectors. Agency is vectored because it is not mere action, but directed action, sovereign action. The direction is important and not only echoes Barad's emphasis that the distance is important between entangled pieces of the universe but also is an admission that there is separation between the particular pieces that comprise it. To accept radical entanglement, the integration of all things, requires that we also accept radical separation, the existence of meaningful distance between all things. This combination of radical entanglement and radical separation forms a *complexio oppositorum*, or complex of opposites that are simultaneously true without logical contradiction (Schmitt 1996).

RADICAL SEPARATION: WEINSTEIN'S EXISTENTIAL POLITICAL PHILOSOPHY

Weinstein's ocuvre provides the structure for a novel approach to metaphysics and ontology: being, while singular, presents itself in multiple realities. Man engages himself and his other(s) in four systems: material, social, psychic, and temporal simultaneously and without contradiction. These realities are not mutually exclusive but are, rather, interactive and interpenetrate one another axiologically; value and meaning represent the tools of relation and thus form and frame how man engages himself, his surroundings, and others. They are also the tools by which man encounters who and what he was and develops his intention to project what he desires to be. Weinsteinian reality provides the argument for not only a multiplicity of being but also a multiverse of social realities.

Weinstein's intention is to illuminate that "existentialism is a political philosophy" (Weinstein 1977, 93). His agonic, existential-phenomenological paradigm precisely and sincerely reflects lived experience in social and political life, providing the "ultimate justification of anarchism" (Weinstein 1977, 93). Reveling in agony and contradiction, the Weinsteinian school of thought embraces lived experience and vitality at the expense of any singular, butchered worldview. He sees a world of radically separated individuals who, when viewed in aggregate, exist and live socially. Although he does not construct the puzzle for us, he has provided all of the pieces for a holistic understanding of reality. For Weinstein, the individual engagement is everything; man acts within the world that is. Those *realms of action* define the places within which corresponding *complete human actions* present themselves as social fact (Weinstein 1973, 56–58).[7]

Weinstein, similarly to Barad, rejects the Cartesian epistemology but replaces it with Pascalian activity rather than Bohrian agency. He explores "active transcendence or authentic existence" as a mystery of ontology that reveals the relationship of the data to the problematic itself (Weinstein and Weinstein 1978, 41). He sees the individual man as Heidegger's the One who is exists already as part of the mass *à la* Karl Jaspers's life-order but authentically projects himself through the domain(s) of his reality with action that engages said reality as an active participant (Weinstein and Weinstein 1978, 42). Active participation with the domains within which the self may project requires judgment regarding where or in what direction said projection should be directed. As Cassirer tells us, judgment always contains "an element of universality and particularity" (Cassirer 1944, 206).

Reality itself is a realm of domains; its universal nature of encompassing everything that exists requires that it include all material and ideational domains. The (social-) fact of existence reflects this dualism; to be the domain within which activity is being observed is to literally *be* reality. However, this does not in any way interfere with, negate, or diminish the activity that takes place in said domain. Reality *is* existential; the material existence occurs in a material domain and is beholden to the laws of the natural sciences, yet ideational existence is dependent upon the domain in which the act of projected will is directed. All domains interpenetrate one another.

In his earliest published works, Weinstein situates his sociopolitical inquiry into the rank and file of the existentialists, "to outline in general terms an existential theory of the political relation. . . . an existential political science and normative theory are both possible and meaningful" (Weinstein 1970, 214). His work begins by negating experimental consciousness in favor of personal consciousness, which "allows the individual to go beyond the experimental life and attempt to order his existence in other ways. It also permits him to be trustworthy, which is the first condition for his trusting others. Finally, it is the basis for reconstructing the political relation" (Weinstein 1970, 210). The problematic that he confronts throughout his oeuvre extends from these: I exist and the world exists and we are not one; we are in this, but are we in this together?

His question, therefore, becomes how does man exist authentically? Weinstein and Weinstein examine authenticity as active transcendence, "a being in the world that focuses attention not on future participation, but on the appearance of the world," to be an objective attitude from which one can intend anything other than itself, which is the objective position (Weinstein and Weinstein 1978, 44–45). For the authentic being, society is "an aspect of one's own life." Moreover, social phenomena present themselves to the authentic being as both problematical and necessary: they define a terrain within which the authentic being may act, becoming agential, but by so acting, the agent participates and loses his objectivity and is no longer experiencing an authentic moment (Weinstein and Weinstein 1978, 45). Therefore, though "an individual is known by his projects," which are "only satisfied through the use of cultural objects and within relational processes" (Weinstein 1973, 56). Weinstein apprehended, however, that human action was both social and relational: Weinstein's existential political science would require that individual men with individual projects oriented on cultural objects and acted with reference to the other individuals toward a goal that is a shared vision of a future; empiricism could be redeemed if social fact could usurp the unit of analysis (Weinstein 1973, 57–58). The study of complete human actions, the social facts that comprise the core of Weinstein's desired political science, hinge upon the project-object relational process as the unifying field.

Weinstein and Weinstein continue to struggle with the Newtonian empiricism of social science and ultimately reject man's ability to engage with the social objectively. They present a series of contrasts that reflect their rejection of any singular positivism that attempts to control the objects of existence through the techniques of scientific inquiry, making objects "manageable and manipulable, bringing them under conscious control" (Weinstein and Weinstein 1982, 2). In this, the Weinsteins begin to construct a position that man's relationship to the natural world, the physical environment, is radically different from man's relationship to other men. They present man as a self to whom there are at least two external realms: nature and society. Objective detachment is denied, however, and the puzzle-solving activities of natural science, rooted in "wondering doubt," including the search for laws, emerge as disrespectful intentions onto the objects of inquiry by the scientist. Scientists cannot remain objective because the manipulation of data is an act of engagement that disallows them objectivity (as it cannot take place in an authentic moment; Weinstein and Weinstein 1982, 3–4).

Weinstein's vitalist ontology depends upon the agony of contradiction. "Agony is authentic existence" (Weinstein 1977, 20). He laments, "I want to realize contradictory values, living them simultaneously. Yet in order to act politically, I must adopt one of these partial perspectives and collaborate with others who believe that it is true" (Weinstein 1977, 21). Purposeful action is necessary to live:

> Life is apprehended neither as a stream of vital experience or will, nor as the inscription of codes by an alien culture, but as an objective structure with a subjective reference, as the diversity of the flesh extended into the world and then springing back into the flesh, penetrating the psyche, and superintended by the spirit.
>
> (Weinstein 1995, 103)

Purposeful action takes time and requires commitment. Life being a temporary state of affairs, the commitment to any action is predicated on a decision (not a choice) to do X rather than Y, Z, or simply not X at a given moment. When man acts, however, he encounters opposing wills and resistance against his living in his own way. Man gets denied, diminished, and disenfranchised, but it is only when he rebels against his finitude and rejects the vitality of life that he plunges into the torpor of ressentiment (Weinstein 1982, 150).

Weinstein finds that the radically separated being is desirous of entanglement, of purposeful action that is meaningful, a committed relationship with something(s). Separation itself is only possible in a world of multiples; even separation of self from self (to be of two minds) requires that the self be divisible. The project-object orientation of Weinsteinian existential phenomenology is not the opposite, but the flipside of Barad's agent-object orientation of her agential realist onto-epistemology. They form, in tandem, an ontology that is premised on existence as tension.

PRAXIS: THE FAILED ATTEMPT[8]

The tension of reality is maintained through failure. The Baradian agent's activity results in finite moments of self-and-other distinction before being drawn back into the entangled matter of the universe. The Weinsteinian actor projects himself through his world within the universe, constantly separated, always purposeful, which requires external engagement. Barad's agent fails to separate herself and be rendered distinct from the universe in her search for critical distance. The Bohrian epistemology is predicated upon universal interiority of every particular—absolute separation is impossible. Weinstein's existential phenomenology is predicated upon individual interiority—being trapped in a Stirnerian bag of bones that both allows and requires the self's failure to fully engage with externals. It is in Zizek that we can achieve praxis between the Barad and Weinstein as well as the universal and particular.

Zizek's synthetic ontology is nothing less than an attempt to understand the real as the failed attempt. Failure penetrates the entirety of the text and is reminiscent of Doc Hammer's take on *The Venture Brothers*: "It's about the beauty of failure. It's about the failure that happens to all of us" (Publick and Hammer 2006, 2). For Zizek, the real is inseparable both from the radicalized material reality that forms everyone and everything from stardust as the heavenly bodies explode and collapse in the creative destruction of our ever-expanding universe and the social meanings of our unique presentation, as Nancy would say, as being(s) singular plural.

The material realm of Zizek's ontology is derived from Barad's take on Bohr's epistemology. He keys in on radical diffraction, "Diffraction itself is thus diffracted into combining and splitting [much like the universe's dual process for expansion] into overlapping and spreading" (Zizek 2012, 949). Zizek then likens radical diffraction to parallax, "the shift of perspective needed to produce the effect of the depth of the Real, as if an object acquires the impenetrable density of the Real only when its reality reveals itself to be inconsistent" (Zizek 2012, 949).[9] Zizek asserts that there is a price to be paid for something to appear out of nothing; his sexual encounter is explicit:

> In Lacanese, the idealist position is "masculine," it totalizes the universe through the observer as the point of exception, while materialism is "feminine"; that is, it asserts the "non-All" of every measurement. However, it would be too easy to simply privilege the "feminine" non-All and to reduce the "masculine" totalization-through-exception to a secondary illusion—here, more than ever, we should insist on (sexual) difference itself as the primary fact, as the impossible Real with regard to which both positions, "masculine" and "feminine" appear as secondary, as two attempts to resolve its deadlock.
>
> (Zizek 2006, 934–935)

The Real for Zizek is the coinhered singularity of the idealist-materialist dichotomy. This ontological position is the agential cut or parallax gap from which both classical realism and quantum realism emerge as explanatory constructs.

Zizek's Real issues forth from his theory as a nexus between Barad's radical entanglement and Weinstein's radical separation (Barad 2007). Reality is the tension of the void that is nothing but is capable of holding everything. The nothingness presupposes the sublimation of an emergent something, which will give meaning to the void as the Real that encompasses the somethings and nothings but IS both of them simultaneously and without contradiction, a pre-ontological proto-reality (Prozorov 2012, 2014a, 2014b).

> The Real is thus an effect of the symbolic, not in the sense of performativity, of the "symbolic construction of reality," but in the totally different sense of a kind of ontological "collateral damage" of symbolic operations: the process of symbolization is inherently thwarted, doomed to fail, and the Real *is* this immanent failure of the symbolic.
>
> (Zizek 2012, 959)

Tension is the key. What Zizek does not do an adequate job illuminating, however, is that this tension is necessarily between the ontic In-itself (the Void) and the ontological Thing-in-itself, which emerges spatio-temporally within the void. The (inter)action of objects located in space and time are also symbolic gestures with meanings dependent upon the coordinates of the transcendental subject that is critically engaging that interaction and searching for meaning.

Less Than Nothing provides a powerful reminder that philosophy is an abstraction of reality and that we philosophers are inherently always-already situated within a web of social networks that affect, effect, and infect us. Progressing Zizek's sexual metaphor, we can accept the "feminine" objective reality as void that only has meaning, including what it means to be a void, when it is filled with the totality of objects as subjects that both fill and fail-to-fill it. This philosophical discovery of zero, or the void, is an important addition for political practice, which Zizek helpfully points out in his conclusion, "The Political Suspension of the Ethical," in which he posits that the goal of eliminating class inequality involves the organized politicization of a class to self-negate. Zizek's proletariat can only find equality with the bourgeoisie by eliminating the relationship and its meaning that renders each distinct; for class equality to emerge, classes themselves must no longer exist or have a meaning perpetuated by a relational identity (Zizek 2012, 1010).

Zizek's political agent is a dignified rebel, an individual who operates outside the logic of appropriateness and focuses instead on the freedom of action proscribed only by what Zhao would call personal talents (Oprisko 2012a, 2012b). This normal, limited human being is a harbinger of annihilation, "the apocalyptic subject," whose in/action that, in a true Camusian sense, is always both a "no" and a "yes," *is* the symbolic gesture that binds the individual person with the infinition of humanity (Zizek 2011, 395).

MULTIDIMENSIONAL REALITY

Weinstein clearly presents the radically separated being as an individual situated in three domains of specific relational activity: self, others, and material (Weinstein 1985, 10–11). Projects, however, occur within the domain of time, encompassing one's assessment of who one is, reflecting on who one has been, and contemplating whom one ought become (Weinstein 1978). The sovereign individual is authentic and accepts himself in his power and limitation, avoiding ressentiment. Authenticity provides freedom for the individual, placing him within his contexts such that he not only reflects upon his situation with a mind to potentiality and possibility, but also prepares to engage his world in the anticipation of action, the precession of commitment to his unified and indivisible act as a nontransferable being and the "center of originality, responsibility, and choice" (Weinstein 1973, 52). With this first absurd dilemma faced by man, Weinstein begins to conceive of reality as a complex-system of real domains within which authentic actions are taken rather than as singularity. Direct life experience reveals "a oneness that is always changing," a unity in flux (Weinstein 1982, 142).

The unity that is the radically separated individual/person confronts the absurd in all things. Weinstein quotes José Ortega y Gasset, succinctly laying his foundation: "My life is the radical reality" (Weinstein 1985, 10). Living, then, in all of its forms and processes constitutes reality, as radical, complicated, or contradictory as it may be. Philosophy that presents man with how life ought to be is striving to contain life—an impossibility. Life, as we shall see teems with potentiality and possibility; "it is inalienable, insubstitutable, and intransferable" (Weinstein 1985, 27). For Weinstein, man has to confront and engage his world singularly, as a unified individual with a personality. The process of living, of confrontation and engagement, is what constitutes reality, not a mere existence of being. This is what drives Weinstein to focus upon ontology and to eschew metaphysics because *being* is not living and only life is real.

Focusing on the level of analysis as the core of actuality is what Weinstein refers to as the "lived present," a "vital space and time," which is the "context in which the primary responses of the self to its environment are occurring" (Weinstein 1985, 32–33). Life happens within an environment, and within said environment, the self actualizes according to the values that the solitary person has internalized to be important. These values are, to Weinstein, virtues—that which makes personal existence worthwhile—and though they are experienced personally, the concepts are universal and reflect the individual's situation within a lived present.

The vital spaces for man are the natural world, the social world, his personal psyche, and time. The first three are explored within *Finite Perfection*, the last in *Meaning and Appreciation*. Nietzsche sees them as places where the individual person projects his intentions through action in an effort to overcome obstacles; success produces feelings of power. Weinstein adopts Nietzsche's premise but suggests that man need not seek out obstacles in order to attain glory and thus "the good life," but rather may overcome obstacles as they appear, enjoying both virtuous moments and erotic hedonism—finite perfections (Weinstein 1985, 44).

> A virtue may be understood as a perfection of experience, there being three general virtues in correspondence with the three kinds of entities to which the self refers: itself, objects within the environment, and other selves. The perfection of the self to itself is self-control . . . the perfection of the relation of the self to objects in the world is artistry . . . the relation of the self to others selves is perfected by love.
>
> (Weinstein 1985, 44–45)

Life is reality. The agony of uncertainty provides the impetus to drive us forward on a quest to be, realizing ourselves through the culmination of actions and reflecting on the patterns. The authentic individual emerges by embracing reality as life and determining his position as situated in a moment of time and space. In this way, lived experience obeys the Heisenberg uncertainty principle: if he knows where he stands, he cannot know where he's going because once action is initiated, the current moment vanishes and the self is projected into a task. The unity that is the person is a collective that sets forth, purposefully risking everything for one goal until the individual ceases his action for reflection once more.

This view is not new in Weinstein's work; it came before and it has come after. Tracing Weinstein's thoughts leads us invariably back to Max Stirner. Stirner echoes and foreshadows Weinstein's focus on the unity of man as a singularity, "everything I do, think, in short, my expression or manifestation, is indeed conditioned by what I am" (Stirner 1995, 164). For Stirner, man's bag of bones was his reality, his property with the ego as the owner, and his social roles mere spooks that qualify his reality (Stirner 1995, 159–221). Stirner precedes existentialism when he cries out to "raise the value of myself, the value of ownness," to be unconditionally valued and respected—to be a whole person rather than a part, an image of it in action (Stirner 1995, 224–225).

Simmel's engagement with reality is very similar to Weinstein's. He divides lived-reality into "comprehensive provinces of life," which are "everywhere enmeshed in . . . dualism" (Simmel 1964, 16). Simmel's provinces of life are personal, objective, and social.[10] They conform very well to Weinstein's vital spaces: personal/psyche, objective/material, and social. Simmel suggests that man lives always showing two contrasting parties of his self in opposition. For Simmel, life is a "central vitality" that grows out of neither pure optimism nor pure pessimism but from both simultaneously (Simmel 1964, 16). Each action can manifest simultaneously opposed results. He shows that an action of conflict has both integrative and disintegrative forces (Simmel 1964, 16–20). Again, he foreshadows Weinstein, but while both are accurate, neither is comprehensive.

The dyadic form of analysis and dialectic is inherently flawed because it focuses only on diametrically oppositional forces. We can ask ourselves whether this integration and disintegration happens with only two opposed parties, or whether it is more complex than that? Can I, with one action, integrate with multiple others to form stronger unions to varying degrees just as I disintegrate with multiple groups of others to whom I am united? Can I with one action alter my union—strengthening certain bonds and weakening others? Synthesis of multiple theses is inherent within the complexity of lived reality, of province(s) that is/are comprehensive. As the catalyst for change, action emerges as nothing less than the radically altering force that makes a given space comprehensively vital. In order to ascertain the real, it becomes necessary to reject the dialectic in favor of the *multilectic*, or collection of competing theses that produce a synthesis; philosophy must allow for life's complexity in order to present an ontological theory that is comprehensive, parsimonious, and accurate. Rather than to envision life as being in tension between two opposing forces or motivations—to do or not to do, and so forth—it is perhaps best to radicalize Simmel's web of group affiliation. Each individual is a fulcrum point with diverse motivational forces, Buchlerian procepts, and impulses vying for immediate dominance (Buchler 1979, 1995). As the motivational forces wax, the scales tip, the balance shifts, and man acts. Once action is taken, the situation changes and a new status quo emerges. This process is necessarily continuous; however, the action based upon the decision is not necessarily in line with the single dominant force but represents a judgment call regarding the balance as presented at that critical moment.

Zizek echoes the multilectic engagement of man as a radically separated individual who is situated in a complex of realities simultaneously within *The Parallax View*. For Zizek, it is the connections between the subject and its object premised upon observational position and the actions that accord with their nominal values: to subject (submission) and to object (opposition). Every subject is the object to all others; the relationship is mediated by the meaning that links two beings together, though the point of view necessarily alters the ontological markers of who counts as what (Zizek 2006, Location 244 of 7574). He recognizes an "irreducible parallax gap between the ontological and the ontic," emphasizing that "the great Heideggerian political temptation" is "to forget this gap and endeavor to impose an ontic order that would be adequate to the ontological truth" (Zizek 2006, Location 4751 of 7574). Zizek argues against Meillassoux's "naïve ontology of levels: physical reality, life, mind" advocating for an engaged philosophy with a political project (Zizek 2012, 908). Finally, he uses quantum physics to parallel ontological reality as a means by which to premise Heidegger as the appropriate philosophical vehicle from Kant to Hegel; "reality is 'in itself' non-All . . . reality itself is ontologically 'incomplete,' indeterminate . . . it is our very epistemological limitation which locates us in the Real: what appears as the limitation of our knowledge is the feature of reality itself, its 'non-All' " (Zizek 2012, 908).

We, finite beings that we are, must be located in domains of reality because we cannot *be* reality itself. We are not all that is because if we *were* reality writ large, we could no longer engage others as there would be no other; nothing would exist that was not part of the self. We would *be* the field of domains into which diverse parts of our totality would engage one another. The spark of life that distinguishes the conscious awareness of self and existential radical separation propels living beings into a more complex reality than exists for purely material fragments of the universe. "The distinguishing feature of a human as opposed to merely biological life is a meaning that integrates various pursuits and dynamisms" (Weinstein 1978, 25). Man strives to find patterns of meaning and places them within the context of action. The domains of reality that are engaged in the human condition represent the arenas in which man (inter)acts. They include time, materiality, society, and the psyche.

TEMPORAL DOMAIN

"Among many other distinguishing characteristics, human beings are marked off from other creatures by the activity of creating time" (Weinstein 1978, 25). Existential philosophy introduces the multiverse of possible futures. The individual's project is nothing more or less than a personal strategy to alter one's reality from the present less-desirable state to a potential future that includes a more-desirable state. Projects presuppose motivation, and Weinstein suggests that meaning, being placed within the context and holding value not only with contemporaries but holding a position that is valuable and, therefore, valued by those who came before and to those who will come after, is an activity that transcends any single individual will. Time, and one's position in it, is negotiable, not while navigating through it as a domain of action but in shaping the reality of a self with regard to the narrative of one's holistic contribution within particular domains.

There is, therefore, an uncertainty principle similar to that for which Heisenberg is famous. Man can either consider where he is at within a given [set of] domain(s) or he can project himself into a domain in order to alter the inertial progress of the domain and his meaning within it. Therefore, man cannot know with any certainty both where he stands in a particular domain and where he is going. He may either strive for clarity regarding the value that others inscribe upon him and thus his meaning as value or he may seek to persuade others to perceive him as embodying a particular value and thus gain meaning that he feels is lacking, whether that is a correct sentiment or not (Kornprobst 2011).

Zizek argues that Heidegger's greatest achievement is "the full elaboration of finitude as a positive constituent of being-human . . . finitude is the key to the transcendental human. A human being is always on the way toward itself, in becoming . . . far from limiting him, this exposure is the very ground of the emergence of the universe of meaning" (Zizek 2006, Location 4724 of 7574). As Sartre illuminates, individuals are trapped in a nontransferable presentation of awareness that is linked to a corporeal, material form (Sartre 2007).[11] Although the progression through time is, as of yet, constant and decidedly moving forward, the historic self is negotiable. There are lies that individuals incorporate into the narrative of their social relational-identities that emerge as social-truths without being social-facts. One's past presents difficulties, but not necessarily limitations on our present and may not limit the self as project. Our epistemology is not necessarily different from either Descartes or Bohr here, as factual statements regarding the past are premised upon observations that reflect the best theory of how to comprehend our reality and the best practice of how to assess vital statistics of valuable evaluative descriptors of an object or life-form (Oprisko 2012a).

Similarly, the future is filled with numerous possible future presentations of the self in variation from miniscule to massive (Pratchett 2002).[12] As we desire to change our present circumstances for the future so as to alter the meaning that we have within the domains we project, we decide upon how to cultivate the myth of our own existence, and we must negotiate these alterations with others upon whom our desired future-selves hinge. The alteration of identity requires that others so identify an individual as such in order to grant them the benefits and honors of said relational position. Academics know this only too well; we are our production of work, and said work must be peer reviewed in order to be included in the body of work that counts toward the defense of claiming the identity of an academic. In fact, one may work toward the goal of being a professor and have others arbitrarily deny the attainment of said identity, thus denying the individual the right to claim such an identity regardless of the work that he has done; the activity of the self represents nothing more than an argument that may or may not be found to be persuasive by others who may or may not be receptive to such persuasiveness. There are multiple futures in which this sentence was never written, this paper never presented, and you the reader skipped ahead of this sentence for reasons ranging from boredom to an emergency phone call or the distraction of an attractive passerby.

MATERIAL DOMAIN

Systemic forces rule the material world. We study them via the natural sciences. Chemical, biological, and physical limitations ground the flights and fancies of all living creatures, including man. The material domain evokes the political realism within consciousness, ascribing significance to that which man does not and cannot control. Anxiety over this lack of control floods the cognition of man and politicizes the world: that which is me [ego] versus that which is other [alter]. When extrapolated into groups, us reflects the ego and them the alter, but this is nothing more than the continuous (re)drawing of lines in the sand. Weinstein's material reality is rooted in Stirnerian egoism; he sees us as concrete, durational beings.

It becomes impossible to grasp reality as a whole because of its totality. The finitude of man's existence presents a problematic to skillfully articulating what is and what is not. The struggle to encapsulate everything into one abstraction has led some thinkers to reject parts of it as mere illusion or as fantasy. Max Stirner's wrestling match with reality becomes apparent in a deep reading of "The Owner." He begins with a confrontation between man as he is and man as a concept (Stirner 1995, 155–166). Stirner is experiencing life encapsulated and limited by his corporeal self, the self through which he encounters the world around him. He rejects the conception of man as a "spook" and posits himself as un-man which contains, "my quality, my own and inherent in me; so that man is nothing else than my humanity, my human existence, and everything that I do is human precisely because I do it, but not because it corresponds to the concept 'man' " (Stirner 1995, 150). Stirner's man is un-man because of his finite self, because he does not and cannot measure up to the image of Christ that is the exemplar par excellence of man.

Stirner's separation of his self from the ideal image is the first division of reality for man. He acknowledges that the separation is conceptual and limited because he remains un-man as well as man:

> I am really man and un-man in one; for I am a man and at the same time more than a man; I am the ego of this my mere quality. . . . Against the egoists "human society" is wrecked; for they no longer have to deal with each other as men, but appear egoistically as an *I* against a *You* altogether different from me and in opposition to me. . . . Therefore we two, the state and I, are enemies. I, the egoist, have not at heart the welfare of this "human society." I sacrifice nothing to it, I only utilize it; but to be able to utilize it completely I transform it rather into my property and my creature; that is, I annihilate it, and form in its place the Union of Egoists.
>
> (Stirner 1995, 159–161)

Stirner rails against the rules on life dictated to him by others defended by the aegis of society. He despises those who stand crowded together within the group as failing to grasp the truth of life in its base, nontransferable materialism. However, by rejecting the spooks and spectres of the social realms, Stirner's materialism helps to illuminate the primacy of dualism, especially when he states that to cut off his hand is to alter the extent of his ownness, as the hand would no longer be something he owns. The importance of vitality and life-in-the-present emerges as the central theme to Stirner's paradigm—man is nothing more than his bag of bones, but the bag of bones is negotiable and does not diminish the vitality of man.

Strict materialism divides the world/universe into two realms, the interiority of the self, one's physical manifestation versus the exterior forces of other beings and systems that limit the individual will and absolute egoism. Artistry is Weinstein's virtue within the material domain, valuing the material that one finds and engaging it to the best of one's ability, however limited one may be.

SOCIAL DOMAIN(S)

There are multiple social worlds within which each person is forced to act (Oprisko 2012a). Weinstein finds social realities to be confining, limiting possibility away from a comprehensive intrahistory in favor of the official history of each group: "From the outside I may appear to be a point on a probability distribution, an exemplification of a social character, or a bundle of group affiliations" (Weinstein 1977, 22). According to Oprisko, individuals are affiliates and/or members of groups with whom they identify and are inscribed with value. The archetypes of interaction—individual to individual, individual to group, and group to group—form the relational identities including the inscribed expectations that derive from cultural norms associated with particular relationship types.

Meaning is paramount. A person cannot be something unless he is that something to other(s) (Weinstein 1978; Weinstein and Weinstein 1978). To cultivate and hold onto an identity requires that an individual form a relationship and then persuade others to ascribe to that particular vision of reality, that particular form of social organization. As Kornprobst suggests, there is a continuous (re)negotiation of social relationships predicated on experience and engagement wherein individuals seek to be as persuasive as possible and seek for others to be as receptive as possible to them (Kornprobst 2011). Herein lies the contestation of Nietzsche's blonde beasts, each seeking to shape the world in their image, trying to will their ideal reality into power (Nietzsche 1968, 1989; Petersen 1999). Power in this sense is socially manifested, which means that the individual must have power over something else, internalizing that which is other into the self.

The social nature of power illuminates both the symbiotic nature of relationships and the parasitic nature of political authority. Political authority is a form of power wielded by an individual or group that claims sovereignty over others. To be sovereign, one must be exceptional. To be exceptional is to stand out/apart from the crowd, to be a border-savage. This requires that there be a crowd to which one belongs and from which one seeks to escape. There can be no separation of the individual without the mass; one cannot be superior without inferiors in abundance around them (Prozorov 2005). Absolute docility is improbable to achieve and even less likely to be indefinitely maintained. Thus there is a need to incentivize docility through rewarding citizens for displaying excellence (for the seminal engagement with docile bodies, see Foucault 1995).

The democratization of excellence comes with the increasing complexity of society. As individuals specialize and as greater feats of prowess are cataloged as societal goods, citizens enjoy a greater ability to distinguish themselves vis-à-vis one another, allowing for larger opportunities to be great in small ways. Adherence to structural authority and its norms, "The citizen . . . has become a constituent and a receptor of rewards and punishments programmed by a hierarchy" (Weinstein 1995, 110). Hierarchy is navigated by unique individuals who comprise humanity, allowing the seemingly concretized structure to show its lack of integrity. In a Badiouian sense, using his set theory, humanity would be the universal category to which all groups and individuals that ever have existed and ever might exist would belong (Badiou

2005). At the other end of the spectrum there are individuals, unique presentations of humanity that operate as radically separated beings but are not individually divisible; they must each act as a holistic entity. They are the particular elements of society, including no other persons within them (or they would lead a group) but belonging to numerous groups that both compete with and nest inside others like warring matryoshka dolls. The groups themselves are negotiable as they are navigable; they exist as the extensions of the egoistic selves of human individuals and reflect their identitarian pluralism (Prozorov 2009).

The multiple overlapping presentations of social reality are derived from the cognitive engagement between lived individuals and their realms of interaction (Badiou 2009). No groups are inherently necessary, none must manifest, but the void presents nothing less than limitless potential to shape and create reality moment by moment (Prozorov 2012). Social reality is the ontology of category theory, determined not as being qua being but being as action, relation, or movement. It is always already in a perpetual state of flux (Badiou 2014; Oprisko 2013). The maintenance of social reality is at the mercy of individual will(s) that seek to reshape it as each individual dances the line between the absolute persuasiveness of a blonde beast and the absolute receptivity of an automaton. The desire to shape is dependent upon the projects that individuals create for themselves as they seek to alter the world as it is into a world they wish to be.

Love is Weinstein's social virtue. It is unidirectional and must be given without any hope of return. It is a Camusian act of rebellion against nihilism, actively willing away one's will in exchange for that of one's loved one—purposefully sacrificing the ego's will to power for the alter's. Love is an act of appreciation, which Weinstein argues is the transcendence over our ambiguity of the other's existence and is used to "express one another to ourselves" (Weinstein 1978, 127).

PSYCHIC DOMAIN

Being what one desires is difficult. Not only is humanity sundered into individual humans, each of whom have their own interpretation of what ought to be, but each human is often also of several minds about what the constitutes The Good. We are torn. As Weinstein puts it, "From the inside, I experience myself as a series of critical choices between my will to actualize and appreciate contradictory ends and my desire to act to help others realize values" (Weinstein 1977, 22). We experience ourselves through our eyes and others, and we seek to shape the images of our engagement. We make being ourselves into a lifelong series of projects.

Cultivating who we are now is impossible. The present is always immediate and there is no possibility for using persuasion to change this momentary state of affairs. Happily, the future is not foreordained, and we may seek to alter our actions and/or the perception of our actions in the eyes of others in order to bring the vision of our ideal self closer to fruition. Sartre suggests that our character is represented by the totality of our actions over time (Sartre 2007). Weinstein believes that "Character becomes intellectualized to the point that it is an image even to its maker" (Weinstein 1970, 207).

Our bag of bones is the draft animal of our unending plans, carrying out our will and dragging our psyche along the way. Weinstein appropriately calls us *concrete durational beings*, stating that we "can only will the mysticism of life in the optative mood: May it not happen that I neglect the other voices that might be raised within me. Yes these voices are constantly being muffled in the process of projecting a *persona* into the past-present-future" (Weinstein 1978, 122).

As we move inexorably forward in time, our consciousness engages with the self as a multiplicity; memories of the past are judged according to present circumstances just as future projects are gauged by a mind that can only estimate likely scenarios. The self falls short as the ideal model of how we wish we were because we suffer our weaknesses and endure our limitations as we revel in our strengths and celebrate our talents. As mentioned earlier, failure to attain the ideal is our reality. Forming ideal images of the self and the self's desired situation and position in time, space, and relationships is the foundation of psychic reality. Weinstein lists self-control as his virtue for this domain; the good is found by balancing the self by the self and by not seeking out absolutes or extremes.

STRING THEORY

Simmel was correct, to a degree, with his choice of the web to illustrate how groups affiliate with one another. The complex weaving of individuals into groups, group with group, and group within group provokes the thought of a tangled interplay of identification woven together and composing the whole of humanity within societies. To understand this visual representation, we must begin with the component parts.

If humanity exists in the abstract and humans exist corporeally, it is perhaps best to define the corporeal and allow it to illuminate the abstract. Individual humans are unique presentations of life, but they are defined via relations. As discussed previously, the definition is produced socially through continuous processes of persuasion and reception between the individual and those he interacts with. It is, therefore, relationships that bind individuals together and form the fabric of social and political reality.

The most simplistic relationship is of singular affiliation, a connection with only one facet to it. The connection that links individual to individual in this singular way can be imagined as a harp string, run from individual to individual. This pure form of relationship would, when plucked, resonate with the pure tone of a single note. Complex relationships, where individuals relate to one another in multiple ways, function similarly; the number of strings increases and sound summoned forth becomes more complex. Notes become chords, there may be harmonic and disharmonic overtones. However, the fundamental concept of human connection via social interaction remains.

If we think of each individual as a string, formed and framed by their simple and complex relational identities, each identity may be more or less important or impactful at a given moment dependent upon the spatial and temporal location of the interacting individuals.

> Each of their identities' individual fiber strands, some thicker and more obvious and some thinner, some almost non-existent at times, some denser and more important to the individual's sense of self, such that the honorableness of the individual's relation to a particular identity could be measured in denier or tex. As the individuals' lives proceed, as their thread lengthens, the strands of their thread wax and wane. Some strands disappear and new strands begin twisting within the thread that makes up the social totality of the individual.
>
> (Oprisko 2012a, 155)

As groups are composed of individuals, the fabric of their reality is a weave of individuals' threads. Social reality is nothing less than the interplay of individuals as they relate to one another; it can only be accurately framed in terms of relational identity, in terms of similarity and difference. The fibers that constitute the weaves of social fabric are not monopolized by any particular group's cloth; the individuals whose identities form that cloth also form the fabric of other groups. As Weinstein points out, it approximates James's pluralistic universe where "all components are related to some others but none is linked to all of the others" (Weinstein 1995, 101). However, the web itself is comprehensive; individual patterns of life connect disparate groups together. The cloths of groups linked together, representing meta-societies, generate the patterns that make up the tartans of civilizations. The social sciences examine these cloths and describe their unique qualities.

The vision of civilization and the cacophony of interaction resonate through time as well as space. As individuals seek critical distance from which to view the world, they look back in time: the further away one is, the further back one sees. Similar to the viewing of stars in the night sky, each heavenly body is a specific distance away, and we, mere concrete durational beings that we are, occupy a mere point in the space-time continuum. Each concrete moment for us contains the vision of plural histories. We see each star as it was and is no longer; the present moment in time contains beautiful visions of the fiction that is my radical reality. Stars I see today and will perceive to exist until my death may have already exploded into supernova.

We are inextricably linked to the universals by being particular elements. We cannot remove ourselves from being simultaneously radically entangled and radically separated from one another. We must relate to one another in groups as failed attempts to bind humans into humanity. Our lived reality is vital and failure to realize a universal harmony of interests in action.

Thus we return to the divestment of Decartes for Pascal and Bohr. The world, the universe, is a necessary combination of stuff and space, things and the void that separates them. However, distance is relative, and the further away you go, the smaller the void between objects. The void is where the music of interaction plays, where the component parts form and frame the universe. However, it takes the separation of the void to define the limits of the component pieces and to represent the space within which they act.

This is politics. All that binds us and separates us, that brings us closer and pushes us apart—the acts of relating—is the political. Globality, the "end state of globalization," is already here (Yergin 1998). Humanity, from the dawn of its existence until its twilight, has been and will continue to be linked by the interactivity between individuals. The difference is that the meaning has changed on an epic scale—the space that separates us from one another is less meaningful because it feels smaller. Globality is not an act of becoming but a reality premised on the recognition of our simultaneous radical separation and entanglement, of life being a complex of opposites (Sirkin, Hemerling, and Bhattacharya 2008). The world is both identitarian pluralistic and generically universal. The world is humanity and the humans that comprise it. It is all of our overlapping realities happening simultaneously, and it is affects us as we affect it. It is what we have done, what we are doing, and what we do next. What will we do next?

NOTES

1. Appropriately, the bodies are buried in the footnotes. Just as there is no theory program at Purdue University, where there is arguably a very productive school of political thought, so the systems of domination and oppression enter the manner in which we as scholars approach our discipline. We cultivate our world, tending a garden in which we plant ourselves.
2. Love-piracy is a method for extracting the best ideas of a thinker and taking them as one's own. It provides the philosopher with the ability to write with enhanced precision and without the shackles of the ideology or paradigm to which it is attached.
3. I owe a debt of gratitude to Sergei Prozorov (2007) for providing the inspiration for this work in his "unfaithful" interpretation of Foucault.
4. I would like to thank Michael Weinstein for his mentorship and guidance in the creation of this work, especially for providing several highly precise concepts that he is currently employing.
5. Adorno's pointed critique of jargon is a marvelous presentation of the difficulty of escaping said jargon. His argument against jargon is filled with said jargon!
6. Carl Schmitt's political ontology is highly useful for understanding the political implications of Barad. His seminal works, *The Concept of the Political*, trans. George Schwab (Chicago, IL: University of Chicago Press, 1996); and

Political Theology: Four Chapters on the Concept of Sovereignty, trans. George Schwab (Chicago, IL: University of Chicago Press, 2005) clearly show that identification, agency, distinction, and exceptionalism are features of sovereignty.

7. Weinstein uses "realm of action" as a more precise term for "level of analysis" and focuses on "complete human action" in lieu of "units of analysis." I find that these phenomenal changes more appropriately reflect Bohrian epistemology.

8. A portion of this section was previously included in "Failure as the Real: A Review of Slavoj Zizek's Less Than Nothing: Hegel and the Shadow of Dialectical Materialism," *Theoria and Praxis* 1, no. 2 (2014).

9. For Zizek's full treatment of parallax, see The Parallax View, ed. Slavoj Zizek, Kindle ed., Short Circuits (Cambridge: MIT Press, 2006).

10. This footnote on page 16 of *Conflict* has made the largest impression on me of all of his works. Within it he constructs an argument for vital life as reality mired in conflict with the hope of union and finds the absurdity to be refreshing rather than agonizing. I am continually amazed by the power of footnotes.

11. Suicide is an option, according to the existentialists, to absolutely reject one's unique existence, but such nihilism is an act of authentic engagement to disengage oneself from the responsibility of being a role model of mankind.

12. Terry Pratchett's L-Space, a theoretical system of libraries that contains all books that have been, are, or could possibly be written, is an excellent example of this engagement with time. It is detailed well in *The Science of Discworld*.

REFERENCES

Adorno, Theodore. *The Jargon of Authenticity*. Translated by Knut Tarnowski and Frederic Will. Routledge Classics. New York, NY: Routledge, 2003.

Badiou, Alain. *Being and Event*. Translated by Oliver Feltham. London, UK: Continuum, 2005.

———. *Logics of Worlds*. Translated by Alberto Toscano. London, UK: Continuum, 2009.

———. *Mathematics of the Transcendental*. Translated by A. J. Bartlett and Alex Ling. Kindle ed. London, UK: Bloomsbury, 2014.

Barad, Karen. *Meeting the Universe Halfway: Quantum Physics and the Entanglement of Matter and Meaning*. Kindle ed. Durham, NC: Duke University Press, 2007.

———. "Posthumanist Performativity: Toward an Understanding of How Matter Comes to Matter." *Gender and Science* 28, no. 3 (2003): 801–31.

Buchler, Justus. *Nature and Judgment*. New York, NY: Columbia University Press, 1955.

———. *Toward a General Theory of Human Judgment*. 2nd ed. New York, NY: Dover, 1979.

Cassirer, Ernst. *An Essay on Man: An Introduction to a Philosophy on Human Culture*. New Haven, CT: Yale University Press, 1944.

Churchland, Patricia. *Brain-Wise: Studies in Neurophilosophy*. Cambridge, MA: MIT Press, 2002.

———. *Braintrust: What Neuroscience Tells Us About Morality*. Princeton, NJ: Princeton University Press, 2011.

———. *Neurophilosophy: Toward a Unified Science of the Mind-Brain*. Cambridge, MA: MIT Press, 1986.

Churchland, Paul M. *Matter and Consciousness: A Contemporary Introduction to the Philosophy of Mind*. Revised ed. Cambridge, MA: MIT Press, 1999.

———. *Plato's Camera: How the Physical Brain Captures a Landscape of Abstract Universals*. Cambridge, MA: MIT Press, 2012.

Davis, Murray S. "Georg Simmel and the Aesthetics of Social Reality." *Social Forces* 51, no. 3 (1973): 320–29.

Foucault, Michel. *The Archaeology of Knowledge and the Discourse on Language*. Translated by A. M. Sheridan Smith. New York, NY: Pantheon Books, 1982.

———. *Discipline and Punish* [in French]. Translated by Alan Sheridan. Vintage ed. New York, NY: Random House, 1995.

Kornprobst, Markus. "The Agent's Logic of Action: Defining and Mapping Political Judgement." *International Theory* 3, no. 1 (2011): 70–104.

Luhmann, Niklas. *Theories of Distinction: Redescribing the Descriptions of Modernity*. Translated by Joseph O'Neil, Elliott Schreiber, Kerstin Behnke, and William Whobrey. Stanford, CA: Stanford University Press, 2002.

Nancy, Jean-Luc. *Being Singular Plural*. Translated by Robert D. Richardson and Anne E. O'Byrne. Crossing Aesthetics. Edited by Werner Hamacher and David E. Wellbery Stanford, CA: Stanford University Press, 2000.

Nietzsche, Friedrich. *On the Genealogy of Morals and Ecce Homo*. Translated by Walter Kaufmann. New York, NY: Vintage Books, 1989.

———. *The Will to Power* [in German]. Translated by Walter Kaufmann and R. J. Hollingdale. Vintage Books ed. New York, NY: Random House, Inc., 1968.

Oprisko, Robert L. "Entropy Versus Thought Traditions: I. R. Theory Isn't Dead Yet." In *IR Theory and Practice*, edited by Robert W. Murray. London, UK: e-International Relations, 2014a. www.e-ir.info/2014/06/16/entropy-versus-thought-traditions-ir-theory-isnt-dead-yet/

———. "Failure as the Real: A Review of Slavoj Zizek's *Less Than Nothing*: Hegel and the Shadow of Dialectical Materialism." *Theoria and Praxis* 1, no. 2 (2014b).

———. *Honor: A Phenomenology*. Routledge Innovations in Political Theory. New York, NY: Routledge, 2012a.

———. "I. R. Theory's 21st Century Experiential Evolution." *e-International Relations* (2013). Published electronically May 25, 2013. www.e-ir.info/2013/05/25/the-fall-of-the-state-and-the-rise-of-the-individuals-ir-theorys-21st-century-experiential-evolution/.

———. "The Rebel as Sovereign: The Political Theology of Dignity." *Revista Pleyade*, no. 9 (June 2012b): 119–36.

Petersen, Ulrik Enemark. "Breathing Nietzsche's Air: New Reflections on Morgenthau's Concepts of Power and Human Nature." *Alternatives: Global, Local, Political* 24, no. 1 (1999): 83–118.

Pratchett, Terry. *The Science of Discworld*. Kindle ed. New York, NY: Random House, 2002.

Prozorov, Sergei. *Foucault, Freedom, and Sovereignty*. Burlington, VT: Ashgate, 2007.

———. "Generic Universalism in World Politics: Beyond International Anarchy and the World State." *International Theory* 1, no. 2 (2009): 215–48.

———. *Ontology and World Politics: Void Universalism I*. Interventions. Edited by Jenny Edkins and Nick Vaughan-Williams. New York, NY: Routledge, 2014.

———. *Theory of the Political Subject: Void Universalism II*. Interventions. Edited by Jenny Edkins and Nick Vaughan-Williams. New York, NY: Routledge, 2014.

———. "What Is the 'World' in World Politics? Heidegger, Badiou, and Void Universalism." *Contemporary Political Theory*, no. 12 (2013): 102–122.

———. "X/Xs: Toward a General Theory of the Exception." *Alternatives* 30, no. 1 (2005): 81–112.

Publick, Jackson, and Doc Hammer. "Home Insecurity (DVD Commentary)." *The Venture Bros.—Season 1* (2006).

Rosen, Lea. "'I'm Not a Boy Adventurer Anymore': Success and 'Failure' in *The Venture Bros.*" *Journal of Venture Studies* 1 (2012): 1–8.

Sartre, Jean-Paul. *Existentialism Is a Humanism.* New Haven, CT: Yale University Press, 2007.

Schmitt, Carl. *The Concept of the Political.* Translated by George Schwab. Chicago, IL: University of Chicago Press, 1996.

———. *Political Theology: Four Chapters on the Concept of Sovereignty.* Translated by George Schwab. Chicago, IL: University of Chicago Press, 2005.

———. *Roman Catholicism and Political Form.* Translated by G. L. Ulmen. Westport, CT: Greenwood Press, 1996.

Simmel, Georg. *Conflict and the Web of Group-Affiliations.* Translated by Kurt H. Wolff and Reinhard Bendix. New York, NY: The Free Press, 1964.

Sirkin, Harold L., Jim Hemerling, and Arindam Bhattacharya. "Globality: The World Beyond Globalization." *BCG Perspectives* (2008). www.bcgperspectives.com/content/Classics/globalization_strategy_globality_the_world_beyond_globalization/.

Stirner, Max. *The Ego and Its Own.* Cambridge Texts in the History of Political Thought. Edited by Raymond Geuss and Quentin Skinner. Cambridge, UK: Cambridge University Press, 1995.

Weinstein, Deena, and Michael A. Weinstein. "An Existential Approach to Society: Active Transcendence." *Human Studies* 1, no. 1 (1978): 38–47.

———. "On the Possibility of Society: Classical Sociological Thought." *Human Studies* 5, no. 1 (1982): 1–12.

———. *Postmodern(ized) Simmel.* Routledge Revivals. New York, NY: Routledge, 2011.

Weinstein, Michael A. *Culture/Flesh: Explorations of Postcivilized Modernity.* Social Philosophy Research Institute. Edited by John A. Loughney. Lanham, MD: Rowman & Littlefield, 1995.

———. *Finite Perfection: Reflections on Virtue.* Amherst, MA: University of Massachusetts Press, 1985.

———. *Meaning and Appreciation: Time and Modern Political Life.* Google E-book ed. West Lafayette, IN: Purdue University Press, 1978.

———. "New Ways and Old to Talk Politics." *The Review of Politics* 35, no. 1 (1973): 41–60.

———. "Politics and Moral Consciousness." *Midwest Journal of Political Science* 14, no. 2 (1970): 183–215.

———. *The Structure of Human Life: A Vitalist Ontology.* New York, NY: New York University Press, 1979.

———. *The Tragic Sense of Political Life.* Columbia, SC: University of South Carolina Press, 1977.

———. *The Wilderness and the City: American Classical Philosophy as a Moral Quest.* Amherst, MA: University of Massachusetts Press, 1982.

Yergin, Daniel. "The Age of "Globality." *Newsweek* 131, no. 20 (1998): 28.

Zizek, Slavoj. *Less Than Nothing: Hegel and the Shadow of Dialectical Materialism.* Brooklyn, NY: Verso, 2012.

———. *Living in the End Times.* Kindle ed. New York, NY: Verso, 2011.

———. *The Parallax View.* Short Circuits. Edited by Slavoj Zizek. Kindle ed. Cambridge, MA: MIT Press, 2006.

Part II
Contemplation

4   This Flesh Belongs to Me
Michael Weinstein and Max Stirner

Justin Mueller

INTRODUCTION

Following Plato, Western philosophy has been predominantly occupied with the pursuit of crafting enduring symbolic substitutes for immediate and limited lived experience. The unseemly and irreducible particularities of discrete individuals have historically fallen by the theoretical wayside or, more accurately, been intentionally buried there. In a powerfully contrasting affirmation of finite, conflictual life, Michael Weinstein develops throughout his work a sophisticated, process-oriented "critical vitalism" for "concrete durational beings" to use toward furthering their own self-understanding and self-direction in the world. To this end, Weinstein draws from a variety of more recognizable process philosophers, naturalists, and vitalists, including Henri Bergson, Miguel de Unamuno, William James, Samuel Alexander, and Josiah Royce. He also, however, draws critical inspiration from the oft-neglected nineteenth-century figure of Max Stirner. From Stirner, Weinstein takes and adapts the concept of "ownness," deploying it as a critical reflective position to be dwelt in when assessing, critiquing, and revising one's own axiology and orientation toward the world.

Weinstein's use of Stirner's concept of ownness is significant in two major respects. First, it provides a powerful support for the "critical" aspect of Weinstein's project of critical vitalism. Stirner's "ruthless" (Weinstein 1978, 84) and reflexive phenomenological tools provide a means of assessing and analyzing the makeup of one's values, belief systems, and composite worldview. Second, it provides a more practicable and positive conceptual framework (though certainly not the only possible one) for Stirner's ideas than Stirner himself provided, balancing out the preponderantly "critical" orientation of Stirner's work. The precise manner in which this is accomplished will be discussed more fully later.

This chapter will begin by providing a general overview of Weinstein's project of critical vitalism, sketching its major concerns, concepts, and aims. Then it will provide a brief introduction to Stirner and his work, with a partial focus on his concept of ownness and the role it plays in Stirner's thought. Next it will elaborate on how Weinstein appropriates and integrates Stirner's concept of ownness into his overall project and explore the consequences of this for understanding both Weinstein and Stirner's projects. Finally it will position this innovation and its significance within current philosophical literature.

WEINSTEIN'S PHILOSOPHY

Weinstein's philosophy of "critical vitalism" provides a sharp and powerful contrast with much of the Western philosophical tradition. Following the classical vitalists, critical vitalism presents a strident "partisanship in favor of life" (Weinstein 1979, ix). Life in this context, however, is not to be confused with the simple biological phenomenon (10). Rather, following Henri Bergson's method of intuition especially, it is an inquiry into the experience and structure of being but "grasped from within a body, by a particular organism or self" (ix). Weinstein's vitalism is "critical" in that it restricts its inquiry to the evidence acquired from this intuitional, embodied experience of being. It avoids "metaphysical speculation" and is separated from the turn of the early twentieth century's "classical" vitalist metaphysical concept of an *élan vital* lying dynamically at the heart of all life (ibid.). In its stead, critical vitalism focuses on desire, not as something we "have" but rather as a constitutive, driving element of our very being. Desire or want (11) is especially important for understanding the finite, processual, unique, concrete, and irresolvably "polemical" nature of our being (9) as well as our struggles to identify and understand ourselves and each other and act on all of this in a social context (2).

Rather than macropolitical blueprints or prophecies, Weinstein's critical vitalism gives us philosophical tools at hand for understanding and living life. It is not directed toward the abstract "us" of the Royal We, the People, or the Nation but rather the you and I who read these words, feel that breeze, or crave the touch or recognition of another. Neither are his life tools hidden yokes intended to bind us to a thinly veiled "higher" calling or purpose to which we must defer and pay homage (perhaps even the price of our finite lives, in life or death). Nor are they Procrustean hammers or shears, aiming to stretch, carve, or break individuals until they fit the aesthetic demanded by an abstract ideal or the plans and values of an authoritative institutional apparatus. Both old and new philosophers of state have plied their trade with these tools. They have filled libraries with apologies for dominion, social homogenization, and abstraction from the inexhaustible particularity of real living beings. They have worked very hard at disregarding, diminishing, or absorbing the bodies of flesh-and-blood beings into "contrived systems of transpersonal meaning" and, at their worst, "[reducing] human beings to mere instruments in a social order composed by complex hierarchical organizations" (Weinstein 1978, 132) and suppressing inconveniently ill-fitting experiences and uniqueness through an "intellectual terror" that "goes hand-in-hand with the physical terror of totalitarian regimes" (135).

Even at its most benign, politics (once shorn of its legitimating trappings and fictions) is ultimately still "the process of deciding what will be allowed into space and what will be excluded from it" (137). This process pertains to social control, to competing concerns for and struggles over where people and things belong, to one's "place" in a stratified social distribution *vis-à-vis* others, and to whether some persons are "in" or "outside" a collective distribution of social roles and parts at all. Political life is an unavoidable part of collective human experience, and Weinstein does not argue otherwise; he is not positing an idealized individualist order that can truly divest itself from struggle and conflict over values and power. But, premised as it is on the "denial of complexity" at a basic level, political life and thus political thought (at least in their traditional systemic, reductive, and formalistic approaches) are necessarily incapable of incorporating the "concrete durational being" of flesh and blood as their subject of analysis. While certainly not ignoring or attempting to negate the political, Weinstein's critical vitalism embraces a recognition of its limitations and sets about attempting to reclaim and bring to light the real "concrete durational beings" that are hidden or engulfed by conventional social and political theory while simultaneously reanalyzing the (conventionally) political from this vantage point of individuated, embodied, lived experience.

The primary methods that Weinstein explicitly uses to guide his inquiries draw from the works of Henri Bergson and Miguel de Unamuno, two classical vitalists writing at the beginning of the twentieth century. Driven by persistent, productive, and sometimes painful suspicions regarding the adequacy of our views of ourselves and the world, both Bergson and Unamuno sought to better explain lived human experience and consciousness and shared the "project of vindicating our existence" against proponents of reductive and mechanistic scientisms,[1] as well as metaphysical idealisms and historical teleologies (Weinstein 1979, 39). Each of them, through his own unique theoretical innovations, attempted to get behind or below the veneer of conventional life perspectives, assumptions, and modes of living in order to bring submerged and ignored life processes to the fore.

From Bergson, Weinstein borrows the method of "intuition" (Weinstein 1978, 56). Bergsonian intuition is not simply a gut feeling, a hunch, a sudden insight, or a moment of Zen-like *satori* (let alone a flash of divine inspiration) as with the colloquial uses of the term. These everyday meanings do suggest part of what Bergsonian intuition embraces and attempts to uncover—a better glimpse into the real nature of things, especially into "what makes our everyday life possible" (133). They are limited, however, in the accidental and passive character through which such insight is supposedly achieved. Conventionally, one is set upon by an intuition as if one were the unexpected recipient of an urgent secret from an anonymous messenger. Bergson's intuition, on the other hand, is far more deliberate and directed than any of these other meanings of the term suggest. Not only is it intentional, it takes a substantial amount of effort, involving the highly "unnatural act" of abandoning and inverting (at least temporarily) the consistencies, order, and solidity of the conventional, "practical" viewpoint under which we all normally operate (Weinstein 1978, 57).

One of the major points of Bergson's philosophy is the observation that time and space are constantly being conflated and confused, not simply in terms of our understanding of the ontological character of the universe but throughout our everyday experiences. Time (understood as *durée*, not "clock time"), for Bergson, is the force of change and newness itself. It is heterogeneous and is the "ground" of immediate lived experience. Space, on the other hand, is homogeneous. It is not simply a given dimension of the world but involves an "act of the mind" that places and juxtaposes some objects within an imagined homogeneous medium (Bergson 2001, 94).[2] Imposing this homogeneous medium onto the world entails a conversion, then, of time into space, of difference into sameness, and change into stability. Language, identity, and much of thought itself depend on the "spatialization" of time—our imposition of a simplified, ordered homogeneity over and in the place of the radical difference inherent to the processes of time and the world itself. We invest a lot of personal psychological energy in the maintenance of these "symbolic substitutes" for the complexity and "confusion" of reality (Bergson 2001, 139). They give us a sense of security, direction, and value for our lives and are necessary for us to actively live at all.[3] Social life, Bergson admits, can only exist through the generation of some shared perception of homogeneous space. It requires the construction of a "practical viewpoint"—especially a sense of being "a part of" something in common, shared expectations for behavior, and the upholding of conventional myths that consolidate these homogenizing procedures—in lieu of the radical mutability, particularity, and heterogeneity comprising real individuals and their complex relations with each other. Nevertheless, always remaining comfortably within the practical viewpoint leads to "difficulty after difficulty" when attempting to actually understand our lives (139). It also entails potentially problematic consequences for our attempts to live them. Consequently, Bergson offers intuition as a method that attempts to look behind the "thinly woven veil" of conventions that we depend on to sustain our day-to-day routines and that structure social and political life. Intuition entails a rigorous inversion of the practical viewpoint. It attempts to momentarily reestablish perceptions of duration, time, and processes of change in lieu of our impositions of stability, sameness, and space in order to better understand our experiences and, perhaps more importantly, help us orient the direction of our lives.

From Unamuno, Weinstein makes use of the method of "agonic doubting" (Weinstein 1979, 4). This form of introspection and visceral doubting of one's own existence is consciously used by Unamuno in the spirit of René Descartes. Descartes posed a question mark toward all objects of human experience, bringing a "methodical doubt" to bear against not only the precepts of beliefs and the validity of claims about the world but also against the accuracy of our own senses. Yet ultimately, his doubting floundered once he approached the shores of his own existence, and Descartes found himself clinging to the dry ground of his (in)famous *cogito*. He had "allowed himself the luxury of doubting the world but paid the price of remaining self-confident" in the solidity and unity of his own being and the necessity of obedience to "convention and authority" (Weinstein 1979, 4–5). Unamuno, however, makes no such compromises or assumptions of secure foundations in his visceral and totalizing "self-inquisition." Rooted in nascent doubts about the accuracy of his own self-understanding, the recognition of the possibility that "I may not be who I tell myself that I am," the tendrils of Unamuno's agonized doubting crept relentlessly inward. Ultimately, these doubts extended to "the bottom of the abyss," carrying with them Unamuno's comforting beliefs about the world, his certainty in his own existence and his ability to comprehend it, his confidence in the authenticity of his own motives for doubting, and thus even his ability to be confident that he was truly doubting in good faith at all rather than feigning doubt for unknown or suppressed motives or drives (5).

Rather than an implicitly reserved, conditional, and formalistic Cartesian doubting that balks at its own doorsteps, agonic doubting serves as a driving motive for Weinstein's inquiries into the structure of human experience. When carried out fully, it "opens up subjective insecurity and brings forth the person," revealing the unique autobiography and constitution of the self-inquisitor (5). At the bottom of his abyss and undergirding his beliefs about himself and the world, Unamuno discovered his own unremitting "hunger for immortality" (Weinstein 1978, 86–88).

> I do not want to die—no; I neither want to die nor do I want to want to die; I want to live forever and ever and ever. I want this "I" to live—this poor "I" that I am and that I feel myself to be here and now, and therefore the problem of the duration of my soul, of my own soul, tortures me.
>
> (Unamuno 1954, 45)

When faced with this reality, he made a Kierkegaardian leap of faith in an attempt to overcome the abject disharmonies and lack of apparent unity and durability of his own self. While other concrete durational beings will discover hidden motives and assuaging beliefs unique to their own constitutive histories and devise their own life strategies for existing afterward, Weinstein concludes that they also share a common, comprehensible "structure of existence" beneath this diversity (5). Uncovering this structure is one of the principal, guiding aims for the critical vitalist project.

Through his reappropriations of Bergsonian intuition and Unamuno's agonic doubting, Weinstein draws several important conclusions regarding the structure of human life and the nature of our individual and collective existence. These conclusions stand in stark contrast to much of ancient and modern philosophy, challenging notions of the unity of the self over time, the priority of reason in will, the character of desire, and the possibility of harmony or completion, either collectively or in the oddly crowded solitude of our own minds. Ultimately, his conclusions stand as a defense of finite, disharmonious, mutable, and embodied life and against "death," alienation from existence, and those who "purchase their resignation cheaply by devising symbolic substitutes" for the limitations and contradictions of real, lived experience (x).

The history of Western philosophy from Plato to the Moderns is littered with attempts to develop a harmonious, unified, and stable account of the self. These attempts even include Bergson and Unamuno in their ranks, both being thoroughgoing—if a bit odd—Moderns. While Bergson is fundamental to developing Weinstein's understanding of the incomplete, polemical nature of our being, the impetus and focus of his work shifted over time. While *Time and Free Will* and *Matter and Memory* are rife with new, critical inquiries into intuition, duration, and memory, his later works became increasingly conventional in their turn toward speculative metaphysics and moral philosophy, especially through his attempts to establish life as "an absolute reality, a vital impetus" that ultimately bound all beings together underneath the "superficial" conventions of everyday life (Weinstein 1979, 92–93). Unamuno's desperate grasping for certainty and a harmonious self, on the other hand, wasn't a product of slow theoretical ossification. Rather, in *The Tragic Sense of Life*, Unamuno finds some satisfaction for his desired unity and stability in a self-confessedly nonrational leap of faith, reaffirmed rather than discovered in the wake of his agonic doubtings. Each of these efforts has sought to provide accounts of our existence that render us sufficient and whole, at least potentially. In contrast, Weinstein argues that such efforts to "complete" our being and conceptualize a stable and noncontradictory notion of the structure of the self are doomed to constant frustration and failure. To ignore the contradictory and irreconcilable processes and drives at the heart of our existence and instead attempt "to center one's life around a meaning which arises out of that life and which represents but a fragment of it is to deliver oneself to the inert, to make of life a practice for death" (x–xi).

Rather than stable and unified, our being is irresolubly "polemical," "divided by warring selves," finite, and changing (13). For Weinstein, to be alive is to want. Want is not something we have but something we are at a basic level, something that possesses us, drives us ever onward with resurgent dissatisfactions, and indicates the incompleteness that characterizes the structure of our very foundations. This incompleteness manifests in the form of a variety of binaries in our experience, revealing that we are internally and externally divided among disharmonious life processes. Life and awareness, finitude and infinity, relatedness and nothingness, desire and fear, analysis and synthesis, and appreciation and control, among others, are divergent poles of our experience that we inevitably alternate between (cf.: 1978; 1979, 17–37). At times we are open to the world and immersed in the kaleidoscopic particularities of this body, this sensation, this moment, washing over us. At others we sort, structure, and categorize the world around us, fleeing from our own immediate limits and reaching for a sense of the universal and the timeless. We navigate both our urge to be appreciated by others and a corresponding dependency on those around us, as well as the demands of our psyche to throw up walls and levees against the threats to our uniqueness and security that such dependencies and vulnerabilities might pose. Such experiential binaries are fluid and enable the richness that is life as we understand it, but they are also responsible for rendering life both a pleasure palace and a "chamber of horrors" (1979, 19). While many do attempt to shed or negate one or another pole of these binaries in their own life philosophies in an attempt to surmount the difficulties they pose, Weinstein does not, instead preferring to understand and come to livable terms with their persistence.

Our polemical and finite nature also reinforces the fact that we are historical (and contingent) beings. Our uniquely developing autobiographies are inextricable from our social and material circumstances that structure those experiences and condition our life possibilities. In spite of our historicity and the continuous changeability it implies—or rather, because of it and the fear this reality instills deep within us—we are continuously attempting to define ourselves: "ever coordinating disparate experiences into a temporal unity that we call character or personality," and trying to seize universal, certain meaning (1979, 13). We grasp at something to ward off our own vulnerabilities and fears, yet "each time we reduce ourselves to the outcomes of efficient causes or deliver ourselves to the service of an ideal we diminish our lives in order to gain a specious security" (40). While this specious security may provide some temporary relief from our fear, it is always a contingently maintained illusion, since "in our infinitely complex particularity we are greater than any of our self definitions" (15). For Weinstein, while we may attempt to flee from our finitude and polemical incompleteness, it is always there, ready to frustrate our most powerful denials.

Rather than despairing when faced with this fact, Weinstein's critical vitalism attempts to understand and affirm the contradictory finitude of our lives and experiences. In lieu of meaning, however, whether of the objective or subjective sort, Weinstein argues for the importance of appreciation and the cultivation of finite perfections in the form of private virtues. We regularly exercise the motive of control when we sort and order our world, exercising judgment and skepticism and warding off external threats. It is fundamental to our sense of independence, but being driven by fear, it also isolates us from the recognition we crave. Appreciation dispenses with this controlling disposition and opens the individual for "receptivity to life," as well as compassion for other concrete durational beings with their own precious, irreplaceable, polemical, and incomplete uniqueness. Practicing appreciation relaxes our defenses, opening us up to the uniqueness and experiences of others as well as to the limitations of ourselves. It cannot remove the stings of life—indeed, by lowering one's defenses, it can invite them—but it can make possible the practices of reciprocal sacrifice, trust, and loyalty to other particular beings as a means of life fulfillment in full recognition of our shared finite, unique, polemical, and incomplete nature (cf.: Weinstein 1979, chapters 3–4).

Weinstein's critical vitalism is original and unique, but, like all original works of philosophy, owes a debt of inspirational gratitude to others. The contributions of Bergson and Unamuno have already been discussed, but a less obvious—yet still critical—contribution to Weinstein's vitalist project comes from the enigmatic nineteenth-century figure of Max Stirner. Stirner provides Weinstein with the notion of "Ownness," a concept and method of radical self-possession and ruthless interrogation of oneself and the world. Locating the place of Stirner's Ownness in Weinstein's vitalism and the changes it undergoes in translation are important for understanding the projects of both Weinstein and Stirner. The often-troubled reception of Stirner in wider philosophical traditions and his resulting marginalization, however, make a more explicit overview and interpretation of Stirner necessary before we can make sense of the connections between his ideas and Weinstein's.

UNDERSTANDING STIRNER

Philosophy, political and otherwise, has had a rather ambivalent relationship with Max Stirner. His single major theoretical work, *The Ego and His Own*, has been regarded as one of the most strikingly critical works of political theory. At the same time, Stirner is relatively unknown or, more frequently, known about but misunderstood. He is sometimes situated as a curious secondary figure within the timeline of the early Marx, owing (if nothing else) to the acerbic style and tremendous volume of writing in *The German Ideology* that Marx devotes to attempting a line-by-line rebuttal of *The Ego*. He is also frequently counted within the anarchist tradition in pertinent anthologies owing to his uncompromising critiques of the state, religion, and authority. Even this positioning, however, has been a contested and uncomfortable one owing to common readings of his work as a sort of prescriptive psychopathy or at least too self-interested in its "egoism" to be compatible with the broad anarchist tradition (cf. Van der Walt and Schmidt 2009).

In *The Ego*, Stirner provides us with a radical critique of much of the Western intellectual tradition. God, Law, Morality, Rights, Mankind,

Society, the State, Freedom, and a host of other regular artifacts of political philosophy are simply obliterated in his epistemology as symbolically potent but ultimately empty abstractions that, to the extent they are taken seriously, mask concrete power relations and potentially do violence to real "flesh-and-blood" individuals (Stirner 2005, 13). Saul Newman is hardly exaggerating when he describes Stirner's efforts as that of "taking a wrecking ball" to the foundations and structure of Western philosophy (Newman 2011, 1). It is in part this wholesale dismantling of so many common points of reference that were assumed to be secure that has likely contributed to the persistent misunderstanding of his work. Where, then, does Stirner ground his critique if not in traditional axiomatic concepts?

The nodal point within Stirner's critique is *der Einzige*, or, "the Unique." *Der Einzige* is not, as many critics have suggested, simply another human nature account of our lot as ultimately selfish creatures run amok. It is not, as Paul Thomas suggests (following Marx's lead), a confused new essence and categorical normative ideal in poor mock-Hegelian trappings (Thomas 2011, 129). Nor is it simply Stirner himself, as Marx mockingly characterizes it, writing a defiant and narcissistic love letter to his own misplaced sense of greatness. Neither, as some liberals like Isaiah Berlin suggests, is the Unique simply a figure of neurotic skepticism invariably leading to madness (Berlin 2000, 144–145). Each of these criticisms misunderstands the role of the Unique in Stirner's thought, taking it to be in some form or another a new reduction of concrete individuals to just another partial account of our being, a subsumption of their particularity into a wider movement or whole, or something comparable to a new abstracted notion of a general political subject. This is the general aim of their own projects (differentiating details aside) and precisely that which Stirner is attempting to circumvent.

The Unique is rather an "empty" placeholder term that recognizes that while individuals are certainly embodied and embedded in the world, they are also constantly in a process of becoming, fluctuation, self-definition, and self-creation and carry their own unique histories (5). As Widukind De Ridder notes, it is "extra conceptual" (De Ridder 2011, 150) and a consequence of Stirner's refusal to falsely reduce the particular individual to the Procrustean bed of a "fixed" internal essence or dissolve their uniqueness and particularity into a "higher" abstract Subject. Within Stirner's project, it functions as a means of referencing the discrete individual without falling into reductive trappings of traditional notions of the Subject, simultaneously giving the discrete individuals making use of his work a set of tools that they can deploy (or not) for themselves. Thus, within the context of his wider thought, it can be understood as a null standpoint to be occupied by the flesh-and-blood individual using Stirner's ideas, particularly as a means to try and "get behind" the ideational and linguistic fog in which we find ourselves in modern society, both internally and in relation to each other (9).

Once we accept Stirner's invitation and step within this standpoint of the Unique, we encounter something curious as we think and act in the modern world. In *The Ego*, Stirner (following Hegel's example) takes us on an individual and social-historical *bildungsroman* in order to analyze themes and phenomena that he wishes to underscore, problematize, and explain regarding humanity. In the not-so-distant past of this narrative, individuals—indeed, whole societies—quite openly believed that ghosts, gods, devils, and spirits haunted the world and ourselves. Humanity lived in deference to these otherworldly forces and entities and, indeed, celebrated them as "higher" and greater than the mere material and "earthly" (11). The Modern age of the Enlightenment, however, is supposed to be different from the Ancient in its celebration of science and inquiry. Indeed, in expelling old religion and superstition from the world and championing Reason, how could it not be?

Instead of vast difference from the Ancients and their superstitions, Stirner finds that "the moderns never did nor do make their way further than to theology . . . Even the newest revolts against God are nothing but . . . theological insurrections" (Stirner 2005, 27). Modern thought has all the more fully adopted the concern for the spirit bequeathed by the ancients. We all the more enthusiastically find ourselves compelled to believe in, internalize, and subordinate ourselves to a host of noncorporeal abstractions, of "spooks" or "fixed ideas" (39–43).

> What is not supposed to be my concern! First and foremost, the Good Cause, then God's cause, the cause of mankind, of truth, of freedom, of humanity, of justice; further the cause of my people, my prince, my fatherland; finally even the cause of Mind, and a thousand other causes. Only *my* cause is never to be my concern.
>
> (3)

Stirner declares further that

> Man, your head is haunted; you have wheels in your head! You imagine great things, and depict to yourself a whole world of gods that has an existence for you, a spirit realm to which you supposed yourself to be called, an ideal that beckons to you. You have a fixed idea! . . . What is it then, a fixed idea? An idea that has subjected the man to itself.
>
> (43)

These spooks are not benign but rather, in so far as we believe and act as if they are "sacred" and meaningful, exercise real power over our thoughts and lives. Perpetuated by the State, schools, family, religion, and myriad other institutions, these spooks for Stirner serve an internalizing disciplinary function that facilitates self-subjugation and submissiveness, in many ways anticipating Foucault's work with governmentality (Newman 2011, 197). What is most incredible about this situation for Stirner is that these powerful abstractions are simply imagined and illusory, empowered solely to the extent that we give them power by failing to recognize our own power and aims as concrete individuals.

In order to fully conceptualize his opposition to the possession of concrete individuals by the ubiquitous spooks of the world, Stirner develops the concepts of "own" and "ownness." Ownness is conceptually tightly related to the Unique and its egoistic attempts to rid itself of that which is alien to itself and that which attempts to possess it. As Kathy Ferguson observes, ownness is a "way of being oneself, of having oneself within one's power" (Ferguson 2011, 169). The spooks that possess us and limit our ownness are those that we deem to be sacred, to be unquestionable, and that compel us for their ends. Most importantly, they possess us *because we abandon our primacy and self-direction as concrete beings* to their direction and demands.

Ownness is not an abstraction of individual freedom in a vacuum, akin to the self-ownership of classical social contract theories of autonomous individual subjects. Neither is it synonymous with freedom or autonomy, understood as the lack of constraints or "negative liberty" in relation to an institutional power structure. One's own is a positive, holistic account of the concrete, worldly condition of that which is under my power and control and "is my whole being and existence, it is I myself" (Stirner 2005, 157).[4] One's own therefore comprises an expansive notion of one's self that includes one's context, individuated developmental history, and the power and capacities one has in relation to oneself and one's world, while ownness entails a way of living this fact, of carrying, recognizing, and relating to one's own. To engage in ownness and thus be one's own is not to throw off all obstacles the world puts in your way. One can never be totally rid of obstruction, limitation, and counterpowers.[5] Even when facing abject physical domination, however, as with the case of slavery, one can defend the scope of the own one has by maintaining a stance and practice of ownness. Ownness involves a refusal to place oneself in one's own evaluations and concerns in a subordinate position to something sacred, something alien to yourself, something that places demands upon you that you comply with *because the demands have been placed* rather than because you actively judge those demands to be valuable or worth complying with (or at least value avoiding the consequences of noncompliance).

In considering the Unique, ownness, and the project within *The Ego* as a whole, the purpose of Stirner's project then can be read as one of epistemic desanctification, of dispersing these illusory, haunting ghosts and spirits of modernity so that we can begin to act in recognition of ourselves as concrete, particular individuals, for our own empowerment and enjoyment. Stirner's critique provides the foundation for an *applied incredulity* toward the legitimacy claims of any other entity, whether conceptual and symbolic or corporeal, attempting to subordinate a concrete individual. Through this, it makes possible a radical rending and reordering of one's relationship to oneself and the world. In part, it is this method that makes Stirner's work so amenable to Weinstein's own project, though not without some requisite alterations. Stirner is not easily categorized into any fixed belief system. Indeed, and much to the vexation of his early critics, his very ideas make any attempts to fix or "crystallize" his thought in a closed or systematic fashion problematic (Newman 2011, 1–2). Unlike the conventional political theories and traditions, Weinstein's critical vitalism itself, however, is highly resistant to rigidity and closure and maintains a distance from theoretical attempts to enclose, subsume, and reduce concrete durational beings. Consequently, it is precisely this intensively critical and unruly aspect of his thought, alongside his concern for concrete individuals, that makes Stirner useful for critical vitalism.

WEINSTEIN APPROPRIATES STIRNER

Stirner makes frequent though often auxiliary appearances in many of Weinstein's works. Across these appearances in his published texts as well as in contemporary and unpublished commentary, Weinstein's assessment and use of Stirner's thought undergoes refinements and adaptations. Throughout, however, the primary concept that Weinstein appropriates from Stirner is, as previously mentioned, his concept of ownness. This concept provides a vital grounding for one facet of Weinstein's critical vitalism, providing an impetus for its critical reflexivity and practically contributing to the possibility of adjusting one's direction in life in an intentional fashion.

Even though Weinstein seizes upon Stirner's idea of ownness, this is not done without a critique of Stirner's perceived limitations. In particular, Weinstein critiques some of the ambiguities that Stirner leaves in regard to the application of his thought and the feasibility (and desirability) of the sustained achievement of its aims. Within Weinstein's understanding of human life as a process in dynamic tension with itself, alternating between expression and reflection, openness and solitude, appreciation and control, Stirner's "militant" and "merciless" effort to expunge all that might possess him is problematic if left to itself (Weinstein 1978, 83–84). Stirner's "ultra-utilitarian" use of the idea of ownness runs parallel to the other "philosopher of contradiction," Miguel de Unamuno's "ultra-existentialist" concept of the "hunger for immortality" (83). Viewed between the experiential poles of expression and reflection, these efforts attempt a reduction and collapsing of both poles of self-process into a unitary process that, for Weinstein, inevitably "falls into deep contradiction" (84).

The application of Stirner's critique in a sustained fashion, as he demonstrates in *The Ego*, is a continuous process of drilling down through the layers of possessive spooks that one has acquired (or rather, been acquired by) through living in the world. This pursuit of ownness, to strip off all things "alien," eventually leaves one in a seemingly "ragamuffin-like" condition as "naked-Man" (Stirner 2005, 139). On Weinstein's reading, this quest eventually contorts the original idea of ownness into an aversion to all social relationships that involve sacrifice, vulnerability, or dependence and a kind of proto-Nietzschean ethic of the strong and independent being averse to weakness (Weinstein 1978, 84–85). Even this "ragamuffin" condition, however, is not the end of the pursuit.

The last possession, the last "rag" to be disposed of, is that of the idea of a fixed human essence or nature and the dissolution of solid identities (Stirner 2005, 139). The quest for ownness in one's concrete self, to be free from possessive objects (both internal and external), leads not to a Cartesian core self but rather to the discovery that one is a "creative nothing" (5). Left with just our flesh and bones and our embodied experience of the world, there is "nothing" underlying who or what one is in any ultimate or transcendent sense, and in this way we are free from the constraint of fixed essences and identities. Yet with this, we are still "self-positing" creatures and thus are actively "creative" in each moment of our own self-definitions and understandings (150). Weinstein observes that ownness entails "for Stirner the ability to get rid of any object, whether it be material or ideal. Yet there is no self in the absence of a self image" (Weinstein 1978, 85). Further,

> The notion of being one's own is the ideal of expression, which is perpetually assimilating the contents of experience. However, in order for expression to persist from one present to the next, it must despoil reflection of any specific content and use it for its own purposes. Reflection, which is the root of possession, exacts the toll of making expression itself into an ideal . . .
>
> (ibid.)

While ostensibly comprising the critical heart and ethos of Stirner's entire project, ownness becomes an invariably temporary and often quite fleeting experience in the life process. The creative nothing creates new objects, while the pursuit of ownness then casts them off. Ownness operating as a project to pursue and a goal to be enduringly achieved represents, for Weinstein, a "contradictory concept representing a contradictory life" (ibid.).

At first glance, this seems like a rather damning critique of Stirner's entire project. Of what value can ownness be for Weinstein if it stands within a fundamental contradiction to our internal life processes? The problem, however, has less to do with ownness itself and more to do with the implicit linkage of ownness with a regulative project as an ideal to be pursued. Instead of an alleged absolute to be actualized, Weinstein retools ownness into a position that can be occupied or taken up within the dynamic life process. This retooled ownness is a position wherein "I have discretion over my disposition towards life; my judgments are in my hands when I am in that position" (Weinstein 2012). The life process contradiction that Weinstein identifies within Stirner's project of ownness makes the unbroken implementation of ownness seemingly impossible. Understood as a critical reflexive position that can be entered into, however, ownness retains its critical edge without becoming knotted in processual contradiction.

One is their own in this view when they are engaged in what Weinstein refers to as the "home discourse"—talking to oneself in a way that is both comprehensive and critical—and are "reviewing [their] life—[their] engagements, [their] attitudes—reflectively" (ibid.). Following Justus Buchler, Weinstein understands that we are "summed-up-selves in process" (Weinstein 1979, 122). At a given moment, what constitutes "you" is a summed-up account of the processes of your proception, what Buchler describes as

> The interplay of the human individual's activities and dimensions, their unitary direction . . . The term is designed to suggest a moving union of seeking and receiving, of forward propulsion and patient absorption. Proception is the composite, directed activity of the individual.
>
> (Buchler 1979, 4)

Importantly, our proception is not simply our "experience." For Buchler, this carries far too many "mentalistic overtones," since the constitution of what we are may be composed of events and objects about which we have no awareness. Our proception is the aggregation and summation of all that has made us what we are. This is not a static still-frame but rather the collection of interconnected and moving processes, objects, and events that have effectively shaped and constituted what we are as complex living beings.[6] As we live and move through the world, we are inflected, created, and changed by myriad elements of the universe that affect us in some way ("procepts"), and our "proceptive direction" through the world can be altered (leading to further, new elements to our proception and a potential shift in the boundaries of our proceptive domain; 3–8).

Ownness, with this context in mind, provides the means of intentionally "taking stock of," "[adjusting] and [readjusting]" one's axiology and proceptive direction through the world as "conditions within and outside [one] change" (ibid.). The impetus for entering into a position of ownness is not something that can necessarily be predicted; it is a consequence of the unique experiences of a concrete durational being and their reactions to their encounters with the world (with their reactions also being a semiflexible constitutive part of their proception). An event that, for one person, may be a simple, unremarkable fact of daily routine could very well be the instigation of a deep moral or existential crisis for another, setting their new feelings, desires, or understandings at war with their existing self-definitions and accounts of their self and creating genuine inner turmoil. Regardless, while in this position, one's life is intentionally subject to critical review and assessment, with the outcome of this review constituting or reconstituting one's axiology (the conscious element of one's proceptive direction).

In the rhythm of one's life processes and proceptive direction, there will be alternation between expression and reflection, acceptance and rejection of the makeup of one's internal and external relations, openness to the world and a desire for solitude or internal life. Stirner's understanding of ownness is at best rather ambiguous in relation to these unavoidable vacillations and tensions in lived experience. The nature of Stirner's inattention to these complexities, especially his allegedly narrow preference for an autarkic, use-based disposition toward the world and all social relations, has, however, I think been highly overstated and its implications misunderstood. In large part, this overstatement has been dependent upon a very narrow reading of Stirner's meaning of terms like "selfishness" and "use" and the character and motive of his rejection of dependence of various sorts. At least within his earlier published readings of Stirner, Weinstein repeats this very common reading of the implications of Stirner's thought as comparable to a Nietzschean ethic of celebrating the strong at the expense of the weak and denying the legitimacy of sacrifice and mutual dependence on others (Weinstein 1978, 85). In both *The Ego* and his less popular rebuttal against his critics, Stirner responds directly to such interpretations with clear resistance. While his rhetoric is certainly highly critical of what he considers to be our propensity to allow ourselves to be dominated by hollow symbols, as well as the servitude he believes attends being totally overcome and possessed by other persons, feelings, or convictions, he also peppers his writing with meditations on the value and experience of a truer and more immediate love and affection among individuals.

> If I cherish you because I hold you dear, because in you my heart finds nourishment, my need satisfaction, then it is not done for the sake of a higher essence whose hallowed body you are, not on account of my beholding in you a ghost, an appearing spirit, but from egoistic pleasure; you yourself with your essence are valuable to me, for your essence is not a higher one, is not higher and more general than you, is unique like yourself, because it is you.
>
> (Stirner 2005, 42)

It is not affection and mutual dependence or the want of another concrete individual that Stirner finds problematic. Rather, it is the process of rendering one's affections dependent upon a "haunting" and "higher essence" such as duty or in order to affirm them as valuable and worthy that Stirner finds repulsive. Similarly, the transformation of love into a possessing infatuation or obsession renders it a higher calling that removes one's ability to actively love another as a particular individual at all; one becomes instead a thrall to a sanctified representation (292–293). This plea for a more direct, immediate expression of value and affection (or even revulsion or hate) is itself in the spirit of Weinstein's own laments. As Weinstein sees it, the very purpose of philosophy is to "leave us without any recourse but one another," a goal that only makes sense by virtue of our "proclivity to devise barriers that separate ourselves from each other" (Weinstein 1979, 3–4). Stirner's efforts at desanctification also carry this goal of defending more direct, carnal, and immediate relationships and breaking down the emotional and psychological barriers to this immediacy posed by the creeping influence of the demands of social obligation or tradition, religious myth, or other enemies of the uniquely personal.

Here, a more skeptical reader familiar with Stirner might object: surely this emphasis on unmediated affections and—gasp—*dependence* and love goes too far! This is *the* philosopher of the unique, radical particularity of our selves, after all, with practically an allergy toward any whiff of being dominated, rendered weaker, or carried away by the throes of . . . well, anything, is he not? It is true that throughout *The Ego*, Stirner very clearly states his opposition to these things in hardly veiled language. After all, he ends his introductory chapter with the defiant declaration that "Nothing is more to me than myself!" (5) and closes the book with the claim that "All things are nothing to me" (366). Yet, by glomming onto such seemingly unequivocal statements and isolating them from the rest of Stirner's claims, we miss out on the nuance of their meaning and the ethos of Stirner's project as a whole. Yes, Stirner is against sacrifice of a certain sort, especially to an unquestionable concept or entity held as "higher" than or primary to oneself *a priori*. But he also defends sacrifice in the service of self-direction, self-fulfillment, and joy:

> Am I perchance to have no lively interest in the person of another, are *his* joy and *his* weal not to lie at my heart, is the enjoyment that I furnish him not to be more to me than other enjoyments of my own? On the contrary, I can with joy sacrifice to him numberless enjoyments, I can deny myself numberless things for the enhancement of *his* pleasure, and I can hazard for him what without him was the dearest to me, my life, my welfare, my freedom. Why, it constitutes my pleasure and my happiness to refresh myself with his happiness and his pleasure. But, *myself, my own self*, I do not sacrifice to him, but remain an egoist and enjoy him . . . I do not sacrifice my peculiar value, my ownness.
>
> (290)

It is not the act of sacrifice itself, then, but the motivating source and purpose behind the sacrifice that matters. The act of sacrificing some particular thing is simply part and parcel of the existence of social relationships, especially personal ones. As long as the sacrifice does not consist of one's own self-direction, active valuation and judgment, and consideration of one's own wants, then the sacrifice is in no contradiction with ownness. Similarly, he is against individual dependence of a certain sort, especially upon a sacred idol or concept that negates the use of one's own judgment. But, as with sacrifice, it is not the material dependence upon others in any particular way that is the problem for Stirner, but rather the acquiescence of one's valuations, judgments, and ability to challenge the propriety or sanctity of that which no longer accords with one's values or goals.

Stirner is against being possessed by spooks and advocates the practice of ownness in shedding these "rags" in a ruthless way. In actuality, though, and in spite of the apparent mercilessness of his demeanor in this ghost hunt, it seems that he does recognize the fleeting nature of the practice of ownness. We drill to our empty core, but he doesn't offer us a steady resolution or see it as necessary. Ownness rids us of rags and illusions, but the creations of the creative nothing form new (temporary and disposable) ground for us to walk on, and in walking, we are as unique individuals each "a world's history" (365). Making new symbolic or conceptual grounds on which we can walk is not a problem for Stirner, as long as these creations remain useful, furnish us with joy, or strike our fancy. Ownness demands not that we live without thoughts or language or that they be actually *alienated*. This would indeed be an absurd regulatory ideal, and Stirner says as much. It simply demands that they be *alienable* rather than sacred, unquestionable, and served for their own reasons rather than for your valuations and needs.

Stirner lacks a fleshed-out theoretical framework for conceptualizing the polemical structure of lived experience as sketched out by Weinstein, and this leads to plenty of confusion and a lopsided emphasis on the removal of illusion and barriers over the "creative" facet of the creative nothing. But, arguably, Stirner's work still carries an implicit understanding of the divergent poles of experience that are fundamental to living. This implicit understanding comes to the fore, however, only once we appreciate ownness as a practice—particularly in service to pleasure and joy—rather than a new sacred ideal to be followed in solemnity.

In spite of what I consider to be limitations in his earlier, published interpretations of Stirner, Weinstein's use of Stirner's concept of ownness still provides us with a double boon. Rather than posing a problem for the critical vitalist project, a more sensitive reading of Stirner's oft-hyperbolic and rhetorical language and his expressed intent (including his later responses to critics) further buttresses the cross-compatibility of Stirner's concept of ownness and Weinstein's philosophy. We have already surveyed the role that Weinstein's reading of ownness plays in his philosophy of critical vitalism. Similarly, Weinstein's critical vitalism can provide a correlatively useful theoretical framework to further the implementation of Stirner's concepts and concerns. The eclectic and antisystemic nature of Stirner's work makes it useful for the generation of critical conceptual tools for individual use but provides little in the way of a broader theoretical framework through which they might be situated, interpreted, and deployed. Stirner's sentiments on the matter suggest that he himself valued precisely this kind indetermination and interpretive autonomy for his readers, declaring about his ideas and writings that one should "Do with [them] what you will and can, that is your affair and does not trouble me"

(Stirner 2005, 296). Discussing the Bible as an archetype for the traditional use of literary and philosophical works in clear opposition to his own approach, Stirner declares that

> In fact, the child who tears it to pieces or plays with it, the Inca Atahualpa who lays his ear to it and throws it away contemptuously when it remains dumb, judges just as correctly about the Bible as the priest who praises in it the "Word of God," or the critic who calls it a job of men's hands.
>
> (335–336)

In making conceptual tools at hand for discrete individuals to do with what they will instead of a closed system of truth production to which a subject must display fidelity, it should be clear that Stirner does not oppose transformations of and elaborations upon his proffered ideas. Rather, he seems to welcome it, tendentially preferring to leave undeveloped open ground for diversely situated individual appropriations and experimentations with ideas rather than cordoning them off.

Weinstein's critical vitalism can provide a particularly fertile framework for future elaborations on Stirner's thought given that they share several overlapping concerns. Regard for philosophizing through concretely experienced individuality over "God's eye" system building, a sensitivity toward the power of symbols, concepts, and language, and an actively critical and reflexive disposition are all shared between Stirner and critical vitalism. Contemporary efforts to bring Stirner into conversation with Foucault and Deleuze or generally reassess his value for contemporary Continental and critical theory and radical politics (cf.: Bargu 2011; Newman 2011) could also be usefully enhanced and facilitated by concurrently taking a page from Weinstein's critical vitalism and Stirner's relationship to it. In particular, Weinstein's enrichment of and elaboration upon the structure of experience provides a place wherein Stirner's philosophical methods can find a practicable home and also from which the ambiguities and complexities of Stirner's thought can be translated into other discourses and given a greater sense of completion and practicability.

SIGNIFICANCE AND NEW CONNECTIONS

If critical vitalism involves a partisanship in favor of life, it is worth asking whose or what sort of life is having the banner raised in its name and what benefits that partisanship provides. What (on this reading) does Weinstein's project allow us to do? What is its value? Perhaps most pertinently for this collection, premised as it is on the importance of making connections between Weinstein and other theorists, how can we best situate his work with other contemporary persons and projects?

Weinstein's own stated goals for situating critical vitalism among other philosophers and traditions provides an excellent starting point. As he sees it, critical vitalism and the tools it provides best operates as a "corrective to all those contemporary modes of thought that prescind from the intimacy of subjectivity in order, as Quebec philosopher Fernand Dumont puts it, to construct systems of 'operations' that can be manipulated externally" (Weinstein 1985, 163–164). While behaviorism, structuralism, liberal corporatism, and Marxism seek to "externalize" the mind, critical vitalism is one way—not THE way—to "reclaim the mind for the unique and intimate center of imaginative expression" (164). It finds "congenial company" with other efforts to vindicate finite life, personality, and concrete durational beings. At the initial publication of *Finite Perfection* in 1985, Weinstein counted among this company the revival of the classical American philosophers of the vitalist and pragmatist traditions, rehabilitations and reinterpretations of Nietzsche and Freud, shifts away from macro-narratives in historical interpretation, and other efforts to focus our attention to "personal existence" and circumstance instead of impersonal structures and historical blocs or timeless universals (ibid.). The continuations and heirs of these projects today continue to provide potential grounds for inspiration and cross-fertilization.

Given the variety of theorists and traditions to which critical vitalism owes inspiration, we can trace a host of webbed connections among it and other contemporary critical philosophies (broadly construed). In so doing, we might open up new and useful pathways for exploration or, better yet, build new tools that might be brought to bear on concrete lived experience and political life in all of its complexities and particularities. One of the more promising areas in which Weinstein's works might establish connections is with other fellow travellers of vitalist, pragmatist, and process philosophies and their contemporary channels of reception. Those who reached, in other words, for Nietzsche and Bergson rather than Plato and Hegel are likely to find resonance with the spirit of the critical vitalist project that could be put to future use.

The reemergence of Bergson and "Bergsonism" as popularized by Gilles Deleuze is a particularly promising source of future theoretical innovation. Especially in *Meaning and Appreciation*, Weinstein himself makes creative use of Bergson and his method of intuition in order to understand—among other things—the urge to find (and the graveyard of attempts to secure) meaning in our lives. He is critical there, however, of Bergson's attempts (especially in his later works) to conceptually ground the structure of lived being in life itself as a metaphysical, generative force. By the time Bergson writes *The Two Sources of Morality and Religion*, he has reverted to an appeal to this life force as a means of unifying he more open-ended and conflictual self-processes outlined in *Time and Free Will* and *Matter and Memory*. Weinstein appropriates Bergson's method of intuition and accepts a processual view of human life and temporality but argues for the continued importance of conceiving of the emergent structure of our being as unavoidably polemical and finite. His efforts here intersect well with contemporary efforts to revive Bergson as a source of vitalist thought and as a resource for thinking in terms of temporality when analyzing society, discourse, and lived experience.

Consequently, Weinstein's thought also intersects well with the efforts of Deleuze and contemporary Deleuzians. This is especially the case in their attempts to bring life, process, embodiment, uniqueness, and change into theoretical focus alongside issues of power and the production of concepts and representations. Deleuze, like Weinstein, also has a closer (yet still critical) relationship to vitalist tradition than most other postmodern philosophers. There are some limitations to their overlap. Weinstein's critical vitalism does take Heidegger's rejection of metaphysical speculation to heart and thus attempts to ground its analysis on human experience grasped from within a living, particular body. Deleuze rejects this end to metaphysics and is far more willing to wed a more imaginative and speculative (if tenuously and experimentally maintained) metaphysical language and collection of concepts in order to explore the problems that drive him. While this isn't a fatal divergence, it certainly presents a difference in style and mood and suggestively raises the question of the role of aesthetics and such speculative forms of concept creation as a form of empirical inquiry into human experience.

Like Stirner, Weinstein's work also has strong affinities with the anarchist tradition, which has seen a serious revival in critical theory and political influence over the last decade and a half. Dismantling the pretensions of official legitimating narratives of political orders, critiquing the powers of language and concepts, and being sensitive to the limits and dangers of representation, institutionally, ideationally, and otherwise are all projects shared by critical vitalism and many strands of anarchism. Also like Stirner, however, any attempt to neatly squeeze Weinstein into that tradition will inevitably lead to some degree of frustration. While both offer tools, methods, and critiques for approaching politics through lived experience, neither accepts the possibility of a realizable utopia of durable cooperation and equality (though they both recognize the power of such abstractions for affecting individuals and collectivities). Such abstractions play a far greater role in "classical" anarchism than in contemporary anarchism. Postanarchist ideas especially, with their incorporation of poststructuralist interpretations of power (especially strained through Foucault and Deleuze), could provide a fruitful avenue for dialogue between the in-depth life philosophy of critical vitalism and the general goals of the anarchist tradition.

Ultimately, Weinstein's critical vitalism is capable of standing on its own as a philosophical and political endeavor. The core kernel of Weinstein's insights, however, cuts across a variety of traditions and could potentially find expression through other unique combinations of theorists and philosophical frameworks. This, appropriately enough, gives it a flexible adaptability for the needs of concrete durational beings. By highlighting the importance of Stirner in Weinstein's thought and the potential importance it could yet have, I hope to offer one such alternative combination and expression of the core impetus driving critical vitalism. It is an exploratory route that happened to provide me with the bridges I required at a previous stage of my philosophical investigations. As evinced by the diverse connections made by others in this project, the adaptations and reconfigurations that are possible with Weinstein's core insights are limited only by the individuated experiences and needs of those who attempt to bring them to bear on their own lives.

NOTES

1. Especially regarding reductive biologisms, psychophysics, and behavioralists of various stripes
2. Bergson provides a variety of examples to illustrate this process. One example he asks us to consider is that of a flock of sheep. Insofar as we imagine each of the particular sheep as consisting of part of the set, we imagine them, in spite of their radical particularities and uniqueness, to share a fundamental homogeneous sameness as sheep of this set. We hold each sheep together in our mind and occlude the differences for the practical expedient of perceiving them together as one set. In our individual lives, we imagine ourselves having an effectively homogeneous and stable identity across time; we hold this as a constant, even though particular identity roles or labels held (more constrained forms of spatialization) may change. Even though we will replace most of our bodily cells in a few years, and even though each moment of "our" existence is an essentially new bodily configuration, "we" persist through complex processes of memory retention and projected narratives of our past, present, and future.
3. The alternative is an inexpressible flow of experience without significance or unity, an impossible condition to maintain for the sustenance of active life.
4. Although not identical, this understanding of ownness is also strongly resonant with Jose Ortega y Gasset's understanding of subjectivity, announced in his famous declaration that "I am I and my circumstances."
5. What George Santayana referred to as "dominations."
6. As proceivers—identifiable and actively accumulating sets of unifying processes.

REFERENCES

Bargu, Banu. (2011). "Max Stirner, Postanarchy avant la lettre" in *How Not To Be Governed: Readings and Interpretations from a Critical Anarchist Left*, eds. Jimmy Casas Klausen and James Martel, 103–122. New York: Lexington.

Bergson, Henri. (2001). *Time and Free Will: An Essay on the Immediate Data of Consciousness*, Mineola, NY: Dover.

Berlin, Isaiah. (2000). *The Roots of Romanticism*, Princeton: Princeton University Press.

Buchler, Justus. (1979). *Toward a General Theory of Human Judgment*, Second Revised Edition, Mineola, NY: Dover.

De Ridder, Widukind. (2011). "Max Stirner: The End of Philosophy and Political Subjectivity," in *Max Stirner*, ed. Saul Newman, 167–188. New York: Palgrave Macmillan.

Ferguson, Kathy. (2011). "Why Anarchists Need Stirner," in *Max Stirner*, ed. Saul Newman, 167–188. New York: Palgrave Macmillan.

Newman, Saul. (2011). *Max Stirner*, New York: Palgrave Macmillan.

Stirner, Max. (2005). *The Ego and His Own*, Mineola, NY: Dover.

Thomas, Paul. (2011). "Max Stirner and Karl Marx: An Overlooked Contretemps" in *Max Stirner*, ed. Saul Newman, New York: Palgrave MacMillan.

Unamuno, Miguel De. (1954). *Tragic Sense of Life*. New York: Dover Publications, Inc.

Van Der Walt, Lucien, and Michael Schmidt. (2009). *Black Flame: The Revolutionary Class Politics of Anarchism and Syndicalism*. Oakland, CA: AK Press

Weinstein, Michael A. (1978). *Meaning and Appreciation: Time and Modern Political Life*, West Lafayette, IN: Purdue University Press.

Weinstein, Michael A. (1979). *Structure of Human Life: A Vitalist Ontology*, New York: New York University Press.

Weinstein, Michael A. (1985). *Finite Perfection: Reflections on Virtue*, Amherst: University of Massachusetts Press.

Weinstein, Michael A. (2012). Interview.

5 Weinstein's American Philosophy
Intimacy and the Construction of the Self

Jonathan McKenzie

One could characterize Michael Weinstein's expressive philosophy as an attempt to reclaim the corporeal self from its own impossibility. This characterization comes to the fore through Weinstein's unwillingness to part with the agonic contradictions of modern philosophy: the self and its constructions, radical solitude and the desire for intimacy, and withdrawal within and with (as well as from) community. Recognizing the impossibility of affirming life in its totality, Weinstein writes in *Culture/Flesh*: "I do not seek to affirm all life but only my life here and now, day by day."[1] Weinstein's sustained refusal to extend his affirmations across temporal bounds indicates the contingency of his philosophical architecture. Instead of negating the modern conundrums of situated selves and the self's mediation through its total institutions, Weinstein embraces these realities and yet yearns toward maximizing the possible self under these conditions. Weinstein's willingness to affirm lived contradiction makes itself clear in his embrace of intimacy as the apex of life in *Finite Perfection* and *Culture/Flesh*. In these two works, Weinstein overcomes a traditional problematic for those who embrace individualism: in order to strategize one's own inwardness, one has to make demands upon love that intimacy cannot supply or keep. In order to sustain one's inwardness, one must sacrifice intimacy.

I was drawn to the subject of this essay through a cursory glance at the dedication to Michael Weinstein's most recent book, *The Imaginative Prose of Oliver Wendell Holmes*, in which he inscribes a note to Deena Weinstein: "To my beloved colleague, who distinguishes me from Holmes." This led me to two interrelated questions: What is the source of the distinction and why would one desire to be distanced from Holmes? With these questions in mind, I reread the book on Holmes as well as Weinstein's broader philosophy (especially *Finite Perfection*) and came across a concept that covers the current of his thought like a film. In this chapter, I suggest that Weinstein's meditative work provides a trenchant entrée into the possibility and fragility of intimacy as a privatist philosophical concept. The move from the self/organization split in *The Tragic Sense of Political Life* and *The Structure of Human Life*, in which the self finds itself railing against the organizational determinants of its identity, to the erotic affirmations of *Finite Perfection* and *Culture/Flesh* exhibit a transformation from the lamentation of mass democratic moves away from intimacy to rethink the concept with all of the attendant problems of radical separation and cultural discourse. In a sense, I see Weinstein's work attempting to rethink the possibility of intimacy by renouncing the necessity of participatory political measures that sever the intimate relations of self to self.

In attempting to rescue intimacy, Weinstein writes himself into an important chapter in American literature and philosophy. American individualism consistently dedicates itself to the conundrum of commitment and its problems. Witness, for example, Thoreau's counsel in the second chapter of *Walden*: "As long as possible live free and uncommitted."[2] Thoreau's invitation to the freedom of carelessness bleeds into his distortion of friendship, making the argument in *A Week on the Concord and Merrimack Rivers* that "[w]e never exchange more than three words with a Friend in our lives."[3] The desire to sustain individuality sacrifices the bonds of ordinary friendship, holding an ideal that insulates the self's enclosures as the standard of intimacy. Emerson, meanwhile, makes the claim to detachment and selfhood in "Circles": "I am only an experimenter . . . I unsettle all things. No facts are to me sacred; none are profane; I simply experiment, an endless seeker, with no Past at my back."[4]

Even pragmatism's inheritance of transcendentalist individualism relies on transforming the utopia of boundlessness into the agony of the necessity of choice, as William James mentions in the "Will" section of his *Psychology: The Briefer Course*. James masterfully paints the deliberative situation preceding choice, attended by "endless degrees of complication."[5] Even upon making a reasoned decision, the background of our deliberation, on the fringe, is all of the possible murdered alternatives to our choice. The uncomfortable space of deliberation reveals the necessity of producing arguments for and against our "live options." James's penetrating insight is to suggest that deliberation itself is not the cause of our misery but the necessity of choice that places us in a bind, forcing us to make decisions based upon unreliable information, improper boundaries, and the complexities of our emotions, our histories, and the others involved. The desire to live disparate and conflicting lives simultaneously is ultimately impossible for James, and this is the source of his tragic sense of life. Weinstein finds himself grappling with similar issues, thus contributing an enormous amount to the discourse of American individualism.

DUAL CATEGORIES AND THE RIDDLE OF INTIMACY

If Oliver Wendell Holmes, Sr., seems an odd choice for inspiration, Weinstein's text reveals the connective tissue between the literary style of Holmes and the trenchant philosophical concern of Weinstein's life. Commenting upon the reception of Holmes's work, Weinstein suggests: "[an] element of complexity in Holmes's imaginative prose is the heterogeneity of his

individual texts."[6] Weinstein is articulating Holmes's method and its contribution to our understanding of American identity, but he also reveals his
own philosophical sympathy with Holmes the thinker. Going further, Weinstein states: "Holmes's texts are complex because he considers many sides
of the same problem and balances contending positions against each other
through various characters and rhetors."[7] Culminating in the claim that
Holmes's works offer often "undecidable" conclusions, Weinstein estab-
lishes the similitude of his thought with Holmes's style. Holmes's ability
to consistently entertain a multiplicity of positions conscientiously, articulated to greatest effect in *The Autocrat of the Break-Fast Table*'s discourse
on death, reveals a philosophical sensibility that responds to the American
desire to maintain individual integrity by choosing not to take sides.

Weinstein centers on Holmes's concept of "disordered volition" as the
key to the self's navigation of its world. Disordered volition is "caused by
conflict among its multiple personae and the tendency of some of them to
rebel against the adversities and limitations of phenomenal experience."[8]
Philosophy attempts to make the most of disordered volition, as Weinstein
recognizes the interminable conflict of its origin: "The fact that my life is
open to that which differs from myself makes communicable and even public
that act of free valuation that is definitive of philosophy, whereas the closure
of my life, its intimacy, makes that act personal and unique."[9] The public
and private aspects of philosophy and philosophizing do not always cohere
in Weinstein's thought. As an individualist in the American vein, Weinstein
recognizes the primary value of "self-possession" as a tool for combatting
the self's desire to rid itself of its inherent deficiencies—loneliness, desire,
death, disease, and decay. Holmes provides a psychological framework that
enables Weinstein to think through the consequences of multiple private and
public personae.

Holmes ultimately fails to experience the intimacy that characterizes
Weinstein's nuanced philosophy, joining a chorus of nineteenth-century
American thinkers whose inability to carry intimacy manifests itself in
failed friendships, bankrupt utopian communities, and the characterization
of interpersonal life as entirely without depth. One thinker, whom Weinstein
does not engage, provides an interesting case in the acceptance of the strains
of individuality and the erotic connections of intimate life in a way that challenges Weinstein. Walt Whitman's *Leaves of Grass*, a mid-century attempt
to push our collective understanding of democracy beyond the political,
embraces the agonic contradictions of existence through the merger of the
body and the soul, and the self and the other:

> I have said that the soul is not more than the body,/ And I have said that
> the body is not more than the soul,/And nothing, not God, is greater to
> one than one's-self is,/. . . And there is no object so soft but it makes a
> hub for the wheeled universe,/And any man or woman shall stand cool
> and supercilious before a million universes.[10]

Whitman attempts to undermine the tensions of the body and the soul, undermining basic questions of philosophy by ignoring their bases. Whitman aims to invoke the United States itself as "essentially the greatest poem," leaning on its promise of "action untied from strings necessarily blind to particulars."[11] For Whitman, the ultimate challenge of equality rests in one's willingness to forgo any existential distinctions of social merit, thereby allowing selves to revel in multiplicity and experience the pleasures of experienced individuality: "Do I contradict myself?/Very well then . . . I contradict myself;/I am large . . . I contain multitudes."[12]

Whitman is the American thinker whose philosophical tenor most closely aligns with Weinstein's. Each aims to dissolve the existential dualisms that bind experience and make it manageable, instead offering an invitation to a lived philosophy of multiplicity that does not give up on the steadying force of a core. The result of Whitman's thought is a thorough domestication of each impulse and judgment, a universalism that strains the credibility of self-discretion. Whitman writes: "I think I could turn and live awhile with the animals . . . /they are so placid and self-contained,/I stand and look at them sometimes half the day long."[13] Whitman injects a self-reliant strain into the animal existence, claiming that the virtues of animals include their imperturbability, their resistance to commercialism, their atheism, and their lack of remorse. Whitman's universal judgment, which begins as a function similar to Weinstein's notion of reflexivity, collapses under the burden of a metaphysical principle of organization. The power of the universal judgment—"not as the judge judges but as the sun falling around a helpless thing"—intoxicates Whitman, thus carrying the necessary discretion useful for a philosophy of multiplicity to its furthest extreme.[14]

Whitman's philosophy of multiplicity ends in a mania supplied by the feeling of power that comes from standing above oneself. Whitman writes: "I help myself to material and immaterial,/No guard can shut me off, no law can prevent me."[15] This attitude signals the definitive nineteenth-century American failure to philosophically capture a livable vision of intimacy. Whitman's choice to democratize intimacy renders the concept vacuous, falling victim to the opposite problem of Emerson and Thoreau. While Emerson and Thoreau idealize the concept of friendship and allow existential realities to wither under its power, Whitman desires to implant a metaphysics of intimacy on everything across boundaries of time and space through the act of writing the poem and becoming the poet. This is most clearly signaled in Whitman's taking of the pain of another: "Agonies are one of my changes of garments;/I do not ask the wounded person how he feels. . ./myself become the wounded person,/My hurt turns livid upon me as I lean on a cane and observe."[16] Whitman's attempt to assimilate the self to its environs in order to form a unified bond ultimately eliminates the other or, perhaps worse, uses the other as equipment for one's ascension to a new level of indirect understanding.

Weinstein's positive philosophy comes in the form of "erotic hedonism," a more carefully construed and personally vigilant form of the individualism that brackets Whitman's thought.

> Love the pleasures of the world: that is the civil savage's imperative for the erotic side of life. Love those pleasures, the delights that the other-than-self offers on its own terms, in full awareness that they can never be fully satisfactory and that they are not necessary. In this vein they will delight just for what they are and they will not deceive.[17]

Weinstein's characterization of philosophy as a strategy of life—"ruthlessly" practicing "the arts of defense"—connects him to the American tradition that insists upon a livable organization for one's thought. But Weinstein's foundation is to love the delights of the world on their own terms, a move that signals a refusal to essentialize or deify fragile and failing selves and objects. Weinstein's insistence upon accepting the reality of things on their own terms is a foundational portion of his thought, for it severs him from the tradition that begins in exultation and ends in the tragic recognition of the always-incomplete other. In this sense, Weinstein apprehends Hawthorne's conclusions without succumbing to Hawthorne's life strategy.

FROM ORGANIZATION TO INTIMACY

In the opening pages of his first meditative work of political philosophy, *The Tragic Sense of Political Life*, Weinstein articulates the philosophical influences that ground his vision of personal clarity. Settling for a short time on George Santayana, Weinstein argues that Santayana's major influence was to incorporate into his naturalist philosophy "a set of dualisms opposing matter and spirit, vital liberty and spiritual freedom, and instrumental reason and disinterested contemplation."[18] Having written a dissertation on Santayana's theory of freedom, Weinstein acknowledges his great debt but ultimately moves beyond Santayana, noting that "I could not settle for a philosophy that boxed my experience into watertight compartments."[19] What Santayana missed, for Weinstein, was "an exit from myself and into politics and history."[20] The flight from Santayana is a critical juncture in the text, which continues with Weinstein's attempt to create and then resolve dualisms by denying their constitutional and semantic qualities.

Weinstein's *Tragic Sense of Political Life* carries a chief motivation grounded in a trenchant philosophical desire: "I want to realize contradictory values, living them simultaneously."[21] This desire is troubling insofar as it problematizes political activity, defined by Weinstein as "the process of constituting a public situation by selecting certain alternatives for human relations and sacrificing others."[22] The crisis between political engagement and withdrawal is a foundational one for Weinstein: "I experience myself as a series of critical choices between my will to actualize and appreciate contradictory ends and my desire to act to help others realize values."[23] On my reading, this is the fundamental contradictory desire of Weinstein's philosophy. Indeed, as I will argue, we can read his thought as a series of concentric circles drawn around the desire to withdraw and to assist others in achieving vital desires. Weinstein's dichotomies in *The Tragic Sense of Political Life*, "Elite and Mass," "Participation and Confrontation," "Collective and Individual," "Organization and Person," exemplify the gravity of this contradictory desire. The desire is not local to *The Tragic Sense of Political Life*, either, as Weinstein's book on American classical philosophy, *The Wilderness and the City*, focuses on the philosophical trope of withdrawal and return; his *Structure of Human Life* vacillates among "Control," "Appreciation," and "Sacrifice"; his *Finite Perfection* assimilates self control and love; and his fourth meditative work, *Culture/Flesh*, attempts to incorporate defensive and erotic life.

Finite Perfection, Weinstein's most meditative work, aims to comprehensively investigate two intertwined questions of the self: First, is self-possession possible or desirable in modernity? And, second, how does self-possession clarify and enhance itself in conjunction with objects of pleasure and other human beings? As a work of freedom, Weinstein carefully constructs a vision of the self, capable of standing over experience with the sharp eye of virtue:

> One may stand above the momentary contents of one's life and entertain possibilities relevant to them, finally making a judgment about the import of those particular contents and possibilities, and then, most often, behaving in accordance with that judgment.[24]

Weinstein's attempt to gain freedom, the recognition of "sovereignty over my life," also maintains that one accept the limitations of one's own existence as a fragile and finite human being. Weinstein relies on the cultivation of reflexivity in order to ground his philosophical work. Reflexivity, for Weinstein, is paramount: "the form of self-consciousness or self-awareness involved in assuming sovereignty over one's life is an act of self-possession which allows distance of the self from any of life's particular contents."[25]

Reflexivity is one of the primary philosophical tools Weinstein uses to solve the sort of problem that vexes the American renaissance. While Emerson and Thoreau cultivate a double consciousness, the second consciousness that stands over experience with the penetration of sharp but disinterested vision is wild and uncontrollable by the managing ego. We can clearly see how reflexivity allows Weinstein to work to overcome Whitman's poetic absorption in everyday life. Weinstein, in fact, describes reflexivity as "acute in the tension between the zero point of pure indifference, at which the self reposes back upon itself and glides from one experience to the next, and the absorption of the self into one of the contents of its life."[26] Reflexivity gives context to the act of judgment—or, as Weinstein wisely terms it, "evaluation," insofar as it allows the self an absorbed and detached vision of life's contents from which to ground the act of evaluation. Understood in the context of American philosophy, Weinstein's careful assessment of the self's evaluative powers allows, for the first time in American philosophy, for a practicable philosophy of intimacy to make itself known.

Weinstein grounds his philosophy of intimacy in a brutal recognition of José Ortega y Gasset's social philosophy, particularly the insight that our life is spent vacillating between periods of extreme inwardness and the loss of the self outward. Ortega writes, "[w]e feign temperaments which are not our own, and we feign them in all sincerity, not to deceive others, but to enhance ourselves in our own eyes."[27] Weinstein himself amends this depiction of modern life in *Meaning and Appreciation*: "[t]he primary implication of an intuitive life philosophy is that we are not essentially free, creative, or meaningful beings, but beings who *express one another to ourselves* . . . We are continually creating contexts for ourselves in the past-present-future."[28] Weinstein's social standpoint makes the question of "how knowledge of the self by the self is possible" an exceedingly personal and profound question. Weinstein's philosophical personae—including the amended free spirit in *Finite Perfection* and the civil savage in *Culture/Flesh*—revels in the continual daily practice of winning battles amidst the losing war for selfhood. Intimacy, then, becomes the reward of a self who has (more or less) successfully tamed the personal and interpersonal beasts that are its nature and managed to reject the desire to "remake the world" and accept its benefits and losses as given.

Weinstein's *Finite Perfection* attends to the contradictions of commitment and integrity, theorizing love in order to correct the "American delusion that life can be made comfortable."[29] Weinstein's departure point of radical separation suggests that individual integrity has to sustain itself as the prime value even when presented with intimate experiences and relationships with the other. The difficult work of love's virtue, for Weinstein, is its "free service," wherein it "makes the other happy in all of the various benign ways it can be done, yet never allowing its service to transform the other into a dependent."[30] The self's ability to manage the other's dependency places limits on intimacy: "The foundation of a philosopher's love will be separation, not union; love will be a joining of the disparate into a fragile solidarity, but that solidarity will never be tight enough to permit the surrender of self-possession."[31] Weinstein moves close to the territory of negating love in order to save the self's integrity but supplies a theory of "free service" that aims to commit the self to the other while maintaining the integrity of both the self and the other.

Placing such importance upon maintaining one's self-possession reminds us that intimacy is superfluous for Weinstein and that the philosophical self must maintain such a firm grip on its ownness that the reality of the continual loss of intimacy must remain a live option. Weinstein offers: "There are multitudes of enjoyments, of heterogeneous pleasures, satisfactions, and joys offered by the world to someone with a vital surplus. The civil savage delights in the plurality of pleasurable unions."[32] Weinstein's aim is to situate the self properly in order to enjoy the other without sacrificing the self's own integrity in order to do so. Rather than absconding from the other upon the completion of one's pleasure, Weinstein leaves open the possibility of "sacrifice for the good of the beloved." The important caveat, however, is that this sacrifice must be done with the vital surplus that originates the cathectic act. Weinstein's belief is that the honesty with which he approaches the placement of intimacy in a table of life values will provide for increased joy and arm the self against anhedonia.

Weinstein's more pressing worry is communion, the identification of the self with the other that is "transient and sporadic" and cannot be made to sustain love over time. Indeed, Weinstein argues, communion can "result in resentment against the other when they end and the other is no longer available."[33] Weinstein argues that communion is the "crown of the life of love," wherein the self identifies with a larger humanity, offering a "mood of acceptance of the other as a fellow sufferer."[34] Communion suffers from its extension into the false edges of communion, wherein the self attempts to fuse itself to an abstraction, like all of humanity. Weinstein argues that the extension of communion to abstractions serves the illusion that life can be made comfortable: "it is not love but a way of evading love's risk."[35] Emerson's extension of the sphere of love to his broad household, his large group of friends, his nation, and all of nature exemplifies Weinstein's fear. Weinstein's demand that love exist only between concrete persons exists primarily to insulate the self against losing its virtue to abstract attempts to wish away its finitude and its disappointments.

Ultimately, love is a superfluous virtue that turns itself toward "the cultivation of individuality in others."[36] Weinstein posits that "once I have become habituated to the philosophic standpoint, I no longer need to love or to be loved."[37] Weinstein concerns himself with the risks of love, being willing to take the risk of rejection. But, in this case, Weinstein's larger risk may be that the cultivation of individuated virtues makes intimacy so unnecessary as to eliminate it as a vital possibility. Weinstein admits this possibility: "I am haunted, and I must be if I am a reflective lover, by the self-sufficiency of a life based on self-control and artistry."[38] This problem recalls Thoreau's conclusion to *Walden*:

> In proportion as he simplifies his life, the laws of the universe will appear less complex, and solitude will not be solitude, nor poverty poverty, nor weakness weakness. If you have built castles in the air, your work need not be lost; that is where they should be.[39]

Thoreau, earlier in the conclusion, mentions that one ought to "explore the private sea, the Atlantic and Pacific Ocean of one's being alone."[40] *Walden* reflects Thoreau's choice to privilege the life of individuated virtue over the equally complicated and perhaps disappointing life of what we might call everyday intimacy. Thoreau's statement "I love nature partly because she is not man" encapsulates the choice to reduce the sphere of potential intimacy and its failures in favor of a retreat to the impossibility of nature's equality with the self. Thoreau's *Walden* depicts the problem of having privileged the cultivation of the self to its fullest conclusion.

Weinstein's virtue of intimacy exists within the space of its failure: "In love the autonomy of the other self opens the possibility that one will be failed."[41] Weinstein carefully articulates the limits of individuated intimacy, offering a theory of loyalty but restricting the possibility of becoming a martyr: "the free judge holds all commitments to be revocable and acknowledges all projects to be finite."[42] The restricted nature of this free service of love complicates intimacy in one important way: it becomes difficult to establish the trust necessary to allow the other self to be loved by the self. To counter this problem, Weinstein offers availability: "it is so difficult to become attuned to the other self. Availability is so central to love because it is the practice of such attunement. It is here that love most frequently fails."[43] Can the practice of availability make up for the resistance of the self to commit to the other to the point of making the self's life "living hell"?

Weinstein's articulation of love refuses to give up on the possibility of love but does so with the insulation of the self's integrity as its primary virtue. Love offers a free service but does so from a position of power. Recalling Hobbes's idea from *Leviathan* that "magnanimity is a sign of power," Weinstein's conclusion to the possibility of love in identifying "leaping in for the other" with the height of love suggests that the other must be similarly individuated in order for philosophical love to exist. In choosing to situate love as a virtue crowning self-control and artistry, the self comes to the other with a reserve of power that, if not met by the other, demonstrates a dependency that perhaps cannot be overcome. By opening the intimate relationship to its free service, Weinstein mitigates the power differential in the intimate relationship but cannot dissolve it. As a result, the failure of love and its result in hate is a live option in every individuated instance of intimacy. Privileging the protection of the self's inwardness and using love as vital surplus offers a deromanticization of love while also keeping its possibility open.

Weinstein does not wish to cheapen love, however. He recognizes that "there is no escape from the conclusion that love demands loyalty and that loyalty requires fidelity in the face of temptation."[44] Further, Weinstein explains that "there is an exclusivity involved in love for a particular self . . . love is graded . . . each is not equally important to each."[45] Intimacy places difficult demands upon the self, and Weinstein's philosophical choice is not to weaken those demands to the point of nonexistence. One way in which Weinstein deals with the problem is by insisting that love remain in freedom: "love is not a substitute for care for oneself but is an opportunity to give and, when love has been perfected, to receive a free gift."[46] The philosophical practices of love are, for Weinstein, located within the self and do not impose upon the other. Rather than falling into the transcendentalist mistake of shielding oneself against the other lest one fall into dependence, Weinstein first cultivates a self that is assured enough to enter into love responsibly, and the philosophical self seeks out those who need its vital surplus—that is, its love is directed to particularly those upon whom one's dependence is not a live option.

Weinstein furthers the cause in isolating the concept of "availability" as a way of managing the relation between the self's integrity and the other's improvement. This concept also signals the care that Weinstein takes to ensure the integrity of the self in the practice of virtue. The self appears at first to place itself into the care of the other: "the available self has decentered itself by entering into the other's field as a reality on the way to being rooted in it."[47] This speaks to the level of intimacy Weinstein employs in individuated intimacy—the self comes to an understanding of the other that is not comprehensive but exceedingly nuanced. However, upon coming to a direct understanding of the other, the self "then pulls back and holds itself ready to judge how to initiate its service for the other."[48] This is a delicate exposition, with Weinstein walking the tightrope between a nuanced understanding of the other and a projection of one's needs onto the other. Weinstein recognizes this, pointing out that availability "shows better than any of the other aspects of love the tension between freedom and deliverance that is always present and never fully resolved in a loving orientation."[49]

If Weinstein is successfully imagining a philosophical rendering of intimacy, he is certainly relying on a robust and careful self to employ the virtue. This is not love for the masses, nor is it a democratic employment of intimacy, as we may find in Whitman. Weinstein's retreat from a widely practicable concept of love suggests both the difficulty in realizing his ideal and the payoff of practicing the life of virtue and erotic hedonism. Weinstein argues that availability "does not mean . . . that the available self has plans for the other or wishes to transform the other into a particular kind of substantial self."[50] This is key to understanding Weinstein's use of intimacy and the way in which he escapes the riddle of love that haunts American thought: while the transcendentalists employ love (idealized in friendship) as a means toward greater philosophical growth, Weinstein reduces love to the employment of the vital surplus; that is, love becomes the outgrowth of one's already completed daily practice of individuation. The type of pleasure seeking explored in *Culture/Flesh* only reveals its sensibility under the umbrella of an individuated virtue.

THE WAR FOR PLEASURE

If *Finite Perfection* presents Weinstein's attempt to rescue the self's capacity to love while maintaining one's integrity, *Culture/Flesh* transforms the intimacy of availability into the war for pleasure. Weinstein's philosophical persona in the text, the "civil savage," "undertakes the war for pleasure in light of the revelations of pessimistic philosophy of life."[51] As in *Finite Perfection*, Weinstein begins *Culture/Flesh*'s discussion of intimacy with the stark recognition of its limitations. Pleasure provides no lasting justification for existence and will not help the self in the "losing proposition" that is the human condition. The reality of death, disease, and decay offers the erotic hedonist entrée into a world of limited pleasures without the desire to redeem the world or one's life from its limits. Weinstein writes, "Let the rest of us be free to direct our attention to our own lives so that we can begin to discern what satisfactions the world offers us here and now."[52] The admission of the limitations of the self's ability to redeem life makes pleasure the most viable option for a meaningful life.

Erotic hedonism absorbs the adversity of existence in its war for pleasure, as Weinstein chooses not to parse virtues from their inherent evils but aims to accept the reality of the formative power of each on one's self-consciousness: "I encounter sin . . . as acceptance, as embrace, of adversity within myself, as collaboration with and participation in evil: hatred of existence, life, and the world."[53] Erotic hedonism differs from love in that love constitutes a superfluous virtue of the philosophical self, while erotic hedonism represents a response to *ressentiment* and the death of God. In *Culture/Flesh*, Weinstein aims to take on Nietzsche's problems without succumbing to Nietzsche's desire to affirm existence. Weinstein wonders "whether it might be possible to be alongside and above existence without any support but one's tenacity and love for what is lovely or what might be made so in one's finite environment."[54] The war for pleasure takes on added significance for Weinstein in *Culture/Flesh*, appearing to advance intimacy from superfluous virtue to "an independent purchase on being."[55]

Weinstein's postontological role for pleasure is carefully crafted, as Weinstein refuses to grant pleasure (or any substitute good) a transcendent purpose. Clearly influenced by the psychology of Max Stirner, Weinstein invokes an optimistic pessimism that allows the self to experience pleasure without deifying it:

> The embrace of finite life as the beginning and ending of comprehensive reflection on existence leads to a keen appreciation of the limits of all human effort to wrest from the relation of self and world any satisfactory fulfillment.[56]

The practice of elective intimacy, wherein the self must keep its own integrity as its primary concern, provides the connecting tissue between the virtue philosophy of *Finite Perfection* and the erotic hedonism of *Culture/Flesh*. Weinstein notes that the "ideal of ascending life shifts concern with pleasure from the circumstances environing the self to the fitness of the whole person to enjoy what the world has to offer."[57] Even within the context of postcivilized modernity, care for the self and the self's fitness remain core elements of Weinstein's thought. In this sense, Weinstein aligns himself with the American tradition from which so much of his thought originates.

Self-construction is the primary concern of American thought from Emerson to William James. Much of the most intellectually honest and important work in American philosophy centers on the difficult tasks of assembling a self, relating that self to others, and avoiding the political engagements that limit the self's autonomy. Perhaps the only full failure of American philosophy is in its apprehension of the relationship between self and other, particularly those elective intimate relationships that provide finite sources of organization and meaning to an individuated life. Although Weinstein finds himself most often within the confines of the Nietzschean problematic throughout *Finite Perfection* and *Culture/Flesh*, it is his attention to the problem of intimacy that sparks a fruitful conversation between his invocation of American thought and themes and the history of American philosophy. Weinstein's tenuous solution to the problem of intimacy—privileging self-construction and holding intimacy dear in its finitude while accepting its disappointments not as loss but as a portion of the experience—confounds transcendentalist and early pragmatist thought on the subject. Simply put, Weinstein's expressive philosophy offers a reinvention of the concept of intimacy, one that is robust, original, and rewarding both as thought and as lived. Attending to the care of its construction, we see the core of Weinstein's existential value structure, and we can understand his reservation in accepting the thought of Holmes as a lifestyle model. Weinstein's refusal to give up on intimacy, despite its attendant fears, speaks to the confidence he places in the integrity of his self-construction.

NOTES

1. Michael A. Weinstein, *Culture/Flesh: Explorations of Postcivilized Modernity* (Rowman and Littlefield, 1995) 59.
2. Henry David Thoreau, *Walden* (Yale, 2006) 89.
3. Henry David Thoreau, *A Week on the Concord and Merrimack Rivers* (Princeton, 1980) 265.
4. Ralph Waldo Emerson, *Essays: First Series* (Cambridge, MA: Harvard University Press, 1979) 188.
5. William James, "Will" in *The Writings of William James*, ed. John J. McDermott (University of Chicago Press, 1977) 694.
6. Michael A. Weinstein, *The Imaginative Prose of Oliver Wendell Holmes* (Columbia, MO: University of Missouri Press, 2006) 3.
7. Weinstein, *Imaginative Prose* 3.
8. Weinstein, *Imaginative Prose* 14–15.
9. Michael A. Weinstein, *Finite Perfection: Reflections on Virtue* (Amherst, MA: University of Massachusetts Press, 1985) 13.
10. Walt Whitman, *Leaves of Grass* (1855) in *Walt Whitman: Poetry and Prose* (New York: Library of America, 1982) 84–85.
11. Whitman, *Leaves of Grass* 5.
12. Whitman, *Leaves of Grass* 87.

13. Whitman, *Poetry and Prose* 58.
14. Whitman, *Poetry and Prose* 9.
15. Whitman, *Poetry and Prose* 63.
16. Whitman, *Poetry and Prose* 65.
17. Weinstein, *Culture/Flesh* 59.
18. Michael A. Weinstein, *The Tragic Sense of Political Life* (Columbia, SC: University of South Carolina Press, 1977) 8–9.
19. Weinstein, *Tragic Sense of Political Life* 9.
20. Weinstein, *Tragic Sense of Political Life* 9.
21. Weinstein, *Tragic Sense of Political Life* 21.
22. Weinstein, *Tragic Sense of Political Life* 20.
23. Weinstein, *Tragic Sense of Political Life* 22.
24. Weinstein, *Finite Perfection* 13.
25. Weinstein, *Finite Perfection* 15.
26. Weinstein, *Finite Perfection* 15.
27. Jose Ortega y Gasset, *On Love: Aspects of a Single Theme* (Meridian Books, 1957) 81.
28. Michael A. Weinstein, *Meaning and Appreciation: Time and Modern Political Life* (Purdue University Press, 1978) 5.
29. Weinstein, *Finite Perfection* 128.
30. Weinstein, *Finite Perfection* 131.
31. Weinstein, *Finite Perfection* 130.
32. Weinstein, *Culture/Flesh* 60.
33. Weinstein, *Finite Perfection* 132.
34. Weinstein, *Finite Perfection* 132.
35. Weinstein, *Finite Perfection* 135.
36. Weinstein, *Finite Perfection* 135.
37. Weinstein, *Finite Perfection* 135.
38. Weinstein, *Finite Perfection* 135.
39. Thoreau, *Walden* 351–352.
40. Thoreau, *Walden* 349.
41. Weinstein, *Finite Perfection* 135.
42. Weinstein, *Finite Perfection* 153.
43. Weinstein, *Finite Perfection* 157.
44. Weinstein, *Finite Perfection* 150.
45. Weinstein, *Finite Perfection* 150.
46. Weinstein, *Finite Perfection* 150.
47. Weinstein, *Finite Perfection* 143.
48. Weinstein, *Finite Perfection* 154.
49. Weinstein, *Finite Perfection* 154.
50. Weinstein, *Finite Perfection* 154.
51. Weinstein, *Culture/Flesh* 58.
52. Weinstein, *Culture/Flesh* 62.
53. Weinstein, *Culture/Flesh* 63.
54. Weinstein, *Culture/Flesh* 65.
55. Weinstein, *Culture/Flesh* 65.
56. Weinstein, *Culture/Flesh* 66.
57. Weinstein, *Culture/Flesh* 69.

6 Irreducible Ends

Michael Weinstein and the Value of Agony and Happy Pessimism

Melba Hoffer

DESPAIR OR BELIEF

Ethics is the locus of a perennial conflict between the one and the many. Weinstein's work is finely attuned to the vital drama that lies at the core of our human lives. The tug between our individual desires and our obligations to others permeates our daily existence perhaps as much as breathing. This Kierkegaardian view of the self as primarily "a relation of-itself to itself" is one of the many existential sensibilities that colors Weinstein's work. Weinstein's relationship to Kierkegaard is nuanced and conflicted though overall sympathetic. He sees Kierkegaard as a member of the dissenting tradition in political philosophy. In his 1976 essay titled "Unamuno and the Agonies," he describes this tradition of dissenters as often not seen as political philosophers at all because their ethical and political projects do not offer either a universal description of the common good or an explanation of existing social structures. Instead, Weinstein notes these dissenters offer something far more valuable: they "pose problems, generate paradoxes, and expose dilemmas" (Weinstein 1976, 40–56). In the case of Kierkegaard, polemics abound.

Kierkegaard struggles to free the human enterprise from complete subjugation to reason. He also problematizes the very quotidian act of communication by positing that there are two distinct types: one that conveys our ideas about empirical facts (direct) and one that conveys our ideas of what we value or what we ought to value (indirect). Kierkegaard does not hold a correspondence view of truth in which language and human understanding can easily get at the essence of objects or persons, at least outside of direct communication. Rather, Kierkegaard points to the relationship we as individuals have with our selves as the most fundamental of all our relationships. Our relationship to our selves, in turn, allows us to develop into making faithful promises and commitments to others and ultimately allows us recognize our own fallibility and incompleteness as we turn to God as the ultimate expression of our self-knowledge and self-love. For this reason, Kierkegaard is considered by many the first modern philosopher of communication. Kierkegaard's problematization of subjective truth and communication reveals a recognition about the complexity and conflicted nature of the human mind and will and a commitment to anchor any ethical project on this acknowledgement. Kierkegaard, ultimately, posits that monologue is as vital a form of communication as dialogue since our internal conversations enable, shape, and preclude our dialogic interactions with others. This claim is provocative by many standards, and it is especially so for a philosopher of Kierkegaard's time, since up until then communication was only studied as a form of persuasion and dyadic interaction. Thus, the very idea that communication with ourselves is of any importance to moral development would have been outrageous considering only dialogue was seen as relevant to this realm of human development. Even more provocative is Kierkegaard's attempt to resolve the paradox of fomenting a Christian practice that both recognizes and nurtures the individuality of its practitioners while at the same time holding up as a model the Christian practice of love, *agape*, in which the love of thy neighbor, as well as the love of Christ for mankind, is undifferentiated and impersonal. This tension between *eros*, or the love of a specific, single, special individual versus, *agape*, or *Christian love*, is a problem that Kierkegaard seeks to resolve by placing unique emphasis on the internal lives of individuals who then come to accept Christ's undifferentiated love while persisting in their quest for self-knowledge and inquiry. This feature of Kierkegaard's work is one Weinstein identifies with and promotes. In Weinstein's view, dissenters like Kierkegaard aim to protect individuals from social institutions. Dissenters place value on individuals as more than contributors to a social order or a given religious practice. They shift the emphasis from individuals as undifferentiated and replaceable to unique. This too is a theme that runs though Weinstein's work.

A second point of affinity between Weinstein and Kierkegaard is the latter's view on anxiety as a positive trait. In the *Concept of Anxiety*, Kierkegaard states, "whoever is educated by anxiety is educated by possibility and only he who is educated by possibility is educated according to his infinitude" (Kierkegaard 1980, 156). This existential attitude that repudiates certainty in favor of a pluralistic openness to otherness can be seen in Weinstein's work, as he too places doubt and uncertainty at the core of an authentic human existence. So far, we have seen the ways in which Kierkegaard's political and ethical project is aligned with Weinstein's, but while it is true that Weinstein's work displays many of the concerns and commitments of an existential stance, there is a critical rejection of Kierkegaard that becomes a defining feature of Weinstein's own critical vitalism. This break with Kierkegaard results directly from Kierkegaard's response to the problem of displacing of reason as the supreme value of enlightenment philosophy. Kierkegaard's answer is to offer the following set of choices: despair or believe. Thus Kierkegaard offers faith as the ultimate replacement for reason. Otherwise, according to this dilemma, we are bound to despair. It is worthwhile to note that Kierkegaard's embrace of faith does not reject the recognition of our limitations or an extrication of anxiety from human experience. On the contrary, to embrace the anxiety that comes from faith still requires us to reject certainty. Kierkegaard chooses faith over certainty as a way to reject the Cartesian project that permeated philosophy in Kierkegaard's view. Still, even though Weinstein recognizes the more complex view of faith that Kierkegaard proposes, his response to Kierkegaard's dilemma is to wholeheartedly and "vivaciously" choose despair.

In *The Tragic Sense of Political Life*, Weinstein reveals his wish to be a precursor to existentialism so he can speak more honestly about his suffering much in the way Nietzsche, Kierkegaard, and Unamuno were exempted from having to account for the numerous commentaries on their work. For Weinstein, agony or agonistic doubt is authentic existence. Agony lies at the very center of an individual's personality as we struggle to join forces with collectivities while avoiding reducing the self to just one aspect of our engagement with said groups. In this way, there is always a tension in human existence, an inner struggle between wishing to unite politically in solidarity with others while preserving our irreducibility to a particular interest group, class, or cause. In this way, Weinstein's ethics are also about the desire to make and keep promises. His focus is on the battlefield where we negotiate our individual selves with our public selves. Weinstein's disenchantment with the political situation can be traced to his reading of Unamuno as one who tried and failed to reconcile individuality with political activity. Unamuno too worried that with affiliation and solidarity to a political cause comes a loss of individuality or a danger that the self becomes reducible to that particular engagement. To thinkers like Unamuno and Weinstein, this simplification of the self is as problematic when it occurs to an activist as when it happens to a bureaucrat. Of course, the implication here is not that we ought to stay clear of political engagement, but this is true for neither Unamuno or Weinstein. The claim is that our activities in these engagements do not exhaust the many facets of our creative freedom or our infinitude, in Kierkegaard's language. In other words, not unlike Kant in this regard, Weinstein and Unamuno see human beings as more than whatever ends they might serve. Individuals are ends of and to themselves and not reducible to a function, limited activity, or task.[1]

Instead of making ourselves into a mere means to something else (even if that something appears to be greater or more noble or divine), we ought to treat ourselves and live as ends unto ourselves. Moreover, the recognition that we are all ends unto ourselves prescribes an acknowledgment that other people's projects are as valuable and conflicted as ours. This recognition calls for individuals to take an interest in other people's projects and to value them equally as our own. Thus, the kind of openness that Weinstein seeks is one that respects the self and others, that chases reflection and self-discovery, and that engages joyfully in agonistic doubt. If this sounds like a paradoxical proposition, that is just the way Weinstein wants it. The idea that one ought to discover and pursue projects while embracing deep, willful doubt might seem like an impossibility or a losing proposition at the very least. For how is a person supposed to embrace the self and manifest the resulting knowledge into the world when one is unsure or conflicted? The answer for Weinstein is that such doubt is not at all an impediment to existence but a fundamental feature of it. This agonistic doubt is not an obstacle to creative freedom but the way to it. In this way, Weinstein's stance is reminiscent of Kierkegaard's embracing of anxiety as the way to infinitude. For it is only by envisioning and pursuing different possibilities that we become boundless.

Agony or despair may have appeared undesirable to Kierkegaard, but for Weinstein, a genuine rejection of certainty requires an adaptation to contradiction, a deep engagement with persistent doubt, and a deliberate appreciation of discrepancy. In Weinstein's work, critical inquiry, humility, openness, and free commitment are vital to human flourishing.

Like many undergraduates at a large research university, I too wandered from major to major looking to satisfy what at the time seemed like a bottomless intellectual curiosity. Things got so crazy at one point, I had four majors going: philosophy, rhetoric, political science, and theater for good measure. This led me to a state of absolute confusion. It is for this reason that I came to Dr. Weinstein seeking guidance. I remember timidly going into his office hours and asking him what I should do since I had no idea which major I liked best and should stick to in order to graduate. I'll never forget he looked me directly in the eyes and said: "I think you should be a critic." I listened to his words and remember feeling a sting of displeasure. Here I thought I had come to one professor who truly understood how much I enjoyed different, even conflicting perspectives, and he tells me to go be a critic! In my mind, and perhaps due to the fact that Spanish is my first language, I thought critics were mean people who found fault in other people's ideas or work. I composed myself and very deliberately retorted: "Dr. Weinstein, with all due respect, I could never be a critic. I am the opposite of a critic. I am someone who lives to see the world how other people see it. My biggest pleasure in life is to try to inhabit other people's experience. I truly seek to understand views outside of my own." Upon listening to my rather vehement reply, Dr. Weinstein sat back in his chair and gently uttered one single word that still reverberates in my head to this day. He said: "Exactly!" And with that I left his office having forever changed my idea of both what it means to be critical and to live critically.

AGONISTIC DOUBT

In Weinstein's ethical approach, despairing becomes the way to sustain belief. In other words, one's individual project becomes enriched when one fully appreciates other possibilities and paths apart from the one individually and freely chosen. Being cognizant of the value and plausibility of other projects will cause personal uncertainty regarding one's choices, but for Weinstein, this commitment to plurality also strengthens one's free commitments and unique pursuits. Central to this way of existing is a vital self-contradiction that not only allows for inner conflict but thrives on it. Inner conflict, or evidence of it, is what signals a proper openness to the world and others in it. Thus, agony and doubt and the continual questioning of our own choices as we encounter others' become the tangible signs that we have not closed ourselves off. In Kierkegaard's language, through questioning, through anxiety, we embrace our infinitude.

Still, some might wonder: What is so appealing about a "vital self-contradiction"? Aren't identities based on some form of willed or actual unity of experience? Isn't the Cartesian cogito an entity that is not only self-aware but consistent in its reflective expression of selfhood? The answer to these questions, for Weinstein, is a resounding no. Weinstein's ethical view is based on a resolve to "live without anesthesia" (Weinstein 1977, 172). Simply put, living without anesthesia is a determination to engage in free commitments and pursue one's projects without the unnecessary pretense of certainty or rigid consistency. Living without anesthesia means that we do not compromise our projects or value because we seek to avoid pain, despair, or doubt. Thus, an acceptance of the discomfort and pain that comes from living without a fixed *telos* is necessary, indeed vital, life sustaining and life affirming. What is appealing about a self-contradiction, then, is that it encourages exploration and contemplation. It invites confusion as a practice that yields reflection and committed openness.

Agonists, according to Weinstein, give themselves over to appearance. They have given up on the pursuit of unquestionable truths in favor of a radical relativism that is still rooted in engagement with others in the world. In other words, rather than pursuing the old Socratic project of transcending *doxa* (appearance) in search of *episteme* (knowledge), they recognize that appearance is all there is. Still, this realization does not yield a nihilistic or even a sophist attitude but a commitment to multiplicity and diversity that places equal value in others' projects as we place on our own. Weinstein's point is not that we should withdraw from ourselves and polity, as we cannot make a claim to supremacy, but that the humbling knowledge that ours is but one of many available projects and worldviews increases our duty, so to speak, to seek and fully engage views other than our own. His view is also far from sophistic in that engagement is not reducible to a zero-sum game of self-interest or winning at any cost. Rather, agonists rejoice in the fact that they can never make a claim to absolute certainty or absolute truth with a capital "T," choosing instead to explore the many truths with a small "t" that surround us. In sum, embracing the Weinsteinian view is to part ways with any desire to live with certitude. Instead, Weinstein calls on us to embrace immanence and contradictions (Weinstein 1977, 178). Interestingly, this is somewhat reminiscent of the Kantian premise that human beings only have access to a phenomenal world and not the noumenal world. Kant's intention here is to make a significant disclaimer to his entire philosophical project by stating that humans, including himself, do not have access to a God's-eye view of the world that would yield a direct access to truth. Thus, according to Kant, if we can only rely on our cognitive apparatus to perceive and make sense of the world around us, then that's what we ought to focus on doing with some degree of rigor. Weinstein, of course, is not focused on the limitations of our cognitive apparatus but still shares Kant's belief that human wisdom and experience is fundamentally circumscribed to experience and, for Weinstein, always in flux.

In a Weinsteinian view, Kant's dedication to reason is replaced by a devotion to what he calls the pursuit of "creative freedom," and this creative freedom is dependent on the relativization of man in every possible way (Weinstein 1977, 182). This relativization is taken to be a fundamental commitment, a dedicated practice, and a guiding principle that is actionable. In other words, this is not a superfluous endeavor. To relativize the self means to "act" in accordance to it. This practice discourages mere contemplation in favor of engagement and action. This is also a rebellious stance, since, according to Weinstein, the Cartesian and analytic approach to philosophy that pervaded idealism has tangible and unfavorable political implications. To be specific, political certainty, which stems from the quest for epistemological certainty, leads to a perception of consensus as the only valid political means of governance (Weinstein 1977, 170). This orientation toward formulating, managing, and, in many cases, engineering consensus often leads to totalitarian regimes that seek to fix meaning and claim exclusive access to truth and rightness. Such a political agenda discourages dissent, creates social stratification based on ideology, and stifles individual and collective freedom.

Still, the lure and power of political certainty is undeniable. The Frankfurt school left us a legacy of warnings against such tendencies, and today, political economists, Marxists, neo-Marxists, and feminists, among others, still labor to, first, identify and then to resist those monopolizing and hegemonic institutions and practices that still aim to amass power by stripping away individual criticality. Weinstein notes that "joining a collective is easier than making a friend," and while this statement may seem puzzling at first, the implication here is that there is something about turning the self into a tool or means for a cause that robs us of the full range of our capacities and possibilities (Weinstein 1977, 172). Making a friend, on the other hand, is posited as the more difficult endeavor, and this is likely because in making and sustaining friendships, we engage the person as irreplaceable. We get to know and appreciate the quirks, contradictions, and virtues of this particular friend, while joining a collectivity by definition shifts the significance of our being to membership in something greater and likely more important than its individual parts. Perhaps for this reason, Weinstein considers dispersed energy and a soul divided as authentic living. This is not to say that we ought not to take part in political action but to remind us that our engagement in such activities does not comprise the totality of who we are. This is because the collectivity only recognizes the consistency and single focus of our actions, something Weinstein resists by locating the substance of our freedom in our enduring moments of doubt and anguish.

A proper Weinsteinian ethical engagement, then, is more aligned with a virtue approach to ethics than with a deontological or consequentialist approach. Weinstein doesn't follow Aristotle's program for virtue ethics, though he recognizes the existence and value of virtues like temperance and justice. Instead, Weinstein's focus is on the portion of a classical virtue ethics that prescribes the free selection of projects, the pursuit of *phronesis* (practical wisdom) by pursuing one's projects with actions, and a singular emphasis on self-control as a fundamental feature of creative freedom. These three features of Weinstein's approach make it resonant with virtue ethics. Furthermore, Weinstein calls on us to practice specific virtues like "ruthless compassion, a combination of corrosive criticism and pity appreciation" (Weinstein 1977, 182). Ruthless compassion deals with the unflinching commitment to a pluralistic engagement with the world, while corrosive criticism appreciation compels us to continually question even our most sacred ideas, and pity appreciation indicates a continued interest in and exploration of new ideas.

By contrast, a deontological approach with its focus on adherence to rules and codes of conduct directly refutes the agonic way of being. The agonic self is not one to be held back by tradition or popularity. Similarly, consequentialism, with its maxim of the greatest good for the greatest number, shifts emphasis away from individual value, replacing it with a calculus of collective happiness. The disjuncture between an agonic self and a consequentialist rubric is only exacerbated by the fact that the very point, indeed the very goal, of a consequentialist ethic is to minimize pain, something Weinstein joyfully embraces. Therefore, virtue is the proper lens through which to understand Weinstein's agonistic view. This ethical grounding combined with Unamuno's political ethic of agony and conflict appear to be two important strands of thought that inform Weinstein's commitment to agonistic doubt.

**Agonistic doubt is something that anchors not only Weinstein's ethical and political views but his teaching. A truly watershed moment in my education occurred when, in the middle of our 300-level course on contemporary political theory, Dr. Weinstein appeared to be overcome by uncontrollable laughter. That's right, he began laughing and simply could not stop. His laughter overpowered him so much that he fell to his knees and lay on the floor holding his stomach as though it really hurt to laugh so heartily. At first, like many in the classroom, I felt confused, stunned, and painfully embarrassed at witnessing these events unfold. To make matters worse, I was the product of a highly conservative and old-fashioned system of Spanish education that would have found it absolutely impermissible for an instructor to lose control, laugh hysterically, or heck, even express any* *kind of joy in a classroom setting. I was mortified and clueless as to what to do. A few moments later, I began to notice, as it often happens, that the fit of laughter had begun to spread to the students. No one knew what was so funny. No one knew how to respond, but Dr. Weinstein's laughter was so infectious, we began to laugh too. I was one of the students who held out the longest, my strict Spanish code of conduct forcing me to repress my increasing desire to join in this confusing moment as I desperately searched for an appropriate response. Well, as you might imagine, I could only hold out for so long. Professor Weinstein was still on the floor rolling around laughing, and by now the entire classroom was laughing loudly and clueless as to what caused this event. Next thing I know, I fell off my chair laughing too, and the entire class shared in this moment of apparent madness. I did not know it then, but that experience changed my view of the role of education and pedagogues dramatically. Today, as a college professor in my own right, I make certain laughter permeates class meetings and discussions. I find that sharing in a moment of joyful confusion soothes insecurities and levels the playing field by reminding us that we are fundamentally alike and connected to each other. Nowadays, it is me who sees the confused, surprised, and agonistically doubtful looks on my students' faces as they try to figure out whether it is okay to join in laughter or repress it. This gift, this experience of happy agonism, is one that will stay with me forever.*

FINALISM

It is not surprising, thus, that the centrality of agony in Weinstein's thought led him to investigate what Western academics might consider fringe philosophy and social theory, such as the finalist ethics of turn-of-the-century Mexican thinkers (*pensadores*) José Vasconcelos and Antonio Caso. Both vitalism and finalism are closely connected philosophies in so far as both philosophies go outside of purely scientific investigation in the examination of living systems. For this reason, both approaches are considered equally untestable in quantitative terms. Finalism searches for the identifiable final cause that directs evolution, while vitalism, the older viewpoint, proposes a creative, purposeful, and nonmaterial "vital force" (*élan vital*) that sustains and promotes life. Finalism arose from the moral revolution promoted by the Ateneo de la Juventud Mexicana, challenging the positivistic dictatorship of Porfirio Diaz with a call to a suprapositivistic logic and public morality. Finalist ethicists sought to replace economic values with aesthetic and spiritual ones that protected individuals from an instrumentalist logic that only recognized the use-value and efficiency of people and resources. For Caso, specifically, good action is a pure act, and for this reason, it lies outside and above the calculus of brute economic concerns. While the positivistic worldview produces a maxim of minimum effort and maximum advantage that actively devalues the humanity of others, the finalist attitude toward human existence calls for maximum effort and minimum advantage. In other words, a finalist ethic privileges charitable actions, appreciation of others, and aesthetic concerns above efficiency, acquisition, and domination. For the finalist, maximum effort is authentic existence. A finalist ethic promotes individuality and spontaneity that must still confront *zozobra*, or continuous vacillation between moral choices. The finalist ethical framework, thus, resembles Weinstein's own emphasis on doubt as a fundamental feature of an authentic existence. It also dramatizes the struggle for freedom and autonomy inherent in colonized spaces where repressive forces seek to stifle creativity and justice, oftentimes through violent means. Moreover, finalist ethics reveal the unexpected ways in which oppressed communities vocalize their suffering and agony while living in *zozobra* and happy pessimism.

Caso and Vasconcelos are paragons of a prolific intellectual Latin American philosophical front that actively resisted positivist philosophy at the turn of the nineteenth century and the early decades of the twentieth century. These philosophers were inspired by the vitalist philosophy of Henri Bergson. We know that vitalism was embraced in many parts of Latin America and the Caribbean as a response to the forty-year reign of positivism as a cultural, philosophical, and economic force. Pedro Henriquez Ureña notes in his *Historia de la Cultura en la America Hispana* that at the turn of the twentieth century, positivism was the presiding philosophy in Latin America (Henriquez Ureña 1947, 114). Moreover, Marta de la Vega, in her *Evolucionismo versus Positivismo*, offers additional support and further historical context by positing that in Latin America, positivism became dominant in many countries that had just overthrown colonial regimes. She describes that between 1870 and 1930, these countries began the uphill enterprise of building a "national culture" while at the same time laboring to adopt alternative political and economic models (de la Vega 1998, 13). It has also been noted that another consequence of the rejection and diminishment of positivism in Latin America is the advent of a new era of philosophical freedom, less dependent on European influences and more reflective of the historicality and reality of Latin America (Sasso 1997, 115).

Philosophers of the caliber and influence of José Vasconcelos and Antonio Caso, both from Mexico, along with others like Raimundo de Farias Brito of Brazil, liberally embraced vitalism. According to Carlos Rojas Osorio in his seminal book on the Puerto Rican philosophical tradition, the sequence of philosophical tendencies in Puerto Rico follows the same pattern as the rest of Latin America (Rojas Osorio 2002, XIII). This research shows evidence of the expansion of positivism to the Caribbean region, although, as Jorge J. E. Gracia points out, positivism took on a variant modality in each individual country since ideas take on new life as they cross the Atlantic and develop according to the sociocultural ecology of each country. Furthermore, while positivism had a powerful influence in Latin America and beyond, the specific brand of positivism in question was, to be precise, conceptually, a combination with another major philosophical strand that was introduced simultaneously in the region, evolutionism (Frondizi and Gracia 1974, 13).

In Puerto Rico, the premier positivist philosopher was Eugenio Maria de Hostos, who, under strong Krausist and naturalist influences, dedicated his efforts to combat what he termed "el escolasticismo filosófico y moral" (moral and philosophical scholasticism), to the betterment of pedagogy—particularly in the sciences—and the struggle for Puerto Rican and Cuban independence (Frondizi and Gracia 1974, 79). While Latin American positivism was focused on creating societies that reflected the latest and best scientific and technological developments—along with other demands of the modern era--philosophers like Bergson, Nietzsche, and James introduced a critique of moral paradigms and axiologies that positivism utilized to direct so called "infant" nations toward progress. Thus, evolutionist vitalism is, in fact, the philosophical impetus that provided the philosophical background for the critical efforts of vitalists throughout Latin America (Frondizi and Gracia 1974, 93).

For these reasons, the critiques of morality, capitalism, and individualism became central themes of this revolutionary evolutionist vitalist approach. This moral and social critique also manifested itself in an increasing scrutiny of the role of the press and the journalist in society. Said critique antagonized vigorously the journalistic values promoted by positivists. One example of such values can be found in Hostos's *Tratado de Moral (Moral Treatise)*. In the treatise, Hostos prescribes an ethical social function for journalists in which duty is a journalistic weapon that "ought to be propagated and imposed; in which the journalistic right to educate should be incited to be exercised; an economic order, so journalists may hold it up against the mistakes of the socio-economic order that hinder or obstruct productivity; a judicial order, journalists should hold up against the clumsiness of the will and reason that continually compel, alter or put it at risk; and finally a moral order, for journalists to present continually as the *desideratúm* of human dignity" (Hostos 2000, 402). Against the backdrop of such a strong moral imperative, Puerto Rican vitalist thinker and journalist Nemesio R. Canales Rivera hit back contra this articulation of the role of the press advocating for a journalistic ethos in which the primary social contribution is to shake the ideologies and expectations of the reader. One prominent example of this debate can be found in the inaugural issue of the *Cuasimodo Canales* magazine in which Canales passionately declares that the magazine will go beyond supplying the public with factual information to shake the spiritual lethargy of his American brothers with the forceful presentation of new ideas. He goes on to reiterate that it is not enough to repeat, as popular journalism does, the trope that the world is changing or ought to change, but instead Canales announces the magazine will deliberately stick its finger right in the gaping wound, in the origin, routines, and attitudes that ought to perish (Montaña 2000, 184). It is easy to see the stark contrast between the two philosophies: while the vitalist call to journalistic service aims to guard against the hegemonization of its readership and to foment the revolutionary impetus, the positivist call to journalistic action is one in which the press, and journalists by extension, are subsumed under the goal of productivity and "progress."

This very attitude of defiance, boldness, and a strong defense of the ever-changing nature of life and individuals lies at the very center of a vitalist worldview. In Latin America, vitalism was popularized through the writings of Henri Bergson. His approach is based on the principle that the dominating ethos of positivism is tied to death (Bergson 1957, 187), while reality lies in continuous change and movement (Bergson 1957, 264). According to the Bergsonian view, positivistic science only contributes half of the human ontology, since the other half is composed of values that are impossible to quantify, measure, or manipulate in the same fashion. Therefore, according to Bergson, the role of the philosopher—and the role of the journalist according to Canales—is to shake the mind, to go against the natural inclination of intelligence. To Bergson, this is the proper function of philosophy (Bergson 1957, 39).

Having introduced the central tenets of a Bergsonian view, I have yet to mention that another important feature of the vitalist view is a chronic aversion to all that, in its purpose to stabilize, ends up "mechanizing" life. In other words, Bergson posits that our very human nature contains a dialectic element that does not allow us to become stuck on one idea and hold on to that idea *ad infinitum*. On the contrary, the more we attempt to remain immune to changes in our biology, social ecology, or thought, the more our innate intuition will obstruct such paralysis. Thus, for Bergson, there is only one reality, and much like for Heraclitus, reality is perennial movement. Still, one might wonder: What are the implications of a Bergsonian vitalism for individual philosophers, including Latin American finalists? For Bergson, as mentioned earlier, the philosopher not only recognizes the ever-changing nature of our existence but navigates comfortably within the swaying of its fluidity. This philosophical function was especially appealing to the turn-of-the-century finalist philosophers who propelled, incited, and witnessed dramatic political, social, and economic change. Of course, this is not to say that the philosopher must necessarily give herself over to chaos or neglect/forget to promote social or ethical theories—which would be useless if society was little more than a senseless maelstrom of events—but the philosopher must find and uphold her truth while creating connections and useful concepts for herself and others.

This engagement with philosophy requires the philosopher to communicate her ideas, and while Bergson did not discount the value and utility of the act of communication, including philosophical communication, he problematizes it in important ways. The first predicament has to do with the fact that a philosopher must admit to herself that that which she values and considers necessary maybe little more than a false belief or a mistaken assumption that may be rendered obsolete by the next wave of ideas. The philosopher exposes herself to the danger that her concepts or theories will be ultimately ephemeral and thus discarded and stripped of their usefulness. The second risk to which a vitalist philosopher is exposed is that, knowing that her ideas and concepts are of her invention and a by-product of her personal experiences, she must consider which method of communication is, in this case, the most effective so as to simultaneously communicate her skepticism—which is part and parcel of the vitalist worldview and approach—and fully participate in a process of persuasion and philosophical communication. In other words, how is it that the philosopher can communicate her ideas while at the same time stimulating a critical reception from her reader or interlocutor?

Søren Kierkegaard hoped to resolve this paradox through his theory of indirect communication. Of course, Kierkegaard is better known for his foregrounding of existential philosophy; however, Kierkegaard's theory of indirect communication exhibits striking similarities to Bergson's vitalist concept of truth. For Bergson, the philosopher is obligated to abandon intuition, once she has felt the impulse, and look only within to continue the flow of ideas (Deleuze 1977, 132). Of course, any comparison between Bergson and Kierkegaard with regard to the concept of truth has to admit without hesitation that in Bergson, we have the concept of intuition, which is simultaneously contradicted and complemented by intelligence. Intelligence for Bergson is that which directs our actions, while the intuition is that which will generate its problems. In the case of Kierkegaard, his concern lies more with the distinction between objective and subjective reality. For Kierkegaard, subjective reality is composed of our experiences and values. This reality is also known as existential truth. Kierkegaard puts a premium on subjective truth and thus creates a dilemma in terms of how it is that we are supposed to communicate a "truth" when our reader or interlocutor has not lived through or shared our experience in an identical manner. Thus, both Bergson and Kierkegaard run into the same problem when it comes to communicating the philosopher's truth. The problem lies in the impossibility of allowing ourselves to be driven by intuition—while becoming comfortable with the swaying of the fluidity of ideas—and then to persuasively communicate with an interlocutor in such a way that our experience will also be true for her. In the case of Kierkegaard, how can we communicate something to another that is only decipherable to ourselves? For Kierkegaard, the solution is to communicate with our interlocutor via pseudonyms, ironies, and other devices that force an interlocutor to be skeptical about our message while at the same time allowing said interlocutor to arrive at their own conclusions. This method of indirect communication (mauetic) is not unlike Plato's own dialectical approach, since Plato also prescribed metaphor, Socratic irony, and aporia in dialogue" (López de la Viela 1994, 36).

Much like the Bergsonian and Kierkegaardian enticement to opening ourselves to the universe and to oneself (in spite of its difficulty), Weinstein finds evidence of a continual effort on the part of the Mexican finalist philosophers to "provide the person with an opening to others" (Weinstein 1976, 110). In particular, Vasconcelos dives into the difficulties of both remaining open to others and pursuing our projects by proposing his own "method of coordination." Weinstein describes Vasconcelos's method as one that stands in opposition to the doctrine of consensus that seeks to reconcile differing points of view through one unifying or universal principle. In contrast, Weinstein describes Vasconcelos's method of coordination as one that "abandons the search for substantive agreement and investigates the possibility that there is a way in which people can learn to appreciate different worldviews and ultimately to create new ones. Eschewing reconciliation in favor of clarification" (Weinstein 2013, 132). Vasconcelos appears to be after a similar problem to Kierkegaard's but comes up with a different approach that is founded on the presumption that each individual worldview rests on analogies or comparisons to others. The coordinating aspect of this approach comes in as we strive to expose ourselves to others' ways of understanding the world, identify the analogies that support their view(s), and try to learn from them. Weinstein describes the process in more detail in his brilliant essay on Vasconcelos and analogy. He says:

> Once the analogies have been comprehended, the appreciator would inspect his experience of social relations and determine whether the world-view made it more coherent. Did it make him aware of new dimensions to his relations, such as subtle forms of exploitation? Did it disclose new values to him, or present new projects? Did it relate aspects of his experience which had hitherto been kept apart? Even if the world-view did not help him coordinate his own life, he would at least comprehend the ways in which others around him might experience their situations. This would not necessarily eliminate or even reduce ideological conflict, but it would clarify such conflict and increase the freedom.
>
> (Weinstein 2013, 135)

This method of coordination relies on a "logic of appreciation" that seeks to comprehend other parts of the whole as opposed to extending one fixed point of view to others. This type of "organic logic" is grounded on the insight that the whole is not the sum of its parts but the "cohesion" of its parts. Furthermore, for Vasconcelos, discourse—one might even say communication itself—is a relating of concepts. Our ability both to be understood and to persuade depends on the very practice of relating concepts. This is another instance in which Vasconcelos's approach differs from Kierkegaard's, as the former situates communication in the sharing of concepts while the latter locates (the superior) subjective communication on subjective experience. Additionally, Vasconcelos notes that analogy is the relating of images through aesthetic forms like "harmony and disharmony" or "consonance and dissonance" (Weinstein 2013, 134). The main objective of Vasconcelos's method of coordination, then, is not to pursue the dubitable task of sharing subjective experience but to promote a logic of appreciation that encourages and sustains diversity. Ultimately, for finalists like Caso and Vasconcelos, among others, the structure of human life is dialectical, and for this reason, our interactions (including communicative ones), and particularly those interactions with others that generate bonds through charitable action as Caso insists, provide the creative force that redeems human existence from degradation. As Weinstein puts it, "one must be willing to both seek the aid of others in confronting one's own suffering and to help others overcome their insufficiencies" (Weinstein 1976, 89).

**It wasn't until I set foot in Dr. Weinstein's classroom that I fathomed that love had anything to do with teaching or learning. Having been a part of his course for some weeks, I took notice of how thoroughly engaged he was in our class discussions. And when I say thoroughly engaged, I mean body and soul, because anytime one of the students made a comment that had some insight Dr. Weinstein's entire body—arms, torso, legs, facial muscles, the whole thing—would react to it! This was a sign that he was fully receptive to us and that we, the students, through effort and engagement, could literally "move" him. This was a new experience for me, as was the day when we were having a particularly lively discussion and Dr. Weinstein abruptly halted the discussion and, as if something was erupting deep within his soul, he exclaimed to the class "I love you so much I can't hardly stand it!." This willingness to be open to others, to allow others to move and affect him deeply, as well as his desire to use love as a way to help students overcome perceived (and in many cases real) insufficiencies, stands out to me as paradigmatic examples of Weinstein's own practice of the logic of appreciation.

IRREDUCIBLE ENDS

As Weinstein puts it, the twentieth century was a time of ideological and philosophical diversity (Weinstein 2013, 132). Mexican finalism was an early response to Western cultural imperialism as well as a turn toward a more autochthonous philosophical movement. Mexican vitalism was intertwined with nationalism, as its proponents sought to create a new social, political, and economic set of ideals. The finalists were also concerned with making a distinctive moral contribution to the world, as they saw positivism reduce philosophical anthropology to the philosophy of science.

For Weinstein in particular, Emilio Uranga is the inheritor of both the metaphysical and the historicist branches of Mexican finalism (Weinstein 1976, 91). In his view, Uranga's greatest contribution to the finalist project may well be his investigations into the problem of reconciling divergent ideas and circumstances. Among his insights into this problematic is the identification of the structure of human experience as *zozobra*. For Uranga, " 'zozobra' is a kind of restless anxiety that results from constant exposure and openness to new ideas" (Weinstein 1976, 96). Other features of living in a state of *zozobra* include not knowing whom to trust, the welcoming of contradictory impulses, and living in a continual state of vacillation between opposite directions. This description is evocative of the Weinsteinian ethic of "agonistic doubt" in that both are an invitation to "coordinate," welcome, and appreciate heterogeneous, competing, and clashing ideas. In short, philosophy itself is *zozobra*.

Weinstein reminds us that "Mexican finalists have believed that future good is best promoted by the example set by those who realize intrinsic values in the present" (Weinstein 1976, 107). Thus, perhaps there is no better example of how a finalist ethic incites us to seize the present as the practice of *"pesimismo alegre"* (happy pessimism). Though the term "happy pessimism" was originally introduced by Vasconcelos to describe the finalist sensibility, Weinstein embraces and translates the term as "vivacious despair" (Weinstein 1985, 192). While Vasconcelos's happy pessimism is anchored on the jubilant acceptance of life—in spite of its essential horror—for the sake of a radical and definitive existence (Vasconcelos 1931, 5), Weinstein offers his own portrait of this seemingly self-contradictory practice as "the opportunity to act freely, unencumbered by the pressure of having to fit oneself into a plan for divine or secular salvation. Liberated from God and progress" (Weinstein 1976, 57). Weinstein also describes vivacious despair as a mood in which we can confront the ever-present sting of our finite existence as well as its "messengers" disease and decay. Through embracing vivacity, we can identify what can be good about life while recognizing its countless misfortunes. Both Vasconcelos and Weinstein promote happy pessimism as part of a larger finalist, Bergsonian and Weinsteinian affinity for humor. The humorist questions human values like dignity, morality, and the values both of one's culture and of the culture that seeks to impose itself through force. Happy pessimism, in this way, is a fitting compliment and response for a finalist philosophy that encourages us to confront our being-toward-death and makes explicit to oneself what that encounter means. It is also a way to remind ourselves that we as individuals are irreducible ends, that we ought to seek a hope without expectation, but a necessary hope (Weinstein 1985, 164). In many ways, and as Weinstein's agonistic doubt shows, this is the proper aim of all philosophy.

***As Weinstein asserts in his book* Finite Perfection: Reflections on Virtue, *enacted love subverts philosophy"* (Weinstein 1985, 140). *He explains that love's gratuity distances it from philosophy. Immediately after this statement, he demands that philosophy recognize love as the crowning virtue. I had the pleasure of learning a great deal about both love and philosophy from this gifted teacher. I remember during my final semester in college*

I took another course with Dr. Weinstein, trying to squeeze every last bit of wisdom I could from him. I enjoyed the semester tremendously, but the last week of classes I could not help but become overwhelmed by the thought that this was my last class with Dr. Weinstein before I was to go off to continue my education elsewhere. I remember going to our final two class meetings and sitting all the way at the back of the room. My demeanor those last of couple of meetings was somber and uncharacteristically quiet as tears rolled down my face for those entire two class periods. I did my best, of course, to not embarrass Dr. Weinstein with my premature nostalgia, but as I sit here today writing this piece and tears once again roll down my face, I realize, perhaps these tears are just a genuine expression of profound gratitude for critically vital lessons. * *

NOTE

1. The only caveat here might be to mention that Weinstein's commitment to vitalism might mean that individuals are part of the pursuit of a greater purpose in so far as they contribute and model the continual life force that continually generates change.

REFERENCES

Bergson, Henri. *La Evolución Creadora*. Madrid: Alainaza Editorial. 1957.

de la Vega, Marta. *Evolucionismo versus positivismo: Estudio teórico sobre el positivismo y su significación en América Latina*. Caracas: Monte Ávila Editores Latinoamericana C.A. 1998. Print.

Deleuze, Gilles, ed. *Henri Bergson: Memoria y Vida*. Trans. Maurio Armiño. Madrid: Alianaza Editorial S.A. 1977. Print.

Frondizi, Risieri y Jorge J.E. Gracia, eds. *El Hombre y Los Valores en la Filosofia Latinoamericana del Siglo XX*. Madrid: Fondo de Cultura Económica. 1974. Print.

Henriquez Ureña, Pedro. *Historia de la Cultura en la America Hispana*. Buenos Aires: Fondo de Cultura Económica. 1947. Print.

Hostos, Eugenio María de. *Tratado de Moral*. Obras Completas 9 Filosofía Tomo 1. Rio Piedras: Editorial de la Universidad de Puerto Rico. 2000. Print.

Kierkegaard, Søren. *The Concept of Anxiety: A Simple Psychologically Orienting Deliberation on the Dogmatic Issue of Hereditary Sin*. Trans. Reidar Thomte. Princeton: Princeton University Press, 1980. Print.

López de la Viela, M. Teresa, ed. *Figuras del Logos Entre la Filosofía y la Literatura*. Mexico D.F.: Fondo de Cultura Económico. 1994. Print.

Montaña, Servando. *Antología de Nemesio R. Canales*. 2da ed. Rio Piedras: Editorial de la Universidad de Puerto Rico. 2000.

Rojas Osorio, Carlos. *Pensamiento Filosófico Puertorriqueño*. Humacao: Isla Negra. 2002. Print.

Sasso, Javier. *La Filosofia Latinoamericana y las Construcciones de su Historia*. Caracas: Monte Avila Editores Latinoamericana C.A. 1997. Print.

Vasconcelos, José. *Pessimo Alegro*. Madrid: M. Aguilar, Ed., 1931 (p.5).

Weinstein, Michael A. *Finite Perfection: Reflections on Virtue*. Amherst: University of Massachusetts Press. 1985. Print.

———. *The Polarity of Mexican Thought: Instrumentalism and Finalism*. University Park: Pennsylvania State University Press. 1976. Print.

———. *The Tragic Sense of Political Life*. Columbia: University of South Carolina Press. 1977. Print.

———. "Unamuno and the Agonies of Modernization." *The Review of Politics*. 38.1 (1976): 40–56. Web. 10 Dec. 2013.

7 Unpacking My Weinstein
Border Thinking and Classical American Philosophy

Ramón E. Soto-Crespo

Finalism, which first appeared at the margins of modernity, has now infiltrated the metropole . . . "Latins" have appeared in youthful Saxon skins.

—Michael A. Weinstein, *The Polarity of Mexican Thought*

Consider nomadism not as originary state, but as an adventure . . . the nomadic adventure begins when they seek to stay in the same place by escaping the codes.

—Gilles Deleuze, "Nomadic Thought"

Is Michael A. Weinstein a border theorist? And, if so, does it change the way that we understand his critique of classical American philosophy? How might this reclassification illuminate, clarify, or contribute to American political philosophy? This chapter explores these questions by engaging Weinstein's early work on Latin American and Spanish thought, arguing that to think of Weinstein only in the context of a U.S. philosophical tradition is to narrow the scope of his impact. Weinstein is not simply an American philosopher but also a philosopher of the Americas. Framed and influenced by Latin American political philosophy, his work exceeds a singular tradition. In other words, Weinstein's philosophy exceeds American and Latin American national traditions yet finds its inspiration in both.

WHAT IS BORDER THINKING?

Weinstein's interventions into border thinking can be best appreciated by considering his book *The Polarity of Mexican Thought*, a study in Latin American finalist philosophy, published in 1976 with the help of a Guggenheim Foundation Research Fellowship. He traveled to Mexico in 1972, 1973, and 1975. "I taught myself to read Spanish with an introductory grammar, a dictionary, and the collected works of Vasconcelos," states Weinstein while on the road heading South (*Polarity* ix). His thinking about finalism and antipositivism derived from a very specific geopolitical location in the Americas. Whereas finalism posits a final causality that motivates its forward-looking evolutionary movement, vitalism believes in life's vital force as that which propels life forward. At the border, finalist thought affirmed vital life and critiqued positivism as an instrumentalization of living experience. Fundamentally antipositivist, finalist philosophy positioned itself as a counterforce to the philosophical positivism dominating Latin American politics. Weinstein's work represents one of the first interventions into finalism—a foundational philosophy that would inform border thinking in the twentieth century. Border thinking uses finalist insights in its politico-philosophical stance against the biopolitical management of life in modern societies.

According to cultural theorist Walter Mignolo, border thinking results from the combination of two interrelated discourses: one described by Foucault as "subjugated knowledge" and another described by Darcy Ribeiro as "subaltern knowledge" ["*conocimiento subalterno*"] (*Power/Knowledge* 82; *Las Americas* 68). Border thinking emerges at the meeting place of "subjugated knowledges"—those knowledges that are disqualified as illegitimate, bastard, or low ranking—and "subaltern knowledges"—the local knowledges that stem from the margins of global Modernity (*Local Histories* 19). Something akin to a Foucaultian critique of biopower from below, border thinking bases its approach on three main components: antipositivist politics (the critique of the instrumentalization of life by the modern state and global corporate power); the vitalist affirmation of life (the critique of postcivilized modernity as an illusion of individual freedom while techniques for the diminishing of life's experience are institutionalized); and the finality of our life experience (the critique of the vestiges of immortality that remain masked under a biopolitics of the management of human life in modern technocracies).

Building on these antipositivist philosophical currents, Weinstein addresses the coloniality of power by introducing a critique of biopower that is framed in terms of border thinking. Consider, for instance, his description of a turning point in the history of Western imperialism, where the colonial impetus reverses course from the margins to the center:

> While Western imperialism was expanding, positivistic methods of control could be imposed on external colonies, giving the citizens of the metropole the luxury of relatively liberal institutions . . . Thrown on the defensive, imperialism turns inward, replacing politics with administration aimed at manipulating markets and preserving internal security.
>
> (*Polarity* 10)

Positivism, having moved from the imperial margins to the center of diminishing empires, acquired new impetus as "a system of instrumental politics, adaptable by any power group that seeks to maintain control in a threatening situation" (*Polarity* 10). Weinstein's brand of border thinking emerges from the margins of the American experience as a response to the global instrumentalization of modernity. His philosophical standpoint challenges the spread of global designs in the management of all planetary life and intuits that its main effect is the impoverishment of human life on earth. No other political philosopher had engaged this turn toward a twentieth-century systematic devaluing of human life in postcivilized society with the fervor of Weinstein. In work after work, from *Polarity* (1976) to *Data Trash* (1994), we encounter a line of thought that confronts the problematic of the ever-greater instrumentalization of life. *Polarity* set the tone of a long career in detecting and deterritorializing the ever-growing authoritarian constructs that devalue existence worldwide. The territories south of the U.S. border promised to Weinstein a critical horizon where life-philosophy continued to provide its vital opposition to those contemporary entities that Deleuze and Guattari called, in *Nomadology*, "despotic forms" (*passim*). As Latino scholar César Hernández-Cela puts it, Weinstein's works show how Latin American thinking "offer[s] an alternative to the predominant technocratic thought of the more 'advanced' Western Nations" (*Polarity* 224).

If on the way to the border, José Vasconcelos's collected writings had framed Weinstein's thinking, then it makes sense that Latin American philosophy had become for Weinstein a source of new critical vitality, one that is fundamentally informed by border knowledge. As Weinstein says of his time in Mexico, "I felt myself moving in my own element" (*Tragic* 14). Not surprisingly, his return from the border took place in the back of a truck with "*braceros*"—the migrant Mexican agricultural workers whose nomadic existence saturates the U.S.–Mexican borderlands. "*Braceros*," meaning "human arms," is the perfect example of the reductive nature of the instrumentalization of life in contemporary modernity. "*Braceros*," the closest to a "bare life" type of existence in the borderlands, are key to understanding the instrumentalizing of those who "cross over the wire" and become nomadic subjects stripped of civil rights and legal protections.

FROM POSITIVISM TO BORDER THINKING

Border thinking is fundamentally antipositivist, for it builds on the scaffold developed by Latin American finalist thought. In the late nineteenth and early twentieth centuries, positivism had extended its influence over Latin American society and began a process of perfecting the administrative apparatuses of the modern state, driven by its key ideological belief that the state should mirror at the national level what had worked for Western political subjects at the individual level, "the self-conscious control of human beings over their material circumstances" (*Polarity* 4). Positivist polities developed as a "set of social structures whose principle is the efficient accumulation of means for collective action, such as wealth, power, influence, and loyalty" (*Polarity* 3). Epitomized by the dictatorship of Porfirio Diaz, in Mexico, from 1876 to 1911, positivism became a primary target of finalist philosophy. Antipositivism contested the scientific rationalization of culture, especially the modernization of society that was at the heart of pro-Western civilization and its dictatorships in the Americas. Accordingly, Latin American finalism rebelled against "a civilization that mechanizes human activity through instrumentally rational hierarchical organizations and behavioristic ideologies" (*Polarity* 15).

Antipositivists opposed the perfection of society via scientific methods, the socialization of production, and economic development via industrialization. They were concerned that "the public situation in the twentieth century was not evolving in the directions of love, justice, and peace, but was marked by the emergence of more refined techniques of domination" (*Polarity* 5). In their view, these technologies of the state "seemed to result in the appropriation of human beings-as-instruments by elites rather than in the liberation of humanity, the proletariat, or the individual" (*Polarity* 5). Thus, finalism represented an "attempt to redeem and rescue intrinsic value from the threats posed by instrumentalist institutions and ideologies" (*Polarity* 4). They condemned the treatment of human beings either as "natural resources" or as functionaries serving ulterior organizational ends (*Polarity* 8). Their treatises represented a "way of encountering the problems of an instrumentalist civilization" (*Polarity* 6). For Weinstein, these philosophers of the Americas had "eschewed liberalism, Marxism, and traditionalism in their search for a 'new humanism,' attempting to forge visions of an authentic community grounded first in vitalism and later in existentialism" (*Polarity* "Preface"). They had absorbed Bergsonian vitalism in their thinking and, as a result, their philosophy defended the vital impetus at the heart of being, the *élan vital*, against positivist (modernists/utilitarian/capitalist) and idealist (communist/fascists) philosophies. In the words of political scientist John Hart, Weinstein's work elucidates how these thinkers challenged "authoritarianism and hierarchy" ("Weinstein" 1395). Likewise, political theorist Howard Wiarda refers to Weinstein's work as "innovative" precisely because he makes perfectly clear that "Mexican political philosophers had initiated a revolt against positivism and instrumentalism long before their North American counterparts and that they had developed an original response to nineteenth century evolutionism rooted in vitalism and personalism" ("Polarity" 256).

Latin American philosophy provided Weinstein with a kindred reaffirmation of his antipositivist viewpoint, given that these life-philosophers had developed philosophical positions that were "strikingly similar to my own" (*Tragic* 12). José Vasconcelos, Octavio Paz, Carlos Vaz Ferreira, Alejandro de Vista, Alejandro Korn, and Antonio Caso all presented in their philosophical meditations unexpected ways of encountering the world. Looking for a way out of the trappings of modern civilization and its sprawling global logic of instrumentalization, these thinkers expanded the scope of their philosophical inspection, venturing inward to their psychic borders, where demons and masked savages inhabited their own personal borderlands. This strategy is of great importance for Weinstein, because he detects at the heart of positivism a strategic negation of interiority. By contrast, Latin American philosophy preferred an existential method: the "sincere examination of the heart" (*Polarity* 13). To this effect, Vasconcelos develops an organic logic, that is to say, a theory of human existence as "a process of coordinating wholes" (*Polarity* 23). In human consciousness, Vasconcelos argues, "all the fragments [are] joined together through coordination" (qtd. in *Polarity* 23).

Although Weinstein is critical of the mystical undertones and utopic endpoints of finalist philosophy, he nevertheless acknowledges "Vasconcelos' major contribution to Mexican thought was to engage positivism as a methodology for thinking" (*Polarity* 12). Vasconcelos, one of the most important Latin American cultural theorists, is central not only to Weinstein's antipositivist thought but also to the intellectual development of border thinking. Vasconcelos's philosophy left an imprint on major twentieth-century Latin American cultural treatises such as Octavio Paz's *The Labyrinth of Solitude*, Gloria Anzaldúa's *Borderlands/La Frontera*, and Walter Mignolo's *Local Histories/Global Designs*. These are three key texts that give shape to the newly constituted canon of border thinking.[1]

Building on Paz's reading of Vasconcelos's cosmic race, Anzaldúa and Mignolo point out that Vasconcelos's philosophy had opened the door to not only a new mythos but also a new consciousness. By thinking through a confluence of many streams of thought, Vasconcelos had structured a different way of encountering the world, one that for Latin American thinkers was better apprehended as a consciousness of the borderlands (Mignolo 78). As the father of a borderland consciousness, Vasconcelos proposed a philosophical counterlogic to twentieth-century political despotisms. At a time when the world found itself dominated by a spectrum of ideologies of purity, Vasconcelos prioritized cultural and racial mixture. In his philosophy, as in Paz's later on, those despised as racial and cultural misfits—as bastards, as border mongrels, as wanderers, nomads, and hybrids—found themselves at the center of an antipositivist political project. Weinstein argues that Julián Marías, a Latin American finalist philosopher, captured this moment of reconceptualizing consciousness from below as a crucial stage in human life: "a state of crisis in human existence occurs when people reach the frontiers of a certain form of life and confront a chaotic cosmos" (*Polarity* 7). Weinstein explains that by developing this border strand of radical perspectivism, "Latin American thinkers provided me entry into the existential tradition" (*Polarity* 14). At the geographical border and into the inner borderlands of the border subject, these thinkers provided Weinstein with a new intensity, a vitalism of the Americas. "So I have wandered between histories," confesses Weinstein (*Tragic* 25). His early works transport the reader to a hemispheric geography of shifting landscapes, to a border consciousness, and to polyvalent cartographies of thought.

BECOMING A BORDER SAVAGE

At the heart of Weinstein's critical antipositivist and vitalist views, we find life, the "*élan vital* or vital impetus at the heart of being" (*Structure* ix). This is a vitalism that repudiates, like Vasconcelos and Nietzsche, "symbolic substitutes" for life's complexity (*Structure* x). If these symbolic substitutes replace "life with meaning" in the form of symbolic harmonies, then critical vitalism would provide a "life grasped without symbolic completions or harmonies" (*Structure* x–xi). Consistent with antipositivism, Weinstein proposes a "critical examination and defense of our being as it is lived from within" (*Structure* xi).

In the spirit of border thinking, Weinstein invites us to accept an understanding of experience that is composed primarily of "conflicting tendencies and incapable of final reconciliation" (*Structure* ix). In this sense, he had developed a particular coordinated consciousness by having adopted the finalist concept of *zozobra*. Against the grain of the American philosophical tradition, Weinstein introduces us to "a mode of existence that refuses to sacrifice values, although the values appear to be contradictory" (*Polarity* 108). *Zozobra*, as he describes it, is "an attempt to 'burn the candle at both ends,' to coordinate heterogeneous elements in their totalities" (*Polarity* 109). Therefore, *zozobra* for Weinstein "describes the ceaseless transit between perspectives on human existence—this transit itself presupposes contingency" (*Polarity* 109). This form of relation between poles, or polarity of thought, seems to be "the most consistent with Mexican finalist thought" (*Polarity* 107). As a fundamental relationality between poles, *zozobra* is something like a dance, a nomadic dance at the borders of instrumentalized culture.

Writing for *The Hispanic American Historical Review*, critic William J. Kilgore (1980) finds that Weinstein's philosophical understanding of *zozobra* provides extreme clarity to one of the least understood concepts originating south of the border. He explains that Weinstein grasps *zozobra*'s primary insights: "a way of attempting to coordinate opposing forces found in human experience without the exclusion of either and with the living in tension between the two" (513). *Zozobra*, located at the heart of border thinking, is precisely where we encounter the polarity of thought that attempts to actualize contradictory values. Akin to Deleuze's nomad thought, border consciousness coordinates a myriad of intensities, and its location is a deterritorialized dwelling in the in-between of cultures, of states, and of other modern despotic inventions. In Deleuzian terms, *zozobra*'s dance is construed as the "play of high and low intensities" that takes place in the plane of intensities ("Nomadic" 257). With his/her play, the border savage keeps a perpetual migration between intensities ("Nomadic" 257). Border thinking thus functions similarly to Deleuze's concept of the rhizome, where "a high coefficient of deterritorialization" works to keep normalizing (or despotic) forces at bay (*Kafka* 16).[2]

Inspired by Vasconcelos, Weinstein's border thinking had transformed him into a border savage: "I want to realize contradictory values, living them simultaneously" (*Tragic* 21). Having predicted a shift in modernity's landscape, Weinstein writes, "Finalism, which first appeared at the margins of modernity, has now infiltrated the metropole . . . 'Latins' have appeared in youthful Saxon skins" (*Polarity* 15). The antipositivist critique that had incubated in the Global South began circulating northward. There it found fertile soil in New Left movements. Both north and south found common ground in devising a series of "intelligible dialectical responses to a positivistic polity that organizes life according to instrumental values and mechanistic processes" (*Polarity* 10).

Founded on finalist insights, Weinstein's border savage engages the instrumentalization of life and its drive to realize other than intrinsic values. The border savage, a "Latin" in spirit masked by a Saxon skin, uses the language of decolonization to critique a territorialization of intrinsic values by modern technocracies. Therefore, decoloniality as deterritorializing refers to that aspect of finalist thought that reaffirmed the vitality of human existence over and against the powers of management over life. As Latin Americanist critic Stanley Ross argues, Weinstein's insights about "'finalism' with its emphasis on ends" adds to our political lexicon "a meaningful alternative to instrumentalism with its focus on means" ("Institutionalized" 292).

DETERRITORIALIZING CLASSICAL AMERICAN PHILOSOPHY

"The most famous North American finalist was George Santayana, whose work resembles that of Caso, Vasconcelos, and Ramos," writes Weinstein in *Polarity*, thereby illuminating a transnational philosophical undercurrent that has penetrated classical American philosophy (104). Tackling the philosophies of Santayana, Josiah Royce, C. S. Peirce, William James, and John Dewey, *The Wilderness and the City* is Weinstein's most serious engagement with the main pillars of U.S. political thought. There, Weinstein proclaims, "[f]or several decades the American tradition of life-philosophy has been moribund" (156). Santayana represents for Weinstein an exception to the geographical movement of life-philosophy from the center of U.S. philosophical thought to areas south of the U.S. border. In his view, Santayana denotes something like an anomaly, for the core of American philosophy had been territorialized by a belief in the instrumentalizing of all life as the outcome of a foundational hatred for existence. According to Weinstein, Santayana "placed himself outside the American cultural tradition" and positioned himself as not an American "except by long association" (109). Santayana's location within classical American philosophy is an ambivalent one given that he "shared the universe of discourse of the other American classical philosophers, but not their 'Anglo-Saxon piety'" (127). Santayana's life-philosophy embodied for Weinstein a refreshing distancing from the "wilderness." In the context of classical American philosophy, the wilderness stood for "the mental space into which the philosopher withdrew in an act of separation from the moral conventions, the cognitive assumptions, and the practical certitudes of the 'city'" (*Wilderness* 5). The retreat to the "wilderness" promised the thinker a "treasure" that will allow him or her "to reenter community with a special gift" (*Wilderness* 5). Weinstein's phrase "'Latin' in Saxon skin" reverberates in his understanding of Santayana's life-philosophy by presenting him as the anomaly among those with whom he shared a discursive world. If, in Weinstein's view, Santayana was "suspicious of any claims that truth could be discovered in the wilderness of pure experience or pure reflection," he nevertheless understood that Santayana believed in the need for "acceptance of personal finitude and an affirmation of the goods that appear in the flux of existence" (109). Santayana's philosophy of "acceptance" was a philosophy at the border of those stemming from the wilderness.

Weinstein's border savage is one who knows that

> there cannot be a mere repetition of the American classical tradition today. The efficient megalomania . . . has worked its way into the center of American culture and will not be easily plucked out. Contemporary fanaticism feeds on the hatred for existence, proliferating weapons and poisons and wastes. The intolerance of existence has issued in the systematic erosion of the basis of life (155).

Border thinking and the concept of *zozobra* allow Weinstein a vantage point from which to examine the erosion of life in instrumentalized society. Consistent with life-philosophy, *Wilderness* proposes a "renewal of individualism in America," and it recommends that this "tradition be deepened and revitalized" (156). For Weinstein, individualism is not the possessive individualism created by moralized society but rather the individualism of those who embrace finitude. Life-philosophy is at the heart of this revitalization process, for it provides a new balance. Inspired by *zozobra*, Weinstein proposes a new recalibration for a tragic being-in-the-world: "The basis for renewal of individualism in the present day is a deepening of inner tolerance to the point at which it becomes normal and not eccentric to live with world-sickness and still to be free for commitment to limited tasks within the public domain" (*Wilderness* 155). The affirmation of personal finitude is key because American pragmatism replaces this fundamental acceptance with morality.

Weinstein's critique of the abyssal foundations of American pragmatism and its moral invention is best elucidated in his chapter on William James. James, he argues, had "advanced to positions that are parallel to those of Nietzsche" (*Wilderness* 22). Weinstein explains further:

> James's resort to a special realm of "practical reasoning" was, indeed, the best diversionary tactic he could have invented for blinding other American philosophers to the existential insights, concepts, and arguments that abound in his works . . . Deeper than the superficial struggle between science and religion, which, as Nietzsche noted, had been won by science at the inception of the modern era, was the effort of American philosophers to center life-philosophy in moral commitment, an effort that may, indeed, have been a continuation of the puritan spirit.
> (*Wilderness* 134–135)

The shift in life-philosophy from a focus on inner tolerance to one in which moral commitment is primary represents for Weinstein a deviation that keeps in place the self-righteous characteristic of the puritan spirit. Like Santayana, the border savage is not blinded by this moral quest. This is the insight that informs Weinstein's argument. When confronted with Nietzsche's abyss, James invents a new realm: "James shows most clearly how life-philosophy has been conceived in America. It has been a means for helping people to live from one day to the next, a way of inspiring participation in the common life, and, above all, a way of accentuating the positive" (*Wilderness* 154). Yet, for Weinstein, this positivism is another mirage that distances the individual from his/her inner tolerance.

Pragmatism had delivered a moral ruse in replacing a life-philosophy founded on finitude. Furthermore, in America, this moral ruse assumes the imperative of producing a moral society: "The community was an abstract totality of voluntary servants who were bound to the social whole, not to the divinity . . . The solution of American classical philosophy to the spiritual problems created by the death of God in the West was the substitution of society for God as the object of life-commitment, deliverance, discipleship, and service" (*Wilderness* 137). Blinded by the promise of a moral society, the abyss of finitude is covered over by a positivism that furthers the instrumentalization of living existence. The disavowal of the abyss propels U.S. culture toward an ever-more-sophisticated and pragmatic technological future. In *Wilderness* we understand the consequences of turning our gaze away from the abyss, for our negation of inner tolerance sets the terrain for a society built further away from *zozobra* and its borderlands. American civilization contemplates neither the wilderness at the frontier of its experience nor the life-philosophy percolating at the edges of its modernity; instead it rushes forward toward a virtual or digital society to be produced, consumed, and inhabited.

FROM BORDER TO CIVIL SAVAGE

When, in *Culture/Flesh* (1995), Weinstein writes, "The civil savage vindicates the finite flesh," we detect the intensity of border thinking in many descriptions of this postcivilized construct that he calls the civil savage (5). If border thinking takes the form of coordinating irreconcilable forces, Weinstein's description of the civil savage emphasizes his strategic geopolitical location at the border of all traditions and civilizations: "it is better for him to live with these doubts and to be free of any particular tradition, to be able to relativize all traditions, to see through the essence of all civilizations, and then to plunder the treasures of each one of them" (*Culture/Flesh* 5). The border savage, with its antipositivist thought and border thinking, had led over the years to the coming into being of the civil savage of postcivilized modernity.

The civil savage results from decades of Weinstein's deep explorations into his border consciousness in order to provide a philosophy of conduct. Weinstein's encounter with finalist thought had pointed to a crisis that emerged with the perception of an "absence of legitimate and acknowledged forms for conducting life" (7). This absence of a philosophy of conduct for postcivilized modernity is a preoccupation that stems from those beginnings.

> The emergence of savagery amidst the ruins of civilization impels me to undertake a meditation on philosophy of conduct if only to draw attention to the horizon of possibilities that individuals might entertain as they seek to hold on to their existence day by day, to survive and, perhaps to flourish.
>
> (*Culture/Flesh* 1)

It is in light of this pursuit that Weinstein states, "this is the book of the civil savage who seeks to live well in the culture jungle" (*Culture/Flesh* viii).

Like Foucault, who in *The History of Sexuality* and in *The Use of Pleasure* sought to understand contemporary culture by studying forms of sexual conduct that preceded the deployment of modern sexuality, Weinstein delves into studying contemporary culture with his "border eyes." In Weinstein's case, he studies the deployment of culture in postcivilized society. This epistemological vantage point allows Weinstein to spell out not only what we have become but also what we, as a civilization will become. In postcivilized modernity, Culture has become king.

He explains further that civilization emerges "in the spiritual act of removing the individual self from its connections to an ongoing community, revealing the self to itself as a strange and fragile being and then reconnecting the self to a reality surpassing in its being and goodness the reality of the particular community" (*Culture/Flesh* 3). If society had replaced god in the creation of American civilization, then in contemporary postcivilized modernity culture had replaced civilization. This cultural world is "dominated by science and technology" at the expense of cultivated inwardness, because it privileges the externally perceptible (*Culture/Flesh* 5).

It is precisely this "cultivated inwardness," found to be unnecessary and undesirable in civilized society, that is finalism's central tenet and border thinking's fundamental premise. For Weinstein, a philosophy of cultivated inwardness stemming from the wilderness follows a pattern that had ruled American classical philosophy from James and Peirce to Rorty. The philosophy of the wilderness had led to the philosophy of the border and then to the civil savages as one of the last stops in the culmination of a long journey.

TOWARD A MINOR WEINSTEIN

Finalism had invited people to a life of "being for perfection" not in terms of authenticity but in terms of a good life (*Polarity* 116). It had directed people's attention to the possibility of "coordinating the heterogeneous contents of existence into acts" (*Polarity* 116). Weinstein's many treatises on self-understanding, such as *Finite Perfection, The Structure of Human Life, Meaning and Appreciation*, and *Wilderness and the City*, share a methodology of self-reflection that stemmed from the coordinated polarity of border thinking. It is in the last pages of *Polarity* where we find those key insights that have given impetus to Weinstein's thinking over the decades. Seeking "unity through coordination rather than through reduction," Weinstein's border thinking shows that he embraces another of Vasconcelos's paradoxical propositions, that is, his concept of "happy pessimism" ["*pesimismo alegre*"]. Therefore, it should not surprise us if this is the same perspective on life that we see at work in *Data Trash*. It is via Vasconcelos's writings that we gain an even deeper understanding of Weinstein's keen observation that when faced with the open solitude of instrumentalized existence, humans are thrilled to "wait for the androids" who will replace them. If finalism had invited humans to a path of "being for perfection," humans have chosen their own future replacement in a digital wilderness. The life-philosophy of "bare life" at the border has led to years of philosophical rumination. According to Giorgio Agamben, "bare life" refers to those "*who may be killed yet not sacrificed*" with impunity (original italics, *Homo Sacer* 12). "Happy pessimism" comprehends the horizon of a postcivilized futurity in which instrumentalization produces a new desire for a digital posthuman existence.

This chapter sought to shed light on border thinking in Weinstein's oeuvre. I have traced a trajectory from border savage to what he calls civil savage. Nevertheless, I acknowledge that there is more to Weinstein's thought than can be made to fit into a single thread. This is because Weinstein's oeuvre is rhizomatic. As Diane Rubenstein pointed out, the Weinstein that I am unpacking here can be considered a minor thread in Weinstein—minor in the Deleuzian sense—where I am reading Weinstein against the grain and where I pursue the thread of the border savage as one of the philosopher's many masks. I see Weinstein's works as a series of critical engagements by a border savage who, like a Deleuzian war machine, learned to spot and deterritorialize the despotic formations of culture.

Weinstein's vitalist critique seeks to dig deeper underneath the despotic codes of postcivilized society. The border savage, as a Deleuzian "war machine of thought," attempts to escape the codes of culture by having them flow through him and by not becoming encoded, or coded over, by them ("Nomadic" 260). Weinstein's border savage is fundamentally an experimental creature in postcivilized culture. In work after work, Weinstein analyzed and decoded the despotic avatars of instrumentalized society. By welcoming codes without being coded and by remaining uncoded while mixing up all the codes, Weinstein has provided a philosophical trajectory for rethinking the border, nomadism, and power.

NOTES

1. There is yet another type of border thinking that develops from the U.S.–Caribbean borderlands, more specifically, from the borderland state of Puerto Rico. I highlight this particular thread in *Mainland Passage: The Cultural Anomaly of Puerto Rico* (2009).
2. Gilles Deleuze develops these ideas with Feliz Guattari in their best-known work *Anti-Oedipus*. But it is in their work on *Kafka: Toward a Minor Literature* that we see the application of their concepts into the field of literary/cultural forms.

REFERENCES

Agamben, Giorgio. *Homo Sacer: Sovereign Power and Bare Life*. Trans. Daniel Heller-Roazen. Stanford: Stanford University Press, 1998.

Anzaldúa, Gloria. *Borderlands/La Frontera*. San Francisco: Aunt Lute Books, 1987.

Deleuze, Gilles. "Nomadic Thought." *Desert Islands and Other Texts, 1953–1974*. Ed. David Lapoujade. Trans. Michael Taormina. Los Angeles: Semiotext(e), 2004. 252–261.

Deleuze, Gilles, and Felix Guattari. *Kafka: Towards a Minor Literature*. Trans. Dana Polan. Minneapolis: University of Minnesota Press, 1986.

———. *Nomadology: The War Machine*. Trans. Brian Massumi. New York: Semiotext, 1986.

Foucault, Michel. *The History of Sexuality. Vol. 1: An Introduction*. 1976. Trans. Robert Hurley. New York: Pantheon, 1978.

———. *Power/Knowledge: Selected Interviews and Other Writings, 1971–1977*. Ed. C. Gordon. New York: Pantheon, 1980.

———. *The Use of Pleasure: Volume Two of the History of Sexuality*. 1984. Trans. Robert Hurley. New York: Vintage, 1990.

Hart, John M. "*The Polarity of Mexican Thought: Instrumentalism and Finalism* by Michael A. Weinstein." *The American Political Science Review* 72:4 (1978): 1395–1396.

Hernández-Cela, César. "*The Polarity of Mexican Thought: Instrumentalism and Finalism*, by Michael A. Weinstein." *Contemporary Sociology* 10:2 (1981): 224–225.

Kilgore, William J. "*The Polarity of Mexican Thought: Instrumentalism and Finalism*, by Michael A. Weinstein." *The Hispanic American Historical Review* 60:3 (1980): 513–514.

Mignolo, Walter. *Local Histories/Global Designs: Coloniality, Subaltern Knowledges, and Border Thinking.* Princeton: Princeton University Press, 2000.

Ribeiro, Darcy. *Las Americas y la civilización. Proceso de formación y causas del desarrollo desigual de los pueblos americanos.* Caracas: Biblioteca Ayacucho, 1968.

Ross, Stanley R. "Institutionalized Revolution in Mexico." *Latin American Research Review* 14:1 (1979): 292–296.

Soto-Crespo, Ramón. *Mainland Passage: The Cultural Anomaly of Puerto Rico.* Minneapolis: Minnesota University Press, 2009.

Weinstein, Michael A. *The Polarity of Mexican Thought: Instrumentalism and Finalism.* University Park: Pennsylvania State University Press, 1976.

———. *The Tragic Sense of Political Life.* Columbia: University of South Carolina Press, 1977.

———. *Meaning and Appreciation: Time and Modern Political Life.* West Lafayette, IN: Purdue University Press, 1978.

———. *Structure of Human Life: A Vitalist Ontology.* New York: New York University Press, 1979.

———. *The Wilderness and the City: American Classical Philosophy as a Moral Quest.* Amherst: University of Massachusetts Press, 1982.

———. *Culture/Flesh: Explorations of Postcivilized Modernity.* Lanham, MD: Rowan and Littlefield, 1995.

——— and Arthur Kroker. *Data Trash: The Theory of the Virtual Class.* New York: Palgrave Macmillan, 1994.

Wiarda, Howard. "*The Polarity of Mexican Thought: Instrumentalism and Finalism* by Michael A. Weinstein." *The Journal of Politics* 40:1 (1978): 256–258.

Part III
Vitalism

8 "I Am the Radical Reality"

Weinstein's "Defensive Life" as a Political Response to Postcivilization

Julie Webber

> My own philosophy, I venture to think, is well-knit in the same sense, in spite of perhaps seeming eclectic and leaving so many doors open both in physics and in morals. My eclecticism is not helplessness before sundry influences. It is detachment and firmness in taking each thing simply for what it is.
>
> (George Santayana 1942, 156 preface to *Realms of Being*)

The above quote is Santayana comparing his philosophy to Dante and Spinoza's. It is relevant to my celebration of Michael Weinstein's philosophy and teaching in the sense that his is so "well knit." It is taken from various philosophers and, though seemingly eclectic, Weinstein's *Culture/Flesh: Explorations in Post-Civilized Modernity* outlines an argument for "defensive life" in the second chapter. It is this thesis that I will elaborate upon in this essay, along with my reflections on his teaching during my time in his classes at Purdue University in the 1990s. When I first met Mike, it was in his Modern Political Theory course held at University Hall, a short walk from the political science building. I was apprehensive about the class, having purchased the books (*The Prince* and *The Revolt of the Masses*) as well as being told by my advisor that his classes were notoriously difficult. When I walked into the classroom, a room that held many people who I now continue to call friends, an older graduate student was sitting in the front row looking around the room, eyes darting to see what kind of person would be taking the course he was no doubt ta-ing. At the moment the clock struck for class to begin, this graduate student jumped up and stood at the front of the room and said, "Okay, we're ready to begin. Welcome to Modern Political Thought." I was shocked: here was this guy who was a professor (or was he?) beginning to teach our class with such seriousness yet complete and total casualness in every aspect of his demeanor. From there, I decided he was probably one of the most interesting characters I would ever meet. In the past twenty years, that has proven true. I have not encountered many people as sure of themselves and yet completely indifferent to inauthentic signs of professionalism as Mike Weinstein. Given the way the world looks today, I doubt I will yet.

In the several years that I took courses with Mike and he served on my dissertation committee, I learned many things from him about teaching and life philosophy. The most important one, I think, was about "social defense." When I first encountered his explanation for this practice, it was in the modern course. However, over the next few years, it would become more and more apparent. Eventually it would come out in print in the book that defined the "civil savage." In it, he writes, "Perhaps the deepest intuition of the civil savage is that life is filled with adversity" (Weinstein 1995, 31). How to engage this adversity in all its manifestations (other people, self-loathing, doubt, and boredom) is addressed in this chapter. In the following pages, I propose to outline Weinstein's justifications for his conclusion that he is the *"ens realissimum"* and how such a conclusion shaped/s his disposition toward other people in postcivilized modernity. This will mean an outline of Weinstein's thoughts concerning this modernity, as well as his detailed examples of how to think about it. In the rest of the essay, I use both the text and my lecture notes and recollections from this period in Weinstein's pedagogical life (1992–96) to accomplish this task. By the end, I suggest that this intervention into postcivilization is profoundly political and challenges contemporary ideologies that struggle to settle the question of existence once and for all. Michael's foray into the culture/flesh problematic is profoundly American. I find his work centered on questions that preoccupied the North American pragmatists and finding a place for them in the pantheon of modern thought, especially where they fit after the death of God. The moral impasse that presents itself between Hegel and Nietzsche is a constant theme in Weinstein's work, especially *The Wilderness and the City*. What is clear is that the conclusions he draws about them in this work find their way into the heart of *Culture/Flesh*, where Mike uses them to diagnose his own (and our) situation. For at bottom, Mike is an American, and he knows the life of the mind in the United States better than anyone else I have ever encountered. This is, no doubt what makes him so seductive to his students. His pedagogy is to take individuals as he encounters them and make sense of their intellectual and vital plights. This means his philosophy and that of the civil savage is a peculiarity, it is a kind of Yankee existentialism. This is odd because Americans cannot be existentialists, at least not in great numbers since the culture works against it. As the author of *Wilderness and the City* admits, he is "a product of American culture," and his philosophy too is "modern in some special way" (Weinstein 1982, 11).

Existentialism often suffers from the charge that it is subjective and apolitical, at least in the United States. Even European thinkers from Husserl to Heidegger to Sartre have had to justify their ontological claims by making reference to a certain freedom or warning of oppression that follows from meditating on the nature of existence. To ponder the nature of existence while keeping in mind the character of one's society and culture can be dangerous. This is especially true in the United States, where, as Mike often intimates, people are averse to acknowledging moral dilemmas except by resorting to found objects like religion or technology as follow-up and often quick-fix solutions. As he wrote of the American classical philosophers,

> The severest criticism that can be leveled against American classical philosophy is not that it was based on a pathetic fallacy, but that it did not think through morality seriously enough. When the consequences of the death of God are squarely faced and absorbed into life, no substitutes for God, whether cultural, social, or psychological are acceptable. There can no longer be, as Nietzsche understood, any taken-for-granted mediations between one human being and another. Each one faces the other starkly as a finite life in the process of corruption and as a center of an absolute demand against being that cannot be met. On the other side of the abyss there is, indeed, as James understood, the moral will, but that will can only be exerted purely if it is grounded in tolerance of the other not as a "rational being" or as an "imperfect logical being" or as a fragment of humanity, but as a finite and individuated life who is here and now an absolute expression of demand. It is an approximation of this image of the individual that is the context of Jean-Paul Sartre's apothegm that "hell is the other person."
>
> (Weinstein 1982, 136)

Avoiding the moment in which you realize that the modern project is over and all that is left is the other in their profound weakness and finitude is the American response to this realization. Even in its only public philosophy, the American pragmatists could do no more than look away. In fact, their philosophy encourages their readers to look away from finitude and ignore an important part of being: "Their defenses of natural piety were primarily a way of making finitude palatable by the old measure of accentuating the positive and eliminating the negative" (ibid., 136). This is what defensive life of the civil savage is at the ready to engage at all times. He must defend against (and respect) the psychological defenses of "natural piety" or "common sense." These two dominant American defenses are illusions (if not held in check) that compromise whatever vitality can be mustered in the "Epicurean garden" of "the streets" (Weinstein 1991, 215). We are in this mess, according to the civil savage, because civilization is over—the modern project has been abandoned *without acknowledgement*—by a liberalism "that has outrun itself, that has lost its footing in voluntary solidarity" (Weinstein 1991, 224). This is the problem: we're all still pretending "Humpty Dumpty" can be put back together again while we all lie around feeling good about ourselves (notes). Defensive life is important if you don't want to end up in emotional cul-de-sacs inspired by these politics (and you cannot avoid them, even if you say you're "not political"—in fact, that may make you even more vulnerable to illusion). Valuing clarity, "self-rule," and avoiding "the good of feeling good about himself," the civil savage invited me to follow him along for a while "on our common journey through and past postmodernism" (book inscription).

DEFENSIVE LIFE

Defense against the illusions of others can take many forms: outright war, hegemonic certainty through the spread of values, religious faith, and even romantic love. What initially drew me to Mike's pedagogy and thinking was his steadfast assertion that to be truly living, one had to be engaged in some form of social defense. From my own perspective at the time, this seemed appropriate given all of the so-called "polite" intrusions I encountered myself as a woman raised in the Midwest. To concentrate on one's own life and happiness while ignoring the almost boorish insistence of other people's values and idealizations was always perceived as a form of selfishness. This meant that social convention always trumped personal happiness, possibly, at times, even sanity. "What" Mike asks, "does it mean to hold a belief, not because (as Nietzsche once said) one 'believes in belief' but because it makes the negotiation of social relations more convenient, because it is judicious, whether or not it is true? The camel and the lion co-exist in an irritating embrace, draining one another of their vitality" (Weinstein 1995, 97). Mike proposes a sense of self-discipline as a response to this social conundrum. I cannot help here but think of his go-to text for Modern Political Thought, *The Revolt of the Masses*, where Ortega outlines the "select" individual who insists on self-discipline. Ortega anticipates criticism,

> When one speaks of 'select minorities' it is usual for the evil-minded to twist the sense of this expression, pretending to be unaware that the select man is not the petulant person who thinks himself superior to the rest, but the man who demands more of himself than the rest, even though he may not fulfill in his person those higher exigencies. (Ortega 1964, 15)

Effort that is self-designed is never rewarded. This means, at a certain point in one's life, whether bound to fulfill the missions of a cultural pragmatism or the demands of Hegelian bureaucrats (the way Mike once described Madeleine Albright's foreign policy), a decision can be made by the person who wants sanity, and possibly more, moments of happiness.

The critical strategy that evolves in *C/F* is intended to deflect these missives. You can, as he always says of his advice, reflections, or philosophies, "take it or leave it;" it's up to you. Circa 1994, the problem with life in the United States was trying to live in a world without civilization, freed from transcendence and situated in the middle of toxic discourses of technocracy. A time that Mike, contrary to many others that came later such as Agamben, Hayles, and others who held fast to the prefix "post–" but attached it to other terms like "human," "modern," or "positivist." The modern and the positivist seem dated and centered on a rejection of Descartes. While the post-"human" seems more recent, it may only be the response to the increasing faith in technocracy that we witness in the aftermath of the decline of humanism. Both signs, and the signifieds that march under them, I think, would be rejected by Mike as inaccurate ways of describing the contemporary political and cultural problems faced in a time of recline and then decline. To stay busy, one can read the "cynical signs" that simulate significance, and one can pretend to believe in something all the while knowing they cannot and therefore decide to redouble their efforts to believe in it. The cynical sign thrives at this time. To it, Mike gives the term "postcivilization."

POSTCIVILIZATION

In many of Mike's courses, I learned a great deal about the importance of periodization. For example, as an undergraduate in his Post-Marxism course, we spent a lot of time discussing different ways of locating, marking out, and describing the "modern" and "postmodern" as well as "modernism" and "postmodernism." Mike was careful to make distinctions among all of these terms and to teach us the importance of understanding the role of aesthetics, praxis, Althusserian practice, and, of course, the term "critical." Of note is Mike's characterization of civilization as a heuristic device: "a dialectical process of consciousness or, better, of spirituality in a broad Hegelian sense, in which human existence comes to be grounded in an inwardly grasped apprehension of being, *an apprehension removed from the specifications of social convention.* Thus, the core of civilization, from which all of the many works associated with it spring, is self-concentration, the seizure of individuality that provides the self with a criterion of judgment transcending custom and artifice, and, compacting aesthetic, cognitive and volitional dimensions of mentality into an *integral strategy of relating self to other*" (Weinstein 1995, 3–4, emphasis mine). This was the Michael I met in University Hall in August of 1992: the civil savage. Michael notes that he may be "romantic" about civilization and that his "master fantasy" may be a "metapsychosis" drawn from his careful study of the "documents that are generally identified as the guiding texts of the world civilizations" (Weinstein 1995, 4). Already here, though, we are met with Mike's "love piracy," for the texts that are taken under advisement are indeed "selected" as among the best "treasure troves" for his purposes and those that promote the strongest elements of those civilizations that Mike needs to build his own: as he calls himself, "the most liberated interpreter, the purest Protestant of all" (Weinstein 1995, 5). Mike's discourse in C/F on defensive life is mindful of standpoint: he is writing in the United States, a place dominated by philosophical pragmatism and its watered-down pedestrian counterpart, common sense. His references to Dewey, James, and Royce throughout clarify what they have accomplished: making a bridge from Pauline doubt to René Descartes, Dewey intervenes to enliven the so-called "American century," providing its inhabitants with a kind of quasi-certitude about the meaning of life by bucking the question altogether and encouraging social activity even while criticizing the idea of certainty itself. The "pragmatists proposed to deconstruct civilization and in their efforts helped to usher in the era of postcivilized life, without, however, understanding the consequence of their reflection, which was to expose the radical contingency within the depths of the individual, the provisional status of all our judgments" (Weinstein 1982, 37).[1] So we are squarely within the realm of twentieth-century questions. In the civil savages' discourse, we are preoccupied with modern obsessions and modernist reactions to them. An anecdote might serve well here. I once remember a student asking Michael point blank, "Doesn't anything ever bother you?" This question was meant to provoke and signified all those things about civilization (especially other people and their political opinions) that make us lose our sanity. He stuck his finger up into the air as if checking to see which way the wind was blowing and thought aloud, "Yes, I have a screen door in my garage that won't latch and keeps banging shut." The class roared with laughter. Mike went on with our "knitting." This refusal to give in to the enticement to "play your tape" is the achievement won from following the "integral strategy." So let's return to this "integral strategy" that Mike evoked in his description of civilization. How does it work and what does it aim to accomplish?

In order to accomplish this task of mastering what can only be provisionally called "self," the civil savage must diligently attend to three aspects of life: the mind, the body, and the psyche. The "individual is a trialistic, not a dualistic being, for whom awareness and corporeality are mediated—a heterogeneous and volatile connective tissue, the psyche, which is embedded in the diverse members of the body through sense and feeling, penetrates the ego through imagination and pacts between the two in what is variously termed attitude, disposition and mood" (Weinstein 1995, 32). There are detailed instructions: "the spirit must be exercised and nurtured intellectually, by freeing it from as many prepossessions as possible, so that it can entertain any hypothesis imaginable" (Weinstein 1995, 34). This one was evident in Mike's classes and relationships with students, especially his mastery of political philosophy and culture of all kinds. Student comments on random newspaper clippings were welcomed and easily fielded by Mike, and he knew how to capture the essence of the student's unformulated argument and turn it into something beautiful enough to make the student blush or, even at times, turn on him momentarily with a look of hot anger—How do you know what I am thinking?—the student's incredulity apparent for a moment. Not for long, though, as Mike would nearly always win them over. This, as I understand it, is part of what Mike means by the arduous and completely thankless task of "preparing for pleasure" that is often short lived and even, at times, possibly aborted altogether by the other. These moments, tense and sometimes awkward, could be mastered only after such careful attention to the self. It is a kind of "care of the self." While it is not the AIDS narrative that critics accused Foucault of embedding in the last three (then published) volumes of the *History of Sexuality*, the "savage essay" nevertheless makes a bold claim: "The famous 'cake of custom' of Walter Bagehot has once and for all been broken beyond repair and mild cases of schizophrenia are increasing at a rate faster than are cases of AIDS" (Weinstein 1991, 214). Morality and sanity are linked (!). I was surprised at how many buried references to morality I found in Mike's writings as I worked on this essay. This insistence on morality, I think, is what marks him out from Foucault in that concern for the other and for a relationship to the world is more important than simple "government" of the self, although in the absence of the important institutions that might make a civil self, it seems one must rely on a kind of fortitude.

I have often wondered how Mike might have revised the ideas from *C/F* over the last two decades. At the end of the book, he charts out three possible reposes to postcivilization: the fetishist, the cultural elitist, and, of course, his own, that of the civil savage. I won't speculate about whether he has changed much about the civil savage, but have these other two strategies perhaps been transformed a bit, even evolved? Is the cultural elitist, who is "nostalgic" and pretends that civilization is not over, perhaps the most victorious political actor of the last two decades? (No doubt this parasitic victory is short lived but has been nonetheless very profitable.) Is this the victory handed to the "shrub?"—the child of the "predator-parasite" (Weinstein & Weinstein 2002). Is this George Will (fired on the day I write this from the *Washington Post*), Fox News, and red-state "America?" I recall once reading a description of Reagan written by Mike in a book edited by Arthur Kroker in which he described Reagan's much-praised "pragmatism" as "not, essentially, an instance of hypocrisy or of self-conscious mendacity, as the liberal mind must understand it, but an evidence of a neurotic splitting, the moral equivalent of a stroke, in which the right hand does not know what the left hand is doing." And this is key, because Reagan is not alone in his pragmatism: "The unity of the Reagan mind is not ideational, but is constituted by his impulse to feel good about himself, to desperately give a hopeful emotional cover to his own inadequacy, and it is this passion that unites him to the public at large" (Weinstein 1991, 220). The title of the essay was "The Dark Night of the Liberal Spirit and the Dawn of the Savage." The words are biting, but they are more directed at Reagan's audience than at himself; even his critics do not remain unscathed in this passage. The civil savage has nothing to gain from denying reality in order to profit from it through a puffed-up sense of superiority, and there's certainly no financial windfall involved for the academic, who is, dare I say it, the ultimate liberal servant. Just what has become of these servants in the last twenty years? How has "participation in the vast external imagination" composed of our own products been transformed? What does fetishism look like today?

Who among us in this liberal audience desperately grasping after vacant freedoms can deny that even we, like President Obama, have a great admiration for Reagan and his revolution in consciousness? Even if we concede that we may live on some hybrid version of fetishism, leftist nostalgia, and disdain for cultural elitists, can a fourth path have been forced onto at least some of the former product worshippers? What we have here in Mike's thinking, in his philosophy of life for the civil savage, is the furthest thing that I can imagine from Christopher Bollas's "normotic individual"—that person who "is fundamentally disinterested in subjective life and he is inclined to reflect on the thingness of objects, on their material reality, or on 'data' that relates to material phenomenon" (Bollas 2011, 23). This is, I think, what Mike calls the "fetishist." Such an individual is said to thrive in our contemporary political landscape: neoliberalism (as the civil savage describes it as a "liberalism that has outrun itself" and is no longer voluntary). Rather, it is "state sponsored community" (Weinstein 1991, 224). The process goes something like this: a fusing of self to market, and from there paradoxically a denial of self takes place (and with it imagination, creativity, and vitality for its own sake), as if an important psychic element has been stillborn, and from there, contemporary illusions of meaning dominate the individual's life. This characterizes the successful or "happy" person today. The civil savage would actually call this "anhedonia," a chronic inability to be happy, and this is fostered in the will that thrives on vital lies. Indeed, it characterizes most of the intellectual work in political science, a discipline that seems to have long ago given up on itself, and with good reason. Bollas speaks of such a person as "unborn," speculating that between parent and child (an important dynamic in psychoanalysis), there has developed "a preference for maintaining an unborn self," and the partnership between them "develops into the child's personality disorder by virtue of the parent's refusal to be alive to the child's inner reality" (Bollas 2011, 28). What to say of a cultural and political landscape that actively encourages people to deny "inner realities" for the sake of the market and technological objects in order to survive? It is no longer your mother, father, and culture that are telling you who to be or playing at simulating civilization for you. Now it is your boss, the human resources coordinator, your doctor, your insurance agent, the investment expert, the health tips posted on the back of the restroom stall—hell, everybody. I cannot help but recall that Mike mentions this as the case when people "worship their products," a problem he finds caused not by capitalism but more broadly, so as to include the cultural and technological aspect (which are mutually exclusive in Mike's thinking) under the sign of *technocracy*. As he says in my notes, there is no "pure" capitalism or science; we only get the science and economy that we "do." Yet under postcivilization, it is nearly impossible to see this as the case. In some respects, Mike's thought in *C/F* has anticipated the not-so-recent turn in theory to regimes of health as mechanisms of power that thrive under the sign of Foucault and Arendt by way of Agamben. Is not *homo sacer* the uncivil savage? More specifically, I think of Alex Galloway's (2012) insight that *we* are actually the gold farmers in the urban legend of exploitation that imagines Chinese workers toiling for virtual gold online in "meager conditions for inferior pay," and the gold is then sold for real money. This, for Galloway, is actually *our* lives online. We are the gold farmers, as he says. I would suggest that Mike thought it was our lives prior to going online, toiling away for "points" or "self-actualization" in the world of culture. Mike always made it plainly clear that he did not watch television (outside of his reference to *Designing Women*). He never judged people who did as "uncultured" or promoted himself as somehow superior because he did not. He kind of just seemed like someone who did not get the point of it. Galloway uses the metaphor of algorithms to explain how our social and political life is mediated, and we participate in the building of them through our important (denial) of social life and finitude by going online. This, it seems to me, is very much the "functional thought" that the civil savage must confront in postcivilization:

> The singular characteristic of contemporary thought is the understanding of thought as a function within life, an incident within a greater process that performs the role of moving experience from one point to another; that is, contemporary thought assents to the immanence of thought to life but refrains from clarifying life in favor of moving it along toward a series of ever shifting goals. (Weinstein 1995, 51)

It is unclear if "thought" is any longer assented the role of immanence to life. Rather, thought is now done for us, as we are shunted along from one experience to another by algorithms. By contrast, while the "civil savage finds himself well adapted to this epistemic environment," he only differs in that he carries "the immanence of thought to life inside himself with critical awareness" (ibid.). This insight, for the civil savage, is very different from the "linguistic therapist" or the "discourse analyst," because it signals the importance of the ideas behind the words that must make sense to the person who is caught up in them. The civil savage is not satisfied with getting by on linguistic glossiness.

Is this not what the civil savage refuses? To become the object that agrees that "language speaks him"? Specifically, the language of the market, of fundamentalism of any form, whether religious or cultural, is a proposition wholly rejected by the "civil savage" who takes on the perspective that in postcivil modernity, "everything is possible but nothing is necessary," the "best and the worst," Ortega might add (Ortega 1964, 33). As I read this now, it occurs to me that Mike meant it as a burden. We can do anything we want, but why would we want to? There is neither a transcendental goal nor a prohibition attached to any of these possibilities, so the pleasure of doing them is diminished no matter which way one might be predisposed. Why do anything at all, one is tempted to ask?

"Everything is possible but nothing is necessary." I heard that phrase a lot twenty years ago in Mike's seminars. I can honestly say that at the time, I had no idea what he was talking about. Still too young (and lucky) to have felt the pull of adversity that Mike designates as singularly important—"the rebellion of the flesh"—and not out of the institution long enough to appreciate just how jungle-like postcivilization really is, I kept it in the back of my mind, knowing it did not mean moral and cultural anarchy, but I was nonetheless confused, blissfully unaware of the constraints it may impose on my own (or anyone else's) existence. There is a lot going on here. Let's backtrack and, to use one of Mike's signature phrases, "knit." Knitting was something that Mike would propose we do when we needed to go back to a text and unpack an author's propositions in order to flesh out their implications for our ongoing classroom topic of conversation. In that conversation, we could have been discussing eidetic reduction, Occam's Razor, or some other topic. Usually, the knitting requirement came after several students raised their hands to "guess," in an educated way, of course, what the author meant or was trying to convey. "Knitting" was Mike's way of saying, "I am now going to teach you something technical: how to read for comprehension and to 'get it.'" Knitting always seemed like a way of helping one take a bitter pill. A recent phenomenon in cities, "Beyond the Stitch and Bitch" and "Knitting as a Life Metaphor" classes now encourage participants "to use the knitting process as a metaphor to examine how we cope with four recurrent themes in life: starting something new, repeating a pattern, changing things, and making an ending" (*Duke Today* 2012). Knitting always seemed like a moment of discipline in Mike's classes, as in, the way one felt when their first-grade teacher got out the abacus, or when your mom said you had to dust the knickknacks on your shelves. *Why even have all these knickknacks?* you thought. Can I just throw them away and start over? Same thing with knitting: it was a way of warning us that we were going to discipline our collective thinking. In Mike's philosophy of defensive life, there is also a lot of work, and I suspect on his part a lot of knitting.[2] I also suspect that the "civil" strategy, if ruthlessly followed and compassionately deployed, can allow the savage to "change things" and possibly even "make an ending;" that was a choice. This is freedom. It must not be made out of fear and ignorance. So I guess the important point here is to understand who is uncivil (all of us) and why this is the case. In *C/F*, the civil savage feels compassion for his "uncivil brethren" because they are alienated and he is not. What are they alienated from? I may be wrong here, but it seems they are alienated not just from civilization (hence our "post" predicament) but even a basic understanding of what civilization was and, possibly more important, how civilization could (have) solve(d) the modern predicament. Why have I used both the past and present tense in the last sentence? Because to be uncivil is really a state of being, the kind of being that animates ignorance, that makes it seem not only desirable but sustaining as well. In order to "do" incivility, one has to participate in the "vast external imagination" that is (usually) the entertainment industry. At least, this is the most pronounced supplier of "feel-good" moments and external-ized objects that can be introjected and cherished as "self" in the absence of critical attention to one's psyche. It is here that a pattern in Mike's seminars arises to throw into relief what this externalized imagination truly looks like, but more importantly, what it does. And here, when we search through other essays, we find that

> People clutch and claw at each other, seek completion in the other, an effort doomed to failure because in the other they confront themselves, though this is the one thing they will not admit. This is not the war of all against all but the ramshackle playroom of the bourgeois man-child, Disneyland after the rides have rusted out and the parents have gone home. (Weinstein 1991, 215)

Key point: we don't know what we are missing. It's not a question of insti-tutional inadequacy or legal reform. We live in a democracy and we hate it. So we do something else but call it "that," and everyone agrees to let the lie stand. Unfortunately, it does not end there. There are a million different ways to express liberal deficiency.

A constant theme in Mike's seminars was a debate about whether to characterize twentieth-century postmodern life as constituted by "lack" with a preference for Lacanian psychoanalysis thrown in here and there, or it was characterized by surplus or plenitude, at the time focused on the Deleuze and Guattari of *Anti-Oedipus* and *A Thousand Plateaus*. For Mike, these discourses coconstituted us as savages and existed in plural; they could come at us from all directions, and we had no control over them. We only had control over how we responded to them. Obviously, this calls to mind the need for civility. From the Lacanian standpoint on language, I believe, the critical difference is in how language plays a role in our lives on an exis-tential level: what we "lack" is the very thing Dewey would like us to forget about: certainty. And for Lacan, this uncertainty of meaning is not only "constitutive" of our being but also what propels us to know and desire in ways that may be contrary to our sense of sanity. For the civil savage, lan-guage is only coconstitutive; the second part of our being is physical—this is the flesh that rebels. We live more or less within the confines of our flesh, more when we are old and less when we are young, and for some, the aware-ness is constant. I think the importance of this statement comes from Paul in Corinthians: "I who tried to subdue his flesh to make himself worthy of God." Beyond transcendence, we have no need of such fleshly discipline. We have no reason to do it for God, so what remains significant about the flesh is different for the civil savage. We savages think we are living a good life, keeping our minds on track, eating right, exercising, and participating in social rituals that affirm our sense of commonality. What to do when the test results come in? Or is it when we, as Mike always said, "begin to feel our organs"? For the civil savage, this is the realization that we have been living in "hospice," one of Mike's favorite metaphors for postcivilized existence, or "liberal society" (Weinstein 1991, 213–214). A hospice is a place where one goes to die in comfort, so the question of vitality is foreclosed altogether. We are already there, Mike argues in many of our lectures. This "good life" has been a series of bargains with predator/parasites (they are both, you see), who tricked us into believing we could transcend our finite being. Not only that, they *kind of* promised we would experience some kind of fulfillment after each bargain. When it left us empty, there was no other choice but to go back to the trough for another helping. In a good Hollywood drama, this would be the compromise formation, where real ideological and moral struggles coalesce around uncertain destruction, reach an arc, and then resolve themselves in the space of two hours. Not so real life.

What happens in postcivilization? Why are we here and how did we get here? Mike takes us on a journey through what seems to be either his favorite or, to him, the most notable ontological claims made about existence. We begin in East Asia, the Indian subcontinent, and on through Muslim thought to the Platonic Socrates and on to Paul of Tarsus. Finally, we meet up with the hegemony of Christian thought, where Mike notes very clearly that Jesus, except as a phantasmatic character—perhaps even as a fairytale—cannot be incorporated due to his last-minute doubt on the cross. Notable themes here are Mike's insistence that people get East Asian religions wrong and, by extension, cultures. From the Koran we find the gem, "Lo! Man was created anxious; fretful when evil befalleth him and when good befalleth him grudging" (Weinstein 1995, 13). Is this not the bargaining mood of the contemporary academic? In postcivilization, we return to the theme that adversity is "what the world is in its most primal and significant state" (notes). Adversity is not just a difference of opinion or people cutting you off in traffic. It is a psychological phenomenon: it is what happens when my being doesn't jive with yours. It is the anxious undercurrent of every existence. Yet one must pretend it's not there. Mike's favorite phrase, "I'm a monkey in a culture jungle," seems important given that in order to experience pleasure while at the same time acknowledging there's no psychological guarantee for it, one has to know those "gems" of past civilizations in order to be able to spot them when these "rents and fissures" appear in the rubble (Weinstein 1995, 53). I imagine that this was how he approached writing for *New City*, talking to students in his office, and attending concerts with Deena, among other pursuits in his long, and (I hope) satisfying life.

PREPARING FOR PLEASURE

"Hedonism," Mike writes, "is the axiological consequence of living without transcendence," or what we are left with (Weinstein 1995, 33). We are all savages, *C/F* makes clear. This is presented not as an opinion but as fact. Objectivity is what has been forsaken at the end of civilization. This is what the civil savage strives to make contact with in his preparations, an objective thought. "Barbarism is the tendency to disassociation," Ortega tells us. Furthermore, the "constituents of civilization" "presuppose the radical progressive desire on the part of each individual to take others into consideration. Civilisation is before all, the will to live in common" (Ortega 1964, 76). The civil savage takes communion with the unreliable other in small, prepared doses. The civil savage, I believe, parts ways with Ortega on liberalism. For "liberalism's immune system," a "sense of duty" is gone (Weinstein 1991, 214). There are no more Ortegas.

Enter the psyche: a sane home discourse substituted for the "self" as understood by modern philosophy. Whereas the psyche is permeable, the self has boundaries. Boundaries do not exist for the savage as s/he is surrounded by discourses that interpellate him/her into one side of the binary predator/parasite. All that the civil savage can do is examine these discourses critically to ensure they do not rule him.

Mike encouraged students to keep a dream journal. "Make note of the first word that comes to mind upon waking (automatic writing) then begin to write about it in sort of free association, until you can unearth the discourses that are presently preoccupying your psyche," he said. These discourses could become full-fledged characters. I think here of Nietzsche's claim that "our organism is an oligarchy" with some voices more dominant than others, vying for control over our ways of thinking, habits, and moods. Mike's answer to this was to establish a "home discourse."

A "home discourse" is a way of speaking to yourself that makes you feel sane. Amid the postmodern world, characterized by intertextuality, we are coconstituted by language or signification. In this, "language is mind and not mind"—both "crazy and chilling." (Insert memory of Mike shivering and smiling while writing with a piece of chalk he holds like a cigarette most of the time.) Because of intertextuality, we are never pure initiators of our thoughts in a world of discourses and we have a different way of speaking for each situation, which can make us seem inauthentic (hence, no self). However, we have "initiative," we can decide which discourses to speak, so life is more like performance art or stand-up comedy than anything else. Language is "born with you." We newbies were confused. What do you mean by the "self" and how is language implicated in it in any way? Mike explains that the notion of the self can shift according to the time in which you are living. In the twentieth century, we learn, this is the postmodern self that changes according to how it is defined within discourses, and these discourses also make explicit reference to the subject or self. Part Althusser and part Derrida, this interpretation of the twentieth-century self, the uncivil savage, is of one interpellated by multiple discourses that may be at odds with one another, creating the very cultural schizophrenia that Mike is apt to use as an example throughout the text. The point at which we are most "normal" is when we are "unemployed." When we are in the position of having no commitments, everything is possible and nothing is necessary, and this leads to a collapse of meaning. We realize that we (and everyone around us) is superfluous—that is, not necessary for anything. In addition, we can always revoke any commitment previously made and, again, we find ourselves unemployed. In my lecture notes, Mike warns us that it is dangerous to go the zero point—for some, not all. One must be careful to adhere to strict self-set guidelines for doing so. Yet the alternative is much worse: when we are "lost in a jungle of meaning, caught in a chain of events—or even several simultaneously—we never question the situation, and this repetitive experience becomes our "prison." The twentieth century, we learn, is characterized by "psychotic politics" through the abject failure of public opinion, which simply records the tone and variance of our collective insanity. What to do about such a state? At this point in the lecture, we had been reading Ortega's *Revolt of the Masses*, and our 1990s Purdue selves were shocked by his arrogance at the "mass man." It was in this lecture that Mike defended Ortega's notion of "arrogant humility" by referencing this existential state and contrasting it with that of the masses, who take freedom on the cheap. They see the world as their "grocery store for self-actualization." Unable to "assimilate the zero point," Mike says, the masses go for a semblance of "total freedom," which is impossible to integrate into a *moral* life. Instead they simulate it through product worship, the mirror of public opinion, and grandiosity. Instead, it is better to use the zero point effectively.

The zero point is a temporal state in which you "disburden yourself in a different discourse; you are outside of yourself" (Notes). It is an existential state brought on purposefully. It may be compared to Santayana's "vacant freedom" and Sartre's "nausea" in order to unearth its difference. For Santayana, vacant freedom is the mistaken belief that freedom is a cause rather than a result of effort. Most political projects of the twentieth century have vacillated around this premise: that we have a right to be free from things such as oppression and fear and a right to things such as food and shelter. Vacant freedom is only possible when a person disavows the psyche, according to Angus Kerr-Lawson, as it brings on the state of "absolute freedom in which the spirit envisages action without any material constraints—the psyche is denied or ignored since it is not a direct object of experience" (Kerr-Lawson 1994, 337). Furthermore, though neither our birth or the "early nurture of the psyche" takes place under conditions of freedom, we "can thrive and be free in one sense only; either the Socratic self-knowledge of our real aspirations and possibilities permits our free development, or we remain distracted and at odds with ourselves" (ibid., 338). Nausea, on the other hand, would be a direct confirmation of life's contingency without any foothold, and the realization that "man the thinker is a by-product, a non-essential component of reality," according to Hayden Carruth (1964, ix). Between wishful thinking and abject misery, we find the "zero point." I don't know if Mike agrees with everything that Santayana said about vitalism, and if the spirit is there for him too. Certainly, the psyche is there, and it has contours, moods, desires, and needs. The home discourse unites the discourses that are useful and discards the ones that are unhelpful to moving on, not to a progressive future (that died with civilization) but to finite pleasures. The work of examining the psyche goes on each day. "My dreams that appear in the night world of sleep and my fantasies that intrude upon the world of wakefulness are the substance of the community of my psyche, each figure in them a personification or symbolization of some desire or fear" (Carruth 1964, 54). How does the civil savage measure what is good? By "self-given standards"—I am the *ens realissimum*.

There is one more thing: truth. This is found in the street. The one thing that the civil savage will not tolerate is to have that essential political liberty expressed by Holmes, "that of stating the laws of his spiritual being and the beliefs he accepts without hindrance except from clearer views of truth" (Holmes 284, cited in Weinstein 2005, 122) foreclosed. For the civil savage, it is most important for the free person be able to "disentangle their real assents from the web of life, and nothing is more important for individuals than to have opinions that are genuinely their own" (Weinstein 2005, 122). I can think of no better way to characterize the goal of the civil savage in navigating postcivilization.

NOTES

1. I recall asking Mike why Dewey wrote the way he did. To my mind, he was kind of a jerk, never getting to the point (and I had read a lot of philosophy at that point, for my age and abilities), allowing himself to be pinned down in an interesting way. In short, why was he so boring and normal? Mike recalled the way Santayana had described Dewey and his circle when they were together at Columbia as like "the Kennedys, playing football on the lawn. Santayana hated it."
2. I think I recall Deena Weinstein once saying that Mike would read an entire book, philosophical or otherwise, just to get even one idea out of it that was worth knowing. http://today.duke.edu/2012/09/knittingworkshop

REFERENCES

Bollas, Christopher. 2011. *The Christopher Bollas Reader*. New York: Routledge.
Carruth, Hayden. 1964. "Introduction to *Nausea*" in *Nausea*. Jean-Paul Sartre. Trans. Lloyd Alexander. New York: New Directions.
Galloway, Alexander. 2012. *The Interface Effect*. New York: New York University Press.
Kerr-Lawson, Angus. 1994. "Freedoms in Santayana: Psychic, Logical, Vacant, Moral, Spiritual," *Transactions of the Charles Peirce Society*, 30(2): 327–348.

"Knitting as a Metaphor for Personal Development," A Seminar advertised in *Duke Today* (9-7-2012), found at: http://m.today.duke.edu/2012/09/knittingworkshop (accessed 9-28-14).

Ortega, José y Gasset. 1964. *The Revolt of the Masses.* New York: W. W. Norton.

Santayana, George. 1942. *Realms of Being.* New York: Scribner's Sons.

Weinstein, Michael A. 1982. *The Wilderness and the City: American Classical Philosophy as a Moral Quest.* Amherst: University of Massachusetts Press.

Weinstein, Michael A. 1991. "The Dark Night of the Liberal Spirit and the Dawn of the Savage" in Kroker & Kroker (eds.), *Ideology and Power in the Age of Lenin in Ruins.* New York: St. Martin's Press, 210–224.

Weinstein, Michael A. 1995. *Culture/Flesh: Explorations of Postcivilized Modernity.* Lanham, MD: Rowman and Littlefield.

Weinstein, Michael A. 2005. "The Power of Silence and Limits of Discourse at Oliver Wendell Holmes's Breakfast-Table," *The Review of Politics*, 67(1): 113–133.

Weinstein, Michael A., and Deena Weinstein. 2002. "Hail to the Shrub: Mediating the Presidency," *American Behavioral Scientist*, 46: 566–580.

9 Weinstein's Methodology for Political Analysis

Robert L. Oprisko

INTRODUCTION

Michael Weinstein, a distinguished scholar in American political thought, began a decade-long foray into international politics in 2005. His initially global engagement quickly narrowed in scope until he focused solely on Somalia.[1] His 108 intelligence briefs, analytic essays, and status updates on Somalia were published in *World Security Network* from 2005 to 2007 and in *Garowe Online* from 2007 to the present.[2] This tenderly cultivated body of work provides scholars with one of the clearest examples of a rigorous method of normative political philosophy in practice.[3] Weinstein's method combines Unamuno's agonic doubting (Weinstein, 1977: 4–16), Simmel's aspectual totalization (Weinstein and Weinstein, 2011: 9–13), and socio-logical process of pressures forming substance from Arthur Bentley (Bentley, 2008: 452) to examine the basic elements of political analysis.[4]

THE METHOD

Weinstein's method for political analysis begins with a *critical moment*, the specific situation and position in time and space that is actively being examined by the person who is doing the examining. At the critical moment, multiple parties will be interacting, and they make up the *conjuncture* or *conjunction of actors*, the actors in a situation in their relations to one another. Each actor brings a combination of *power*, or that which is presently at their disposal, and *interest*, that which they desire, to the conjuncture. The way an actor uses their power to obtain their interest is their *strategy*. The power-interest-strategy represents the core of political analysis and resonates with political realism. Each actor will have at least one *ideology*, or philosophical justification and imaginary, that rationalizes their respective power-interest-strategy. Ideology defends the actor's vision of the good and what ought to be and resonates with political idealism.

The beauty of this methodology is that it is simple but infinitely scal-able, providing the tools to meticulously examine complex relationships.

It follows Dahl's dual requirements for good political theory by being both comprehensive and parsimonious (Dahl, 1971: 33, 162). The rigor of this method comes not from postgraduate statistical or computational modeling but rather from *sincerity*. When examining a situation, it is tremendously important for the researcher to remove one's own agenda from the situation; this form of political analysis requires that the analyst honestly describe what is going on rather than seeking to shape it into a narrative for one's own political purposes, which actors within the conjuncture will be attempting to do via ideology. Weinstein describes this process:

> Read my writings on Somalia and understand that they are based on a methodology that requires me to read dozens of articles each day on Somalia, the Horn of Africa, and the international actors involved in Somalia; take notes on those articles and put those notes into sequential grids that generate timelines of events; and review those grids to discern the power configuration among the conjuncture of actors at a particular time. That basic methodology, which I have practiced regularly for seven years, is supplemented by a wide correspondence with Somali and non-Somali sources who provide me with information that is not available in open sources, and call attention to any inaccuracies or misinterpretations that appear in my analyses, making the methodology self-corrective.
>
> (Weinstein, 2013a)

He also warns that narratives enter into the conversation all too easily. Even at an academic conference hosted by the Center for Strategic and International Studies, he sees the scholarship being forced into the formula of simple narrative structures of single paradigmatic perspectives (Weinstein, 2009a, 2009b).

SOMALIA AS CASE STUDY

The evolutionary deepening of Weinstein's engagement with Somalia presents a tremendous longitudinal study using this particular methodology. The end result is not an ideologically driven narrative that seeks to shape how we see a given situation but rather a historical multinarrative driven by actors with competing ideologies and political motives. It effectively blends realism, constructivism, and idealism while furthering the relevance of Bourdieuian and practice-centric political theory in international relations (Adler-Nissen, 2013). Throughout his writings, Weinstein provides clear examples of the power-interest-strategy and its relationship to ideology, linking political theories to political practices:

> Just as Lenin insisted that goals remain fixed, but that tactics must be altered pragmatically according to the circumstances, Robow said that

whenever al-Shabaab considers taking an initiative, "we always think about whether it is appropriate to do it at this time." Currently, Robow explained, "we believe that we should move forward with caution." In particular, Robow stressed, "it was most important that Al-Shabaab not get ahead of the people (another Leninist dictum).

(Weinstein, 2009c)

Though he is not tied to any narrative or political ideology himself, Weinstein is adept at showing where certain theories and ideas fit within the political reality on the ground.

The narrative of Somalia that emerges from the essays, briefs, and analyses of Michael Weinstein begins with a brief history of Somalia in whole and part(s) from its origins of statelessness, "after insurgent groups overthrew the dictatorial regime of President Mohamed Siad Barre" in 1991 and the failed UN mission and U.S. humanitarian-aid/nation-building venture in 1993 to 1995 (Weinstein, 2005). His analysis illuminates Somalia as a pawn of global and regional powers, each with a stake in Somalia for few reasons other than its strategic location on the horn of Africa. The Somali people experience the anxiety of warfare and strife, initiated with every action as they wait for the other shoe to drop (Weinstein, 2006b, 2006c, 2006e). He shows how Somali provinces began to polarize, then to fracture, moving toward Balkanization (Weinstein, 2006a, 2006d, 2007b). Within this extensive process, Weinstein shows how internal divisions within Greater Somalia influence and are influenced by external forces, most notably Ethiopia and Kenya, both of which sought, unsuccessfully, to partition Somalia as Prussia, Austria, and Russia did with Poland (Weinstein, 2011a), as well as the African Union, the United Nations, and the West (Weinstein, 2011d).

Weinstein's narrative shows both how and why events transpire as they do, withholding judgment or preference. Within the Somali context, one of the most important considerations is the highly fluid alliances between actors (Weinstein, 2011b, 2011c). His analysis also explores the most significant singular events in stages, such as the face-off and eventual deadlock over Jubbaland (Weinstein, 2013c, 2013d, 2013e, 2013f, 2013g), a problem that emerged, "when the Western 'donor'-powers/U.N. rammed through the 'transition' to the Somali Federal Government (S.F.G.) in the late summer of 2012 was that of the form that a permanent Somali state would take" (Weinstein, 2013e). Weinstein shows that much of the face-off over Jubbaland had to do with the conviction of political vision and that the domestic structure would directly affect Somalia in the international political arena,

The stakes are high; they concern the form of political organization that a Somali state will take. The Farole administration knows that and is acting accordingly. If a Jubbaland state modeled on Puntland comes into being, Puntland's vision is very likely to be achieved. . . . The struggle over the form of Somalia's political organization has begun.

The political battle for the south is underway. The proponents of decentralized federalism—Puntland, I.G.A.D., Kenya, and local factions in the south, represented by prominent leaders such as Ras Kamboni's Ahmed Madobe and the Azania group's Mohamed Abdi Gandhi—have the advantage over a weak national government that has not yet found its footing.

(Weinstein, 2012)

Within this single clash of political will, which lasted roughly one year, Weinstein effectively shows how and where the levels of analysis blur. Appropriately, Weinstein prefers the term "realms of action" over "levels of analysis" and favors Bohrian epistemology (Weinstein, 1973: 56–58). Within the procedural shaping of Somalia's structure of governance, external nation states and IGOs can be effective domestic interest groups within the conjuncture but with powers unique to their form.[1]

Weinstein's latest essays on Somalia are from late 2013 and early 2014, during which he reflects on the vote of no confidence in Prime Minister Abdi Farah Shirdon and President Hassan Sh. Mahamoud of the Federal Government of Somalia. He shows the December 10, 2013, speech by Nicholas Kay as "obviously what they [Western donor-powers] wanted to hear—a farce, a charade that alludes to the 'serious questions' and then deceitfully dispels them with a mis-statement of history" (Weinstein, 2013b). For Weinstein, it is the Somali intellectuals Afayare Abdi Elmi and Abukar Arman who correctly see Somalia as being locked in a "vicious cycle of political crises," that is, a "continuation of the political stalemate that has hampered Somalia's political progress for decades" (Weinstein, 2013b).

LIKELY RESISTANCE

The intersection between political philosophy and international relations is an oft-trodden-upon no-man's land where many international political theorists (often realists) make a living declaring that (normative) international relations theory is dead (Oprisko, 2014a; Schweller, 2014; Walt, 2013b). Political philosophy itself has been declared dead (Bird, 2010: 20–21) only to be resurrected, first by Rawls (Bird, 2010: 22) and, later, the postmodernists, critical theorists, formal ontologists, and quantum theorists (Oprisko, 2013). Most recently, R.B.J. Walker has argued that the entirety of international relations is best seen through multiple political philosophies, each with its own strength and weakness, to explain certain circumstances and interactions (1993). The pendulum swings back and forth continuously, suggesting that the most lively theoretical debate in international relations (IR) regards whether IR theory is dead or alive.

Sangiovanni distills the objections against systematic normative political theory down to feasibility, ideal theory is neither necessary nor sufficient, and that projects of "intense moralism" leads to misunderstanding "the nature, limits, and possibility of politics" (Sangiovanni, 2008: 223–232). Each of these objections issues forth from an assumption that the political philosopher is presenting a utopian image or an idealized good that is both universal and timeless.

Colin Bird emphasizes the importance of a realist perspective for ethical analysis and normative engagement. He specifies,

> [N]ormative commitments are shaped by recognition of the constraints placed on action by the character of politics in general and inter-state politics in particular. This constitutes a specific account of the relationship between political theory and political practice, where the former is structured by the possibilities of the latter."
>
> (Bird, 2010: 101)

Therefore, Weinstein's method must place realistic constraints upon normative ideals to shape the projects of actors in order to meet the requirements of a realistic understanding of the nature of politics.

FUTURE IMPACT/UTILITY

To this day, Weinstein continues to diminish the importance of his writing on Somalia, stating, "The present writer is an analyst who engages policy only to assess the probabilities of success of policies forwarded by others." While it is a tremendous virtue for him to be humble regarding his contribution to understanding Somali politics over the past decade specifically and political theory and methodology generally, it is appropriate to celebrate it here. His analysis presents us with a fantastic model of how international relations scholars can produce a major contribution through rigorous, systematic minor publications. It provides a clear example of how political theory and international relations can have exceptional policy relevance (Walt, 2013a). It also exemplifies how blogs are becoming a more important publishing forum (Davis, 2013).

Weinstein's method provides an important tool for normative political theorists. This methodological tool is feasible; it is not concerned either with projecting an ideology across the globe or with forcing every event into its particularly shaped hole. The goal is, rather, to provide an in-depth understanding of how and why political events continue as they are or change into something else. The normative element is within the ideologies of the multiple actors within the conjuncture.

This method's form of analysis presents an understanding of actors and situations, which is realistically complex, which is both necessary and sufficient for effective and accurate political analysis. It is sufficient because it does not propose a transcendental justice, nor does it make absolute statements, but it allows for individuals to seek transcendental justice by taking absolute positions, whether or not they are ever capable of absolute commitment. Instead, it allows "us to compare courses of action, policies, and reforms available to us here and now" (Sangiovanni, 2008: 225). It is necessary because it links the concrete with the ideal, adding context to why actors are pursuing a specific course of action and desirous of specific interests within a given critical moment; with understanding the unique motivational forces of the actors, analysts are making "arguments [that] contain significant *normative* assumptions [and] significant normative *implications*. This is most apparent in terms of foreign policy prescriptions" (Bird, 2010: 97). There is always an element of normative political philosophy within an analysis as it provides meaning and context to patterns of actions.

Due to his commitment to the project, it is apparent that Weinstein's method is capable of producing two important end products. The first is recognized patterns in the behavior of specific actors. Careful documentation of events over a period of time has provided a clear portrait as to when actors will embrace a strategy that adheres to their ideology and when they eschew their values for power politics. It becomes apparent which actors are opportunistic, which are belligerent or jingoistic, which are anxious, and in which situations these actors are more likely to exemplify these traits. The second is the ability to accurately predict events over the short term. The sincerity of Weinstein's method enables the analyst to see the most likely possible scenarios and to calculate the likely responses from the other actors at that critical moment. Although predictions cannot be made with 100 percent accuracy, the depth and comprehensive aspects of this method are of great policy relevance. The responses will be specific and encapsulated within a distinct realm of action. Parties who are in the conjuncture will have clear action items for what they can do to cultivate a desired outcome.

NOTES

1. It is unsurprising that Weinstein so resonated with Somalia that he decided to spend the better part of a decade working on it. Somalia, as a failed state, has become less than a pawn in the international political arena. It is collectively *homo sacer*, living on the fringe of existence and unprotected. Somalia has been bullied by powers great and small that see Somalia as a project, an impediment, or a resource to mine. Weinstein's militancy against domination and oppression clearly influenced his desire to commune with Somalia for so long.

2. Only two pieces were published in both locations in 2007. The originals are Weinstein MA. (2007a) Somalia Completes its Devolutionary Cycle. *World Security Network*. (accessed June 1, 2014); and Weinstein MA. (2007c) Somalia: The Dynamics of Post-Intervention Political Failure. *World Security Network*. (accessed June 1, 2014).

3. It is unfortunate to suggest but realistic to assume that Weinstein's important contribution to normative political theory, political methodology, and

international relations has been missed by many scholars because of where it was published. There is an unfortunate bias for some forms of scholarship and against others based upon the prestige of the outlet rather than the quality of the product.

4. This method of political analysis extends from Weinstein's method of political philosophy, which he characteristically refers to as love-piracy or thought-piracy. He considers it piratical because he reads voraciously and he takes the best, most thoughtful and useful ideas from whomever and uses them where appropriately. He does not cater to a thought-tradition and holds no interest in discipleship to another thinker, choosing instead to ride the wave of political philosophy. This is an important element in his methodology because it revels in complexity and an ever-changing presentation of reality rather than asserting that X must be true dependent on one's paradigm and its gatekeepers.

5. Some authors, experts, and academics are going to balk at the proposition that a sovereign nation-state is a mere actor within the domestic concerns of another nation-state, but that sentiment fails to fully give credit to the meta-capital of sovereignty. States may influence other states but cannot dictate what they will do unless they enjoy an exceptional relationship, such as one being a protectorate of the other or being militarily occupied. The Platt Amendment comes to mind. A more in-depth examination of this argument is made in Oprisko RL. (2014b) Strings: A Socio-political Theory of Multi-Dimensional Reality. In: Oprisko RL and Rubenstein DS (eds) *Michael A. Weinstein: Action, Contemplation, Vitalism*. New York, NY: Routledge.

REFERENCES

Adler-Nissen R. (2013) Bourdieu in International Relations: Rethinking Key Concepts in I.R. In: Little R, Neumann IB, and Weldes J (eds) *The New International Relations*. Kindle ed. New York, NY: Routledge.

Bentley AF. (2008) *The Process of Government: A Study of Social Pressures*. New Brunswick, NJ: University of Chicago Press.

Bird C. (2010) Ethics and Analytic Political Philosophy. In: Bell D (ed) *Ethics and World Politics*. Kindle ed. London, UK: Oxford University Press, 17–34.

Dahl RA. (1971) *Polyarchy: Participation and Opposition*. New Haven, CT: Yale University Press.

Davis J. (2013) The Place of Blogs in Academic Writing. *The Society Pages*. http://thesocietypages.org/cyborgology/2013/04/23/citing-blogs-in-formal-academic-writing/ (accessed June 1, 2014).

Oprisko RL. (2013) I.R. Theory's 21st Century Experiential Evolution. *e-International Relations*. (accessed May 28, 2013). http://www.e-ir.info/2013/05/25/the-fall-of-the-state-and-the-rise-of-the-individuals-ir-theorys-21st-century-experiential-evolution/.

Oprisko RL. (2014a) Entropy Versus Thought Traditions: I.R. Theory Isn't Dead Yet. In: Murray RW (ed) *IR Theory and Practice*. London, UK: e-International Relations. http://www.e-ir.info/2014/06/16/entropy-versus-thought-traditions-ir-theory-isnt-dead-yet/

Oprisko RL. (2014b) Strings: A Socio-Political Theory of Multi-Dimensional Reality. In: Oprisko RL and Rubenstein DS (eds) *Michael A. Weinstein: Action, Contemplation, Vitalism*. New York, NY: Routledge.

Sangiovanni A. (2008) Normative Political Theory: A Flight from Reality? In: Bell D (ed) *Political Thought and International Relations: Variations on a Realist Theme*. Kindle ed. London, UK: Oxford University Press, 219–239.

Schweller RL. (2014) *Maxwell's Demon and the Golden Apple: Global Discord in the New Millennium*. Baltimore, MD: Johns Hopkins University Press.

Walker RBJ. (1993) *Inside/Outside: International Relations as Political Theory*. Cambridge, UK: Cambridge University Press.

Walt SM. (2013a) Breaking Ranks in Academia. *Foreign Policy*. (accessed June 1, 2014). http://www.foreignpolicy.com/posts/2013/09/18/grading_academia.

Walt SM. (2013b) Leaving Theory Behind: What's Wrong with IR Scholarship Today. *Foreign Policy*. www.foreignpolicy.com/posts/2013/01/04/leaving_thory_behind (accessed June 1, 2014).

Weinstein D and Weinstein MA. (2011) *Postmodern(ized) Simmel*. New York, NY: Routledge.

Weinstein MA. (1973) New Ways and Old to Talk Politics. *The Review of Politics* 35: 41–60.

Weinstein MA. (1977) *The Tragic Sense of Political Life*. Columbia, SC: University of South Carolina Press.

Weinstein MA. (2005) Intelligence Brief: Somalia. *World Security Network*. (accessed June 1, 2014). http://www.worldsecuritynetwork.com/Africa/Weinstein-Michael/Intelligence-Brief-Somalia-1.

Weinstein MA. (2006a) Somalia Drifts Toward Fragmentation as Regional Powers Polarize. *World Security Network*. (accessed June 1, 2014). http://www.worldsecuritynetwork.com/Africa/Weinstein-Michael/Somalia-Drifts-Toward-Fragmentation-as-Regional-Powers-Polarize.

Weinstein MA. (2006b) Somalia in mid-November: Sparring and Waiting for Someone to Strike. *World Security Network*. (accessed June 1, 2014). http://www.worldsecuritynetwork.com/Africa/Weinstein-Michael/Somalia-in-mid-November-Sparring-and-Waiting-for-Someone-to-Strike.

Weinstein MA. (2006c) Somalia Remains in Political Stasis Despite Mounting Tensions. *World Security Network*. (accessed June 1, 2014). http://www.worldsecuritynetwork.com/Africa/Weinstein-Michael/Somalia-Remains-in-Political-Stasis-Despite-Mounting-Tensions.

Weinstein MA. (2006d) Somalia's Fluid Politics Move Toward Polarization. *World Security Network*. (accessed June 1, 2014). http://www.worldsecuritynetwork.com/Africa/Weinstein-Michael/Somalias-Fluid-Politics-Move-Toward-Polarization.

Weinstein MA. (2006e) Somalia's Islamists Resume Their Momentum and Embark on a Diplomatic Path. *World Security Network*. (accessed June 1, 2014). http://www.worldsecuritynetwork.com/Africa/Weinstein-Michael/Somalias-Islamists-Resume-Their-Momentum-and-Embark-on-a-Diplomatic-Path.

Weinstein MA. (2007a) Somalia Completes its Devolutionary Cycle. *World Security Network*. (accessed June 1, 2014). http://www.worldsecuritynetwork.com/Africa/Weinstein-Michael/Somalia-Completes-its-Devolutionary-Cycle.

Weinstein MA. (2007b) Somalia Reverts to Political Fragmentation. *World Security Network*. (accessed June 1, 2014). http://www.worldsecuritynetwork.com/Africa/Weinstein-Michael/Somalia-Reverts-to-Political-Fragmentation.

Weinstein MA. (2007c) Somalia: The Dynamics of Post-Intervention Political Failure. *World Security Network*. (accessed June 1, 2014). http://www.worldsecuritynetwork.com/Africa/Weinstein-Michael/Somalia-The-Dynamics-of-Post-Intervention-Political-Failure.

Weinstein MA. (2009a) Current Political/Security of Somalia. *Challenges for Renewed Engagement in Somalia*. Washington, DC: Center for Strategic and International Studies. https://www.youtube.com/watch?v=PmA0fvcCpzg

Weinstein MA. (2009b) No Simple Narrative in Somalia Drama. http://csis.org/story/no-simple-narrative-somalia-drama. (accessed June 1, 2014).

Weinstein MA. (2009c) Somalia's Contending Islamic Ideologies. *Garowe Online*. (accessed June 1, 2014). http://www.garoweonline.com/artman2/publish/Somalia_27/Somalia_s_Contending_Islamic_Ideologies.shtml.

Weinstein MA. (2011a) Kenya's Premature Invasions of Southern Somalia Stalls Balkanization. *Garowe Online*. (accessed June 1, 2014). http://www.garoweonline.com/artman2/publish/Somalia_27/Kenya_s_Premature_Invasions_of_Southern_Somalia_Stalls_Balkanization.shtml.

Weinstein MA. (2011b) Somalia: Al-Shabaab's Split and its Absorption of Hizbul Islam [Intelligence Brief]. *Garowe Online*. (accessed June 1, 2014). http://www.garoweonline.com/artman2/publish/Somalia_27/Somalia_Al-Shabaab_s_Split_and_its_Absorption_of_Hizbul_Islam_Intelligence_Brief.shtml.

Weinstein MA. (2011c) Somalia: Puntland's Break with the T.F.G. and the International Crisis Group's Draft Report. *Garowe Online*. (accessed June 1, 2014). http://www.garoweonline.com/artman2/publish/Somalia_27/Somalia_Puntland_s_Break_with_the_T_F_G_and_the_International_Crisis_Group_s_Draft_Report.shtml.

Weinstein MA. (2011d) Somalia: The West's "Miserable Failure". *Garowe Online*. (accessed June 1, 2014). http://www.garoweonline.com/artman2/publish/Somalia_27/Somalia_The_West_s_Miserable_Failure.shtml.

Weinstein MA. (2012) Somalia: Face-off Over Jubbaland. *Garowe Online*. (accessed June 1, 2014). http://www.garoweonline.com/artman2/publish/Analysis/Somalia_Face-Off_Over_Jubbaland.shtml.

Weinstein MA. (2013a) Somalia: Dr. Weinstein Response to Commentary about Analysis of "S.F.G. Political Strategy." *Garowe Online*. (accessed June 1, 2014). http://www.garoweonline.com/artman2/publish/Somalia_27/Somalia_Dr_Weinstein_Response_to_Commentry_about_Anlysis_of_S_F_G_Political_Strategy.shtml.

Weinstein MA. (2013b) Somalia: Silver Lining or Vicious Cycle. *Garowe Online*. (accessed June 1, 2014). http://www.garoweonline.com/artman2/publish/Analysis/Somalia-Silver-Lining-or-Vicious-Cycle.shtml.

Weinstein MA. (2013c) Somalia: Taking Positions in the Jubbaland Deadlock. *Garowe Online*. (accessed June 1, 2014). http://www.garoweonline.com/artman2/publish/Analysis/Somalia_Taking_Positions_in_the_Jubbaland_Deadlock.shtml.

Weinstein MA. (2013d) Somalia: The Deadlocked Conflict over Jubbaland Ruptures. *Garowe Online*. (accessed June 1, 2014). http://www.garoweonline.com/artman2/publish/Analysis/Somalia_The_Deadlocked_Conflict_over_Jubbaland_Ruptures.shtml.

Weinstein MA. (2013e) Somalia: The Show-down in Jubbaland Begins. *Garowe Online*. (accessed June 1, 2014). http://www.garoweonline.com/artman2/publish/Somalia_27/Somalia_The_Show-Down_in_Jubbaland_Begins.shtml.

Weinstein MA. (2013f) Somalia: The Show-down in Jubbaland Deadlocks. *Garowe Online*. (accessed June 1, 2014). http://www.garoweonline.com/artman2/publish/Analysis/Somalia_The_Show-Down_in_Jubbaland_Deadlocks.shtml.

Weinstein MA. (2013g) Somalia: War Dances in the Jubbaland Deadlock. *Garowe Online*. (accessed June 1, 2014). http://www.garoweonline.com/artman2/publish/Analysis/Somalia_War_Dances_in_the_Jubbaland_Deadlock.shtml.

10 "I Am the God of My Own Tribe"
Weinstein and Islam[1]

Joseph Kaminski

In one particularly memorable conversation about spirituality and religion that I had with Professor Michael Weinstein, he made a comment that seemed contradictory and even absurd at first. He said, "I am an atheist and I firmly believe that when we die, we rot away in the ground. However, if I ever were to adopt a religion, it would be Islam" (Weinstein 2013). It took me a long time to see what he meant, but eventually it started to make sense. This seemingly enigmatic statement ideally summarizes the depth of Weinstein's deeply dialectical and critical thought. It is not as if Professor Weinstein is unfamiliar with the other religious traditions. Intuitively, one would assume a self-proclaimed atheist would most likely embrace some type of Buddhism or animistic religion if they ever were to enter into the religious fold. He could probably be a guru, rabbi, reverend, or spiritual guide for any other religion if he sought to do so. Why then would Professor Weinstein choose a religion that is so antithetical to atheism, if he were ever to choose one?

After talking with Professor Weinstein for just a few minutes about his personal life, one learns that he is not only a tenured political theorist and philosopher but that he was also the singer of a popular underground hardcore punk rock band named Vortis that has released multiple albums. One of the editors of the popular music website allmusic.com described Weinstein's live stage performance as "[. . .] like a cross between Jello Biafra, Ice Cube, and Iggy Pop, at the live shows Weinstein can be found running around the stage, flipping people off, and yelling lines like, 'fuck, fuck, fuck, the human race'" (Morris 2013). Following are a few pictures of him performing live with Vortis that his wife Deena graciously gave to me.

His own song lyrics eloquently summarize his existential position. The punk rock band he was a member of, Vortis, has a song literally titled *Atheism*. The lyrics go as follows:

> That's life baby, you're dealt a hand so play,
> That's life baby, you're idiotic if you pray.

Atheism, atheism ain't a drag, you work to accept it then you've got it in
      the bag;
Atheism, atheism ain't a drag, you give the world the bird 'cause you've
      got it in the bag.

That's life baby, religion is our enemy.
That's life baby, you can't be faithful and be free.
Atheism, atheism. . . .

(Vortis, "Warzone [2005]," *Atheism*)

While these lyrics help shed light on the existential worldview of Weinstein,
they hardly tell the entire story. If one really picks his brain, which I have
had the privilege of doing on numerous occasions since he was my dissertation advisor and he has been my mentor since the first day I started in the
political science doctoral program at Purdue University, they will notice an
incredibly adept and nuanced thinker who is very capable of engaging in
deep conversations about almost any subject matter. As my colleague and
fellow Weinsteinian Justin Mueller once commented to me, "The man is a
walking encyclopedia of philosophy."

Throughout this essay, I will look at the ideas of Professor Weinstein based on his lectures and writings, as well as personal conversations and correspondences I have had with him over the years. I will offer a few hypotheses on why he would find Islam interesting. In the last 10 to 15 years, one cannot help but notice the litany of journal pieces and online works related to the Muslim world. The final section will go in depth, explaining his own explanation of what resonates most with him about Islam.

WHY ISLAM?—FIRST INCLINATIONS

Before directly approaching Professor Weinstein about the topic, based on my own experiences with Professor Weinstein in class and during office hours, I came up with five reasons Mike Weinstein would choose Islam if he were to embrace a religion.

The continuity that immediately came to mind when thinking about Professor Weinstein and Islam is the word "dialectical." Without getting too complicated, I am using the eighteenth-century German idealist Johann Fichte's "thesis-antithesis-synthesis" paradigm to explain Weinstein's own personality and its relation to Islam. I hypothesized that the dialectical relationship between the material order and the spiritual order within Islam was what initially piqued Weinstein's interest in Islam as a discourse.

Islam is quite unique in that it really has two different sides to it. At the one level, Islam is quite doctrinaire. The word of the Qur'an and actions of Islam's Holy Prophet, Mohammed (s.a.w.), are taken by all Muslims as final and binding. Obedience to these holy decrees is essential in Islam. In the words of Bernard Lewis, "It is a political identity and allegiance, transcending all others" (Lewis 1993, 4–5). In the words of the Islamic Republic of Iran's first Supreme Leader, the late Ayatollah Khomeini, "Islam is the religion of militant individuals who are committed to truth and justice" (Khomeini 1970, 8). The identity as "Muslim" is meant to transcend all racial and national bounds. As the Prophet Mohammed (s.a.w.) says in his farewell sermon, "O people, for I have conveyed the Message and understand [it]. Know for certain that every Muslim is a brother of another Muslim, and that all Muslims are brethren" (al Tabari, 1990, 112–113). The communal element of Islam cannot be underplayed. The message of brotherhood and a unique Islamic identity are central to the Islamic belief system.

On the other hand, Islam has a deeply contemplative and esoteric mystical element to it. Often when one thinks of the contemplative and esoteric elements within Islam, the Sufi movement within Islam is the first thing to come to mind. "[. . .] Sufism represents a rare anti-intellectual strain within Islam dedicated solely to esotericism and devotionalism" (Aslan 2005, 200). The practices of the Sufis literally whip their followers literally into a trancelike state of reflection and worship. The Sufi movement sought to detach the individual from the Ummah in order for the individual to master his or her own journey toward Allah (s.w.t.). According to Reza Aslan, "Instead, the Sufis strove towards asceticism and detachment from the Ummah and its worldly trappings through a life of simplicity and poverty" (Aslan 2005, 200). While the contemplative element is undoubtedly a part of the Sufi movement within Islam, by no means is it limited to it.

Even the more doctrinaire Islamic thinkers, such as the Egyptian educator and Muslim Brotherhood member Sayyid Qutb (who considered himself of the *salaf* [سلف] or "the predecessors"), recognized that all Muslims are expected to spend countless hours pondering the nature of Allah (s.w.t.), his book, and his creation. According to Qutb, an individual's reading of the Qur'an and contemplation of Allah (s.w.t.) "equip the soul" with the necessary elements to make him closer to those living in the generation of the Prophet (s.a.w.):[2]

> The issue here, in comprehending the meanings of the Qur'an, is not the understanding of its words and phrases, because they are not a *Tafsir* (interpretation) of the Qur'an, as we are accustomed to saying. It is rather to equip the soul with emotions, perceptions and experiences similar to those that accompanied the revelation of the Qur'an, that prevailed in the life of Muslims as they received it in the course of battles, war against one's own sinful tendencies and against the outer enemy [. . .].
>
> (Qutb 2006, 3)

Spending time contemplating the meanings of the Qur'an and the nature of Allah (s.w.t.) builds *Eemaan*. In the words of the prominent early twentieth-century Saudi Hanbali scholar, Shayk Abdur Rahman ibn Naasir As-Sa'dee, "Furthermore, the believer exalts Allaah [*sic*], declaring Him free of anything that contradicts the perfection of His Names and Attributes. Thus, his [the believer] heart becomes full of *Eemaan*, knowledge, conviction, and serenity, and becomes totally concerned with Allaah [*sic*]" (As-Sa'dee 2004, 58). *Eemaan* [الايمان] is the strength of the individual's belief in what are known as the "six articles of faith." These six articles are belief in God, belief in the angels, belief in divine books, belief in the prophets, belief in the day of judgment, and a belief in God's predestination. The more strongly one believes in these articles, the stronger one's *Eemaan* is said to be. Believers are expected to spend their lives strengthening their *Eemaan* through both contemplation and acts of goodness that are intended to please Allah (s.w.t.).

A second reason I felt Weinstein would personally have an interest in Islam is related to Islam's intrinsic militancy toward truth and justice. Unlike Christianity, which promotes its followers to "turn the other cheek," Islam is adamant about the necessity to fight when antagonized or oppressed. As the Qur'an, in the famous verse 2:216, unequivocally states, "Warfare is ordained for you, though it is hateful unto you; but it may happen that ye hate a thing which is good for you, and it may happen that ye love a thing which is bad for you. Allah knoweth, ye know not" (Pickthall 2:216). One can simply look at his band's song lyrics and note the fight in Weinstein's own demeanor. *Black Helicopters* by Vortis offers a confrontational, in-your-face style response to racists and anti-Semites alike:

> Hail, hail to the oven Jew!
> I'm the son of Satan how do you do?
> The son of Satan wouldn't ever have been if it hadn't been for
>   anti-Semitism.
> So here I am, a fuckin' no account Jew.
> Don't tread on me or I'll stomp on you.
> (Vortis "Take this System Down [2007]," *Black Helicopters*)

I believed it was reasonable to postulate that Professor Weinstein would identify with any movement he deems worthy that seeks to defend itself, even if it means by force, against oppressive hegemony, sexism, and racism. Islam's "militancy toward justice" as articulated by Khomeini seems to fit within Weinstein's own "don't tread on me or I'll stomp on you" attitude toward life.

Another hypothesis I had as to why Islam would be appeal to Weinstein relates to its inclusive nature. Islam extends beyond any specific race or "people." Muslims come from all walks of life and *genuinely* promote racial diversity and harmony within their own religious discourse. The late renowned Marxist-humanist scholar Manning Marable, in his final work, *A Life of Reinvention: Malcolm X* (2011), quotes a wiser and older Malcolm X at the end of his life stating, "The very essences of the Islam religion in teaching the Oneness of God, gives the Believer genuine, voluntary obligations towards his fellow man (all of whom are One Human Family, brothers and sisters to each other) . . . the True Believer recognizes the Oneness of all Humanity" (Marable 2011, 311). The antiracist sentiment in Islam can be traced back to its very origins. The famous farewell sermon of the Prophet Mohammed (s.a.w.) states,

> All mankind is from Adam and Eve, an Arab has no superiority over a non-Arab nor a non-Arab has any superiority over an Arab; also a white has no superiority over black nor does a black have any superiority over white except by piety and good action. Learn that every Muslim is a brother to every Muslim and that the Muslims constitute one brotherhood. Nothing shall be legitimate to a Muslim which belongs to a fellow Muslim unless it was given freely and willingly. Do not, therefore, do injustice to yourselves.
>
> (McIntire 2009, 80)

Based on my own experience with Mike, the inclusivity of Islam would most certainly be appealing. One must remember that Professor Weinstein is of a Jewish background and has witnessed anti-Semitism, bigotry, and exclusion at different points during his life. From his own testimony, he grew up in New York feeling like an outsider in many ways to rather stringent expectations of daily Jewish life in the post–WWII era. Weinstein at a very early age recognized the gilded nature of the 1950s and early 1960s in the United States. Weinstein found solace in jazz and other underground musical and cultural movements during his adolescence and early adult life.

A fourth important element that I believed would resonate with Weinstein is the fact that Islam is one of very few major global discourses that is *not* a product of Anglo-European thought. It is also one that does not particularly cater to nor is it dominated by an Anglo-European audience. During the era of British colonialism in the mid-nineteenth century, those living in the Middle and Far East recognized the hypocrisy of the "Great civilizing mission" of the British Empire. "The ideals of the enlightenment, which the British never tired of preaching, could no longer be separated from the repressive imperialist policies of the colonizing government" (Aslan 2005, 225). In this regard, with more than 1 billion followers worldwide, Islam stands as perhaps the largest, most well-organized discourse that not only is *not* under the control the Anglo-Europeans but actually stands in opposition to European and American cultural hegemony. Going back to the words of Grand Ayatollah Khomeini, "It [Islam] is the religion of those who desire freedom and independence. It is the school of those who struggle against imperialism" (Khomeini 1970, 8). Islam is literally the voice of the ignored and disparate masses in many places. This most certainly would make Islam an appealing alternative to someone like Professor Weinstein, who throughout his lectures and thought stands in firm opposition to all forms of imperialism and hegemony. His research on Somalia highlights this reality in his own scholarship.[3]

Throughout his experience in studying Somalia, Weinstein made many friends and connections to people that normally would be highly skeptical of him not only because of his American background but also because of his Jewish background. Weinstein once joked with me in regard to his research on Somalia that for many of the people he talks with, in the back of his mind he knows he is "the worst of both worlds." He said to me, "not only am I American, but I am an American Jew!" (Weinstein 2013). He said despite this, he was given the honorary title *"gambolle"* by those he corresponded with, which refers to an advisor to a king/emir in northern Somalia who is renowned for his truthfulness.[4]

Finally, I think it is important to look back at the political and philosophical works of Professor Weinstein. In his 1978 work *Meaning and Appreciation: Time and Meaning in Political Life*, Weinstein rails against the dominance of relativistic political and philosophical doctrines that ultimately undermine social cohesion and a greater collective purpose (Weinstein

1978). Professor Weinstein, similar to another great political philosopher I studied with, Wilson Carey McWilliams, recognized the increasingly insular and atomized nature of American society (McWilliams 1971). The loss of purpose for Weinstein is a tragic development. In his 1985 work *Finite Perfection: Reflections on Virtue*, he writes what almost can be described as an atheist self-help book that emphasizes how one can live a purposeful and fulfilling life in an increasingly hopeless world. The last two sentences of *Finite Perfection* illustrate this point. "Can the vivacity of finite perfection provide some compensation for the despair of personal existence? We have our lives here and now to win" (Weinstein 1985, 154). While the inward trek toward "finite perfection" is one approach toward existential fulfillment, I feel Weinstein would accept that the inherent social nature of Islam also can serve as a means of self-actualization and self-exploration; it is through the lens of Islam that individuals can better understand themselves and their own purpose in life.

Despite my belief that Weinstein sees Islam as a route to self-actualization and existential fulfillment for some individuals, by no means do I seek to convey to the reader that Mike secretly is a Muslim! Weinstein in the end of *Finite Perfection* introduces the term "critical vitalism" as the best way to explain his own existential approach to life. For Weinstein, the idea of critical vitalism centers on the notion of the individual and their pursuit of personal fulfillment within the parameters of a finite physical existence.

> The vitalism is the substantive, because it is life on which I base all else, and even further, on momentary experience of life to begin with. But I am not a classical vitalist who believes in a life principle that outruns his own flesh. I take life as grasped from within a center that knows itself to be finite and dependent, and yet, absolute; hence, the modifier "critical," which incorporates the existential component.
>
> (Weinstein 1985, 163)

Islam also recognizes that this world, referred to in Islamic parlance as *dunya*, is passing and finite. It also calls upon the individual to strive toward existential fulfillment. Where Islam most radically differs from Weinstein's critical vitalism is in the ultimate object of existential fulfillment and critical vitalism's belief that life does not "outrun its own flesh." Islam believes that ultimately life *does* outrun its own flesh in the sense of an eternal afterlife in either paradise or hellfire. In *Culture/Flesh: Reflections of Postcivilized Modernity* (1995), Weinstein refers to himself as *the civil savage*. The civil savage does not concern himself with some type of abstract, objective universal truth steeped in metaphysics and an all-consuming concern with an afterlife. In regard to the civil savage, Weinstein states, "As the civil savage, I have no law to guide me but possess only my own wits as I pick through the ruins of civilization and bring the treasures that I discover into the anhedonic culture of subjective and substitute pleasures" (Weinstein 1995, 114).

For Weinstein, individual fulfillment lies wholly within a finite self that is absolute.

While *the self* may be absolute, by no means has it been fully explored and mapped out. "In order to come to myself I have had to surrender only to the wish and the hope that there is some possibility or potentiality of human nature beyond what has already been discovered about it, some essential or saving possibility" (Weinstein 1995, 114). The search for "uncharted territories" within *the self* is an essential element to the beauty and spontaneity that life has to offer. Overcoming the angst of the finality of death is based on the individual's ability to come to terms with death and to not fear it. He goes on to state, "Such surrender is no sacrifice for me, but is instead an opportunity to enjoy what is enjoyable thoroughly and without pretense or contrivance for the first time, perhaps for the first time in history" (Weinstein 1995, 114). In Islam, one overcomes the fear of death and the angst of life by focusing their attention on an absolute that is manifest in the notion of Allah (s.w.t.) and not the individual. For the civil savage, one overcomes the fear of death by enjoying life for all the possibilities that it contains and not being concerned with that which it cannot control, specifically one's own mortality.

Weinstein does reflect on some of the larger global mystical and cultural traditions in *Culture/Flesh*. In this work he refers to a few of the various global mystical and cultural traditions as a part of the tapestry that constitutes "the romance of civilization." In regard to "the romance of civilization" he states, "I call civilization a romance because I believe at its root it responds to the deep human desire for a unity of being and goodness" (Weinstein 1995, 2). While Weinstein is not religious, he still respects and acknowledges those who are, recognizing that such traditions are valuable in themselves. "I am writing to individuals with respect for and acknowledgement of their differences from me, about the lives we lead" (Weinstein 1995, 2). Looking at one of Weinstein's favorite philosophers on the mystical experience helps further expound on Weinstein's point.

The writings of George Santayana take a holistic approach to understanding the mystical experience, which often takes a recognizable religious form. For Santayana, religion is a part of the rational human experience. "Rationality is nothing but a form, an ideal constitution which experience may more or less embody. Religion is a part of experience itself, a mass of sentiments and ideas" (Santayana 1982, 5). Because religion is directed toward something eternal, involving the soul, it can be even more direct in its pursuit of reason. Santayana states, "So that religion, in its intent, is a more conscious and direct pursuit of the Life of Reason than is society, science, or art" (Santayana 1982, 5). In the religious experience, the stakes are higher; thus the practitioner is even more focused on and concerned with the life of reason.

At the end of volume 3 in *The Life of Reason* (1982), Santayana states, "The feelings which in mysticism rise to the surface and speak in their own name are simply the ancient, overgrown feelings of vitality, dependence, inclusion; they are the background of consciousness coming forward and blotting out the scene" (Santayana 1982, 274). For Santayana, there is a direct link between vitality and the mystical experience. Manifest within the mystical experience are vitality, dependence, and inclusion. Unlike his contemporary Bertrand Russell, who was openly hostile to religion because he felt it was dangerous and inherently reactionary (Russell 1927), Santayana recognized positive healthy elements that also come with religion and the religious experience. The mystical experience is a blend of the primordial, or the reflexive, and the rational, or the contemplated.

The way humans are capable of incorporating the primordial experience with rationality is one of the most uniquely human qualities. Other animals incorporate the former into their daily experience, while computers and machines incorporate the latter. Human beings are in the unique position of being able to take the middle road. According to Santayana,

> The Life of Reason, in so far as it is life, contains the mystic's primordial assurances, and his rudimentary joys; but in so far as it is rational it has discovered what those assurances rest on, in what direction they may be trusted to support action and thought; and it has given those joys distinction and connexion, turning a dumb momentary ecstasy into a many-coloured and natural happiness.
>
> (Santayana 1982, 274)

Engaging with the mystical experience does not necessitate irrationality. The rational and critical-minded mystic recognizes the rational elements the mystical experience rests upon. As a result, the mystic can experience a higher, rational form of happiness and self-awareness rather than only a more primitive moment of orgasmic pleasure, or as Santayana calls it, "a dumb momentary ecstasy." It is based on this understanding of the mystical experience and religion that one could understand how a critical vitalist could still find a deep interest in religion and the mystical experience in general.

Like Freud in *Civilization and its Discontents,*[5] Weinstein recognizes the inherent alienation that comes along with industrial capitalist society that constantly commodifies and reifies everything it touches (Freud 2002). As Marx famously stated in regard to the nature of capitalism in *The Communist Manifesto,* "All that is solid melts into air, all that is holy is profaned, and man is at last compelled to face with sober senses, his real conditions of life, and his relations with his kind" (Marx 1972, Section 1, paragraph 18, lines 12–14). Based on my own personal experience with Professor Weinstein, I believe he would be supportive of any reasonable discourse that offers an individual solace in an increasingly alienated world.

WHY ISLAM?—IN HIS OWN WORDS

A workshop was dedicated to Professor Weinstein's thought at the annual 2013 American Political Science Association (APSA) conference held in Chicago, Illinois. During this workshop, the substantive and logistical details of this project were discussed. It was at this event that Professor Weinstein directly addressed my question about why he would choose Islam if he were to ever choose a religion.

Despite my seemingly reasonable hypotheses, my initial inclinations were not accurate. He directly told me that Santayana's explanation of the rationality latent in the mystical experience had absolutely no influence on his interests in Islam. He also made it clear that my meso- and macro-level social hypotheses, such as Islam's commitment to social justice, opposition to imperialism, and unique position as being a global movement that is not a by-product of Anglo-European culture, while all important and relevant truths, nonetheless did not factor into his own appreciation of Islam. Instead, it was the deeply personal and existential elements inherent within the Islamic conception of the attributes of Allah (s.w.t.) that most resonated with him. Weinstein told the panel at the conference that his personal interest in Islam as a discourse and religion comes from his understanding of the ego and the will as embodied in Allah (s.w.t) that is articulated throughout the Qur'an and the Sunnah.

The personality described in the Qur'an of the nature of Allah (s.w.t.) as being a completely unfettered entity is the personality and character that Weinstein most closely identifies with. The writings of Mohammed Iqbal better help explore the idea of man being the vicegerent of God on earth. According to Iqbal in *Secrets of the Self* (1920),

> And wear on thine head the crown of Solomon.
> Thou wilt be the glory of the world whilst the world lasts,
> And thou wilt reign in the kingdom incorruptible.
> 'Tis sweet to be God's vicegerent in the world
> And exercise sway over the elements.
> God's vicegerent is as the soul of the universe,
> His being is the shadow of the Greatest Name.
> He knows the mysteries of part and whole,
> He executes the command of Allah in the world.
> When he pitches his tent in the wide world.
> (Iqbal 1920)

Iqbal believes that every individual has the potential to be a microcosm of Allah (s.w.t.), or the vicegerent of God on earth. At one level, humans are vicegerents of Allah (s.w.t.) in this world simply based on how they are the dominant species on this planet. Human beings both "exercise sway over the elements" and "execute the command of Allah in the world." This places humans in a very special position in comparison to the other entities living in this world. In the corresponding footnote to this stanza, the translator R. A. Nicholson states,

> Here Iqbal interprets in his own way the Súfí doctrine of the *Insán al-kámil* or Perfect Man, which [p. 79] teaches that every man is potentially a microcosm, and that when he has become spiritually perfect, all the Divine attributes are displayed by him, so that as saint or prophet he is the God-man, the representative and vicegerent of God on earth.
>
> (Iqbal 1920, 78)

Iqbal's eloquent stanza in *Secrets of the Self* artfully expresses Weinstein's personal understanding of what he calls, "the transfer of Allah to the individual ego." In regard to the transfer of Allah (s.w.t.) to the individual ego, Weinstein stated at the APSA roundtable that in simpler terms, this can be expressed as, "I am the God of my tribe." He went on to express that this is the key to understanding how he has personally appropriated Islam. The idea of being the God of his own tribe originally appeared in *Culture/Flesh*. In *Culture/Flesh*, Weinstein quotes the medieval Sufi poet al-Hallāj as encapsulating his own existential worldview. On al-Hallāj, Weinstein states,

> Here I encounter the root out of which all of my further thinking and doing will grow, the gift of Islamic civilization: Hallāj's declaration-deed, "I am the creative truth." As I say these words and seek to suffuse my being with them, I wonder how anyone could ever have doubted that subjectivity is real, could have thought that life might be a dream, could have had to retire into solitude in order to make himself an object of study and find something of which he could be certain.
>
> (Weinstein 1995, 44)

Al-Hallāj famously uttered the phrase "I am the creative truth" during one of his mystical experiences. This statement led to accusations of heresy and ultimately his execution at the hands of the more conservative authorities. Articulating Al-Hallāj's words, Weinstein states, "Indeed, grasp yourself as living, here and now, under the revelatory power of Hallāj's words, of his declaration-deed, and you may intuit that the status of being itself is nothing but your current doing: reality is a process of creation and you are a co-creator along with every other center of initiative" (Weinstein 1995, 14). Neither Iqbal nor Weinstein believed al-Hallāj's utterance was heretical like many of the more conservative elements within the Islamic discourse have come to conclude. Rather than heretical, Iqbal views al-Hallāj's statement as a positive affirmation of the human ego. According to Iqbal,

> The true interpretation of his experience, therefore, is not the drop slipping into the sea, but the realization and bold affirmation in an undying

phrase of the reality and permanence of the human ego in a profounder personality. The phrase of Hallāj seems almost a challenge flung against the Mutakallimūn.[6]

(Iqbal 1930, 40)

Weinstein too holds contempt for movements within Islam and outside of it that seek to constrain the human ego. The individual must make his or her own salvation a reality. "Islam makes the perplexity of anxiety extreme by asserting the individual's salvation is completely a matter between God and self: no one can take charge of another's eternal destiny nor is any intercession possible" (Weinstein 1995, 14). For authentic self-actualization, the individual ego must enjoy the same freedom for self-expression as Allah (s.w.t.) is believed to possess in Islam. Mohammed Maruf states that in regard to Iqbal's view of the ego, "He [Iqbal] holds that every act of a free ego creates new situations, each offering 'further opportunities of creative unfolding'" (Maruf 1982, 378).

At the beginning of *Finite Perfection*, on *the self*, Weinstein states, "The self, as manifest in the declaration-proposition, 'my life is the radical reality,' englobes its existence and stands at the center of it, judging it" (Weinstein 1985, 27). Being the God of his own tribe is Weinstein's own unique understanding of a free ego, which in its freedom is constantly in a position for creative unfolding. In the words of another one of my advisors, the late Marshall Berman, on the new possibilities of authenticity and radical self-expression in the postenlightenment world, "It suddenly seemed possible *to be oneself in the world*: to fulfill the self's potentialities not by getting out of this world but by getting into it" (Berman 2009, 57). Like Berman, Weinstein also recognizes how authentic self-expression is best articulated by engaging with the world rather than retreating from it. Weinstein states, "There is no way back to the community from the seizure of the self as creative truth; the only way open is toward the community of Muslims informed by submission to the message, which is a program of obligation for constituting that community backed by the promise of paradise and the warning of hell" (Weinstein 1995, 15). This point is at the crux of Weinstein's understanding of Islam. In order to answer the message of Islam, one must put himself in a position to contribute to the greater good of the *ummah*. One must get into the world rather than escape from it.

Later in *Finite Perfection*, Weinstein goes on to state, "When I declare myself to be the radical reality, I may either be drawn toward the body and through it into the rooted realities, or toward an awareness even more distant from even the promptings of expression and thought" (Weinstein 1985, 129–130). He articulates that the first direction of "being his own radical reality" is that element which gives his life concreteness. It is in this mode of "being his own radical reality" that he recognizes his own physical limitations and ultimately his inevitable decay and death. This recognition is not a bad thing; rather, it is natural and can often facilitate in cultivating compassion and empathy. The second direction of "being his own radical reality" involves the deeper, more esoteric contemplative capacities. This direction, he feels, must be cultivated; within it one can recognize and perfect key virtues such as artistry and love (Weinstein 1985). One can simply look at the breadth and range of Weinstein's research to understand his own constant quest to express his own free ego. The ranges of topics he has written on range from American pragmatism, Somalia, art and photography criticisms, all the way to his most recent intellectual endeavor; the philosophy of NASCAR (for those confused, yes NASCAR, as in the widely popular auto-racing league).

Maruf concludes in his essay on Iqbal and the individual ego and immortality, "His views on the whole present an all-life picture of incessant and continuous struggle—one which is to continue even after death—for the attainment of the highest level of unity and integration of personality, which is one of the necessary preconditions of immortality" (Maruf 1982, 378). This is the real substantive difference between Iqbal and Weinstein. Unlike Iqbal, as mentioned earlier, Weinstein does not have any interest in immortality. "The great undeniable is that right here and now I am at the frontier of being, creating its truth through a synthesis of conscious will and of vitality, which seems in its depth to outrun my awareness of it" (Weinstein 1995, 44). Weinstein is focused solely on the continuous struggle for individual unity and personality integration in this world, and this world only.

The authentic act of submission to Allah (s.w.t.) for Weinstein is an expression of the radical self. Weinstein states, "For the *Koran*, submission is quite the opposite of abandonment, it is self-surrender undertaken and consummated with the most lucid self-consciousness, a free act of will, not a conversation, but rather a response to a plain warning and reminder, not a suppression of self" (Weinstein 1995, 14). Self-surrender *with* a lucid consciousness is a good concrete example of what Santayana discusses as taking a "dumb momentary ecstasy" within the mystical experience and transforming it into something far greater and lasting: "a many-coloured and natural happiness." As the individual frees himself of his worldly constraints and concerns, he is no longer encumbered by the vestiges of *dunya*. These material desires and creations only block the ultimate light of truth and oneness. Submission carries with it a dual burden, that of the submission but also of genuine freedom; Freedom from the material world and unity with the higher order. The self is free in that it has no legitimate worldly overseers. All beings are only subject to the will of Allah (s.w.t.), and that will is ultimately one of benevolence and love. This is the liberating element of Islam and understood in Weinstein's own thought.

For Weinstein, being the God of his own tribe is the ultimate mode for self-expression and individual potentiality. However, it is important to remember that being the God of one's own tribe carries with it a great deal of responsibility. In *Culture/Flesh*, Weinstein states,

The spirit of Allah is ruthless compassion, the thorough acknowledgement of adversity and the need to struggle against it, and the ever greater tolerance of failure. I shall treat myself this way, limiting any desire or fear that seeks to dislodge me from self-command and rewarding those that help me connect to the world so that I enjoy the goods that are available in it. (Weinstein 1995, 55)

Being the God of one's own tribe does not imply acting tyrannical toward one's tribe like some modern-day dictator in the Middle East; rather it means constantly making efforts to act with perfect justice and mercy toward "those in his tribe," just as the *Basmalah* expresses.

Anyone familiar with the *Basmalah* in Islam immediately understands the essential character of Allah (s.w.t.). The *Basmalah* is a statement that all practicing Muslims, Sunni or Shi'a, are supposed to recite before eating, offering obligatory [fard] prayers, or making an important speech or declaration. In English, it translates to, "In the name of God, the most gracious and the most merciful." According to the famous Qur'anic exegesis, *Tafsir Al-Qurtubi* (2003), the *Basmalah* offers protection from the punishment of the hellfire from the nineteen angels of *Jannaham* (hell; Al Qurtubi 2003).Image 10.4 is an image of the *Basmalah* in traditional Arabic calligraphy.

The characteristics central to the Islamic understanding of Allah (s.w.t.) (including mercy and compassion) are what Weinstein seeks to emulate in his own daily life and personal discourse. "These duties, prescribing mercy, justice, and benevolence, are meant to be within the scope of normal human capacity, are offered no in an austere and demanding spirit, but charitably: one should orient one's life to their discharge, but should not be too harsh on oneself if it succumbs to weakness now and then" (Weinstein 1985, 15). The leniency found within Islam has major appeal for Weinstein. While one can look at the list of prohibitions on certain actions and behaviors, Weinstein takes the flip side in his understanding of the central premises of Islam. In conversations, we have mutually come up with a golden rule of etiquette that simply states, the expectation of the individual other than submission at a physical level is simply; "don't be an [insert expletive]."

The simplicity and sincerity of the broader message of Islam deeply reso-nates with Professor Weinstein. In an authentic hadith reported by Imam Bukhari (2002),

> Whoever testifies that there is nothing worthy of worship in truth (no God) except Allah Alone, Who is without (peer or) partner, and that Muhammad is His slave and Messenger, and that 'Iesa (Jesus) is the slave of Allah, His Messenger, and His Word which He bestowed in Maryam (Mary) and a spirit (created) from Him, and that Paradise & Hellfire are realities, Allah will admit him into paradise whatever his deeds might be.
>
> (*Sahih Al Bukhari*, No. 3252)

Once can see from this hadith that Allah (s.w.t.) is all merciful and for-giving; willing to forgive all sins so long as the individual recognizes his authority and believes in him. In Professor Weinstein's own existential and pedagogical approach to the world, he too takes a similar position. Profes-sor Weinstein is willing to work with students and listen to views that he may not agree with so long as the student shows him respect and authenti-cally seeks truth for the sake of truth. As mentioned earlier, Weinstein is not out to create noble minds; he seeks to be a guide in helping students foster their own approaches and understanding of the world.

To a greater extent than the other Abrahamic religions, Islam is truly an individualistic exercise. In this world, commonly referred to in Islamic par-lance as *dunya*, the individual's own will is primary and the individual is in control of their own ego. Despite the fact most Muslim's believe that some-thing can only occur if God wills it to happen, most contemporary scholars believe that this is not an excuse for the individual not being in control of their own will (Kaminski 2014). According to the late influential Saudi Sheik, Muhammed ibn Saleh Uthaymin, "We know that we perform actions by our own choice and decision. We do not feel anyone compelling or forc-ing us to do it. Rather we are the ones who want to do something, then we do it and if we want to abandon it, we abandon it" (Uthaymin 2006, 55). In *Meaning and Appreciation*, Weinstein quotes Jose Ortega y Gasset, who writes on the twentieth-century conceptualization of the individual situa-tion within the public situation. "Ortega y Gasset expresses the image this way: I am I and my circumstances and if I do not save my circumstances, I do not save myself" (Weinstein 1978, 18). I think this quote appropriately addresses a major theme of Weinstein's own vision of engaging with one's own radical reality. "Yet the Koran also announces that Allah 'can do any-thing,' that Allah (s.w.t.) has complete, unfettered command over creation, and that human beings are 'vice-gerents' in the earth, cocreators with God and, therefore, commanders on their own accounts" (Weinstein 1995, 13). As vicegerents in the earth with God it is incumbent upon humans to par-take in the creative process. The important caveat is that the creative process engaged in by man must fall in line with the rules set forth in the Qur'an, which are, as Mike reminds us throughout *Culture/Flesh*, "a clear and present reminder" of God's will.

CONCLUSION

The great French novelist Marcel Proust astutely wrote, "Happiness is beneficial for the body, but it is grief that develops the powers of the mind" (Proust 1959, 237). Even though my initial hypotheses as to why I thought Professor Weinstein would find an interest in Islam were not wholly accurate, I think that it is safe to assume that he would largely agree with Proust's sentiment about happiness and grief. As discussed in this essay, one of the driving forces behind Professor Weinstein's intellectual development is his desire for self-mastery. However, as expressed in his writings, the individual ego, while at one level is constantly reminded of its physical limitations and mortality, is also capable of continual exploration and self-mastery. For Weinstein, then, happiness and grief both have the capacity to help develop the powers of the mind. Weinstein describes his own position in *Culture/Flesh* thus: "I am the civil savage, expelled from Eden and on my own, barefoot on a beach cluttered with the shards of civilization, dancing with a bitter olive in my mouth: I am Nietzsche chastened and sane, willing to be sad and to pity, ready to embrace the pleasures of the world" (Weinstein 1995, 55). Indeed, the critical vitalist often is left lampooned on their own existential island in an era where culture transforms flesh rather than flesh transforming culture.

NOTES

1. In one of my very first meetings with Professor Weinstein, he asked me what I was interested in doing at Purdue. I gave a half-witted, off-the-cuff response that while at Rutgers University and the CUNY-Graduate Center, I did critical theory and that I was interested in looking at social justice from a progressive Marxist perspective. He looked into my eyes and immediately read that I was just saying what I thought sounded acceptable. He then responded, "That is what you said, but I want to know what you *really* want to study." At that moment I lost all fears; this guy actually gets it. He read into my soul. I remember smiling and saying, "Well, honestly, I converted to Islam in 2005, and I would like to study Islamic philosophy. Ultimately I would like to develop an approach to incorporating Islam into a modern state, but I really don't know that much about Islamic political thought or philosophy." He smiled and said, "I can tell that is really what you wanted to say the first time, and I am here to let you know, that is exactly what you will do." Five years and 264 pages later, he was right, it *is* what I did. Thank you again, Professor Weinstein, thank you.
2. Living like the generation of the companions of the Prophet Mohammed (s.a.w.) is very important, because within Islamic tradition, it is universally

accepted that this was the greatest generation to have ever lived on the earth. According to the authentic *(Sahih)* rated *hadith* of Bukhari,

> Narrated Abdullah: The Prophet said, "The best people are those living in my generation, and then those who will follow them, and then those who will follow the latter. Then there will come some people who will bear witness before taking oaths, and take oaths before bearing witness." (Ibrahim, a sub-narrator said, "They used to beat us for witnesses and covenants when we were still children.") *(Sahih Al-Bukhari,* Vol. 5, Book 57, Number 3)

3. See Robert L. Oprisko's "Weinstein's Methodology for Political Analysis," Chapter 9 in the present volume, for more details about Professor's Weinstein's research on Somalia.
4. When I asked Professor Weinstein about the meaning of *gambolle*, he told me to add that along with referring to "a truthful advisor to an emir/king," it also is another word for a woman's headscarf, and that the title *gambolle*, while being an honorary term, also had a more playful connotation and was an inside joke among his Somali friends.
5. Interestingly, the original title of Freud's *Civilization and its Discontents* (1929) in German translates to *Das Unbehagen in der Kultur*. This title actually better articulates Freud's main idea in this work that engaging in modern industrial culture is a difficult and often emotionally painful process for the individual. The literal translation of the original German title is "the uneasiness in culture."
6. *Mutakallimūn* are those who engage in *Kalām* or the study Islamic theology. In the context of this sentence, the *Mutakallimūn* refer to the local scholarly authorities at the time.

REFERENCES

Al Qurtubi. (2003). *Tafsir Qurtubi.* Vol. 1. London, UK: Dar al Taqwa, Ltd.

Al-Tabari. (1990). *The History of al-Tabari: Volume IX: The Last Years of the Prophet.* Translated by Ismail K. Poonawala. Albany, NY: SUNY Press.

As-Sa'dee, Abdur-Rahmaan ibn Naasir. (2004). *Essential Questions and Answers Concerning the Foundation of Eemaan and Obstacles in the Path of Eemaan: Two Treatises by the 'Allaamah 'Abdur-Rahmaan ibn Naasir As-Sa'dee (d.1376).* Translated by Moosa Richardson. Toronto, ON: The Reign of the Islamic Da'wah Centre.

Aslan, Reza. (2005). *No God but God: The Origins, Evolution, and Future of Islam.* New York: Random House Publishers.

Berman, Marshall. (2009). *The Politics of Authenticity: Radical Individualism and the Emergence of Modern Society* (New Edition). New York: Verso Publishers.

Bukhari, Muhammed bin Ismail. (2002). *Sahih al- Bukhari.* Volume 5. M. Matraji and F. A. Z. Matraji (Eds.). New Delhi, India: Islamic Book Services.

Freud, Sigmund. (2002). *Civilization and Its Discontents.* London, UK: Penguin Press.

Iqbal, Mohammed. (1920). *The Secrets of the Self.* Translated by R. A. Nicholson. Downloaded online at www.sacred-texts.com/isl/iq/iq12.htm

———. (1930). *The Reconstruction of Religious Thought in Islam.* Online version, downloaded online 10/6/2014 at http://islamicblessings.com/upload/ReconstructionOfIslamicThought.pdf

Kaminski, Joseph. (2014). *A Theory of a Contemporary Islamic State: History, Governance, and the Individual*. Ph.D. Dissertation. Purdue University.

Khomeini, Imam. (1970). *Governance of the Jurist*. Translated by Hamid Algar. Tehran, Iran: Institute for the Publication of Imam Khomeini's Works.

Lewis, Bernard. (1993). *Islam and the West*. New York: Oxford University Press.

Marable, Manning. (2011). *A Life of Reinvention: Malcolm X*. New York: Viking Press.

Maruf, Mohammed. (1982). 'Allama Iqbal on 'Immortality'." *Religious Studies*, 18(3), 373–378.

Marx, Karl. (1972). The Communist Manifesto, in R. Tucker (Ed.), *The Marx-Engels Reader*. New York: Norton Publishing.

McIntire, Susan. (2009). Farewell Sermon of the Prophet Mohammed, in *Speeches in World History*. New York: Infobase Publishing.

McWilliams, Wilson C. (1971). *The Idea of Fraternity in America*. Los Angeles: University of California Berkeley Press.

Morris, Kurt. (2013). *Review of Vortis- Take the System Down*. www.allmusic.com/album/take-the-system-down-mw0000661375. Last Accessed online 5/14/2013.

Oprisko, Robert L. (2014). "Weinstein's Methodology for Political Analysis." In *Michael A. Weinstein: Action, Contemplation, Vitalism*, edited by Robert L. Oprisko and Diane S. Rubenstein. New York: Routledge.

Pickthall, Marmaduke. (2006). *The Glorious Qur'an* (English Translation). New York: Tahrike Tarsile Qur'an Publishers.

Proust, Marcel. (1959). *The Past Recaptured*. Translated by Fredrik Blossom. New York: Random House Publishers, Modern Library.

Qutb, Sayyid. (2006). *Basic Principles of the Islamic Worldview*. Translated by Rami David. North Haledon, NJ: Islamic Publications International.

Russell, Bertrand. (1927). *Why I Am Not a Christian*. London, UK: Watts Publishing.

Santayana, George. (1982). Reason in Religion. In *The Life of Reason*. Vol. 3. New York: Dover Publications.

Uthaymin, Sheik Mohammed ibn Saleh. (2006). *The Great Islamic Awakening*. Translated by Faisal ibn Muhammed. Birmingham, UK: Al Hidaayah Publishing.

Vortis. (2005). *Warzone*. Self-Released Album.

———. (2007). *Take this System Down*. Thick Records.

Weinstein, Michael A. (1978). *Meaning and Appreciation; Time and Meaning in Political Life*. West Lafayette, IN: Purdue University Press.

———. (1985). *Finite Perfection; Reflections on Virtue*. Amherst: University of Massachusetts Press.

———. (1995). *Culture/Flesh: Explorations of Postcivilized Modernity*. Lanham, MD: Rowman & Littlefield Publishers.

———. (2013). Personal correspondences.

11 A Remarkable Teacher

Kathy E. Ferguson[1]

I was Michael Weinstein's undergraduate student from 1969 to 1972. He was without doubt the most influential teacher of my life. Looking back, I recall his classrooms as "untimely" in the Nietzschean sense of going against the dominant forces of the time and making a space for the unexpected to emerge. In his 1982 book, *The Wilderness and the City*, Michael defines philosophy in a way that also defines his teaching: "The essence of modern philosophy is the expression of an image of human existence and of its major possibilities that appeals to the free judgment of individuals."[2] He expressed to us a variety of images of individual and collective life, and he expected us to bring our free judgment to the task of understanding and critique.

CREATIVE IMPROVISATION

I remember his undergraduate political theory class as a site of creative improvisation: there was no syllabus, no assigned text, evidently no plan at all, other than the requirement that each student write about a political topic of our choice. Students' questions were the spindle around which the classes emerged. If there were no questions on a particular day, Michael asked us questions and provoked us until a question emerged. Students hardy enough to jump into the fray gradually learned to express ideas, to shape a coherent question, to formulate a persuasive argument. He sometimes gave what Jim Stevers recalls as "brief 'lecturettes'" to "prime the pedagogical pump." Upon request, Michael would point us toward a book that would help us refine and extend our perspectives. In these ways, he facilitated our emergence as thinkers, but the questions and commitments that drove our thinking had to be our own.

I was befuddled, frightened, and hooked. This iconoclastic, intense, opinionated professor effortlessly thought about politics and life, and simultaneously thought about his thinking on politics and life, in ways I had never imagined. I did not know it was possible to think like that. That first semester, I recall understanding literally nothing at all of what went on in class, an experience that produced a compelling urge to know what he knew (as well as a life-long sympathy for students' confusions in coming to political theory for the first time). I sat in on that class every subsequent semester until I graduated, and it was different each time.

Students who studied with Michael more recently recount a similar classroom experience, with slightly more structure, yet still created "on the fly" out of the curiosities and urgencies the students brought to the class. Justin Mueller recalls,

> Our seminar structure was similar to yours, but it had a bit more structure. There was still no pre-formed syllabus, and no pre-determined readings. On the first day, however, we would all tell him what it is we wanted to learn or talk about and who we wanted to read this semester. After we did that for a bit, he would tell us to wait a few minutes. Then he would build a syllabus plan from scratch at the front of the room, weaving all of our interests together in a way that, rather than being jumbled or disconnected, made perfect sense in terms of having the ideas flow into each other and build off of each other as the semester went along.

For class meetings after this, someone would distribute a 20-page or less reading passage to the class that was related to the topic or individual they had suggested reading at the beginning of the course. Mike would always open these seminars "relying upon the kindness of strangers" to intervene and get us going in a particular direction in reaction to some part of the text. From there, the meeting could go wildly in any unexpected direction, but regardless, you always felt as if you had taken something significant away.

It has become a cliché in education to call for a "student-centered classroom," a conceit that administrators often imagine can be seamlessly folded into a world of mandated curricula, standardized tests, benchmarks, assessments, and rubrics. Michael's classes were centered on students in a fundamentally radical way: he respected students' independence of thinking. He helped students recognize and articulate their own primary concerns. He sometimes began the semester by asking us to write a paper on what makes life worth living. Peggy Cox recalls that he used those papers "to initiate discussions that helped reveal the impetus for our own personal political philosophies." Michael brought a great deal of ironic laughter to this process, no doubt necessary for making his way through the predictable repetitions of undergraduates but also a consistent element of his philosophical personae. There was a certain amount of danger in that laughter, from the perspective of a bewildered but persevering student, because I was often unsure what was funny. Yet there was a safety net as well—there was no room in his classroom for bullies. As a shy but persistent female member of the theory coterie, I benefited from his quick defense of my hesitant presence when the alpha males got territorial. Others benefitted as well. I recall a notable day when an overconfident Bible-toting student ridiculed one of the campus radicals, a wiry, long-haired fellow named Lucas, for his interpretation of scripture. Lucas borrowed his opponent's Bible, found the passage in question, and read it aloud in support of his analysis. Michael gave them room for their confrontation, at the end offering only this appreciative comment: "Well done, Lucas, well done." It was not lost on the rest of us that Lucas earned praise for making a good argument, while the other fellow was sidelined because his goal had been to shut down an unconventional point of view.

OUTSIDERS

Michael's classrooms—and, more broadly, the conversations that took place while walking across campus, attending office hours, or corresponding about recent work—were places where outsiders could flourish. By "outsiders," I mean those individuals, texts, and ideas that did not have a proper place within whatever approved hierarchy of order loomed over them. This outsiderness affected both whom we read and how we read.

A consequence of my eclectic education in political theory posed a dilemma for me in graduate school, where I arrived knowing a lot about theorists few others had read and nothing at all about theorists everyone else had read. There was no Marx in my library, for example, but a great deal of George Herbert Mead and William James. No Kant, but Josiah Royce and Justus Buchler. Alfred North Whitehead but not Jurgen Habermas. Relatively few European thinkers other than the existentialists, Miguel de Unamuno, Henri Bergson, and Nietzsche, but a panoply of North Americans. One of my regrets, looking back at the learning opportunities Michael made available, was my own lack of interest in the Mexican philosophers he explored in his 1976 book, *The Polarity of Mexican Thought: Instrumentalism and Finalism*. In this book, he invites his readers into an "imaginative synthesis" of a range of Mexican philosophers who contribute to a philosophy of revolt and an enactment of creative freedom.[3] In his introduction, he insists, contrary to "the indifference of intellectuals in the so-called advanced nations," that "the Mexican antipositivists deserve a hearing from contemporary intellectuals sensitive to the crises of freedom and honest human relations in the complex organizations of today."[4] I regret that, as a student, I unthinkingly participated in the imperial dismissal of Mexican philosophy, but I'm grateful that this book was available when I realized my mistake and attempted to rectify it.

Michael respects American political thought and vigorously contests Karl Jaspers's casual dismissal of pragmatism as "cheap optimism."[5] In *The Wilderness and the City*, Michael calls his inquiry into American pragmatism a "recurrence" in Whitehead's sense: "an attempt to make contact with their spirit, to bring into the foreground some themes that have been neglected by most of their successors, to make them live as serious thinkers grappling with fundamental human predicaments, and to draw vitality from them."[6] Similarly, in his 2006 book on Oliver Wendell Holmes, he positions himself as "impelled by gratitude to describe and interpret the complexity and insight of Holmes's thought, because he taught me how to affirm an American identity in a post–9/11 world, where aggressive nationalism and rigid cultural divisions threaten to push individual judgment aside."[7] To make contact, to draw vitality, to express gratitude—these were fundamental to the thinking practices Michael invited his students to engage.

This "methodology," if I can call it that, was in the long run a great gift. I doubt that I would have pursued thinkers such as Simone de Beauvoir, Emma Goldman, or Rosa Luxemburg had I not absorbed an early respect for noncanonical thought along with receptivity to feminism, anarchism, and all manner of critique. Later, I realized that Michael had led us to engage thinkers whose ideas anticipated future directions of political theory. In the 1980s, postmodernism and poststructuralism sounded familiar to me, even though I had no prior knowledge of the relevant texts, because antifoundational, process-oriented ontologies had become a central part of my thinking. In the 2000s, new materialism made sense because it bore a family resemblance to the "comprehensive vitalism" I had met via William James.[8] James's radical empiricism, as Michael presents it, is based on "ontological wonder," a stance that accepts the radical contingency of life and seeks "a reflexive review of the broadest available range of experiences."[9] I took from my undergraduate experience an enduring ontological embrace of excess—life will always exceed our understandings of it—and lack—there will always be something missing—and an accompanying epistemological expectation and endorsement of plurality and contingency. Implicitly, learning the value of excess and incompletion led me to be suspicious of projects of mastery; behind every "desperate attempt to master life,"[10] I learned from Michael to look for a will to power over truth.

Michael's students marveled that he presented every position as though he fully believed it, leading to endless speculation as to what he "really" did believe. His approach taught me a valuable lesson in *how* to read: read a thinker from the inside first, then from the outside. First, do your best to get inside a writer's concerns and imagine the most compelling version of his/her ideas; then bring your best critical faculties to bear on it. It is an element of Michael's teaching that I try consciously to emulate in my own, even if the trials of getting "inside" the thinking of, say, Aristotle or Rousseau tax my intellectual generosity.

I understand from Michael's more recent students that this classroom approach continued: Justin Mueller recounts a graduate seminar

> when we were all supposed to discuss some reading on natural rights and natural law. All of the students were piling on their criticisms of how natural rights were a ridiculous concept, how social contract theory

was stupid, etc. After this goes on for a bit, Mike shakes his head and says that he is disappointed in us for our refusal to critically empathize with the author, and even attempt to see their position from the inside. Mike has always had an enduring dislike for bullies, and while he is more than willing to dismantle and critique the architecture of modern thought, he would not easily tolerate the kind of too-easy intellectual bullying that we were engaging in. It was moments like this that caused me to seriously reflect on my approach and demeanor not only to reading philosophy, political theory, or literature, but also to reflecting on the theoretical implications of the lesson itself as an ontology of human experience, values, belief, and learning.

Michael's classrooms and conversations provided, by example more than explanation, a focus on *how* questions over *why* questions: how to be an individual; how to connect with others; how to form life commitments; how to doubt. He most often taught by showing—he modeled the process of articulating the strongest version of a position, then subjecting that position to critique. He showed me how to organize an argument, a teaching moment that I recall vividly and now try to pass on to my own students. When writing my honors thesis on Simone de Beauvoir, I was struggling to make the transition from summarizing an argument to analyzing it. Michael watched me flounder for a time, then asked, quietly, "Do you want me to show you?" I nodded, grateful for any intervention that would let me stop talking. He took my yellow pad and deftly outlined the argument toward which I had been flailing. Beyond the insight I gleaned into Beauvoir's feminism, the process of watching an idea emerge from its engagements with other ideas, clarify its debts, and seek its trajectory was, as we used to say, mind blowing. I try to reproduce that gift for my own students by modeling for them the work that I expect them to do, not simply giving instructions or pointing at examples but actively doing political thinking with them until they catch on.

Another kind of outsiderness was expressed in Michael's impatient dismissal of professional and educational authorities. His teaching could extend for decades beyond the classroom, but not once was there a hint of what we now call mentoring. His hearty contempt for the instrumentalities of academia created a decidedly "non"-professional intellectual space; there was no professional socialization, no expectations regarding productivity, little talk of careers or even jobs. Instead, there was a relentless critique of authority and normality. I remember Michael denouncing the professional tendency to confuse one's personal identity with the accomplishments listed on one's vitae. He scorned this displacement as "the conversion of the self into an instrument of success or survival,"[11] a move that excuses us from articulating our own political values while hiding the power relations of the profession itself. Decades later, when I became familiar with my colleague Michael Shapiro's characterization of Foucault as a thinker who "leaves power no place to hide," I recognized that impulse, which Michael Weinstein had continuously enacted. Perhaps that is a kind of mentoring after all, a countermentoring that cherishes intellectual independence and honesty over everything else.

His an-archy extended, of course, to governmental authorities as well. After the U.S. invasion of Cambodia and the shootings at Kent State, I was in crisis. I had dabbled in campus radicalism: I was strongly opposed to the war, attracted to the counterculture, persuaded by civil rights and feminism. Yet I had not seen past the alibi offered by apologists as a sop to critics: the war in Vietnam was a "mistake." The invasion of Cambodia was a "mistake." Racism and sexism were "mistakes." In an otherwise fair and reasonable political order, "mistakes were made." The language of error positioned me, an emergent critic, as a supplicant trying to talk sense into people who had temporarily lost their way. In Michael's class, during those freighted days when even Purdue, dubbed by *Newsweek* the "hotbed of student rest," was in turmoil, we worked out a different analysis. He punctured the language of "error" and insisted on a language of power. I remember the Kent State killings in the same way that people remember where they were when President Kennedy was killed or the Twin Towers were hit. It was the day I stopped being a liberal and started understanding that violence and oppression have a systemic logic, that they are not oversights or aberrations of an otherwise reasonable political system.

Michael Weinstein resists summing up, perhaps because he resisted summing us up, instead expecting us to be independent and to cultivate the capacity to surprise him, to surprise ourselves. While his students often loved him and were nearly always in awe of him, he discouraged anything that hampered our own migrations. I recall a time when he abruptly ceased holding office hours because they had become a site for dozens of adoring undergraduates to literally gather at his feet and hang on his words. I remember feeling bereft of an opportunity I had come to cherish but at the same time dimly understanding that his actions were requiring us to learn a more intimate lesson about intellectual independence.

Michael often invoked Josiah Royce to the effect that "we are sources of ideas for one another" and that philosophy at heart is spiritual autobiography.[12] I am confident that many of his students share my gratitude that my ideas could pass through his, and perhaps vice versa as well. Tim Soots aptly characterizes Michael's classroom as a place hosting "the mutual exchange of gifts." Aviral Pathak similarly recalls Michael's "remarkable ability to recognize and sympathize with the questions that were troubling his students." He gave our concerns dignity and modeled an intense and respectful engagement with ideas and with each other.

The haunting picture by Don Carter on the book jacket for *Meaning and Appreciation: Time and Modern Political Life* (pictured below) suggests the process that Michael places at the heart of human existence: "we express one another to ourselves."[13] A man stands in profile, facing left, looking into

a full-length mirror. But he does not see himself; he sees someone else. Out-side the room's window, a second man stands, also in profile, facing right. In the mirror, the man outside reappears, looking back at the first man. They express one another to themselves. I appreciate Michael encouraging us to cast a wide net in the process of expressing others to ourselves, to be recep-tive to unorthodoxies, to welcome untimely ideas and practices. I learned that there is more than one time. His classroom was a living embodiment of a different time, a time worth emulating, a time worth fighting for.

NOTES

1. My thanks to Peggy Cox, Justin Mueller, Aviral Pathak, Troy Smith, Tim Soots, and James Stever for sharing with me their recollections of Michael Weinstein's teaching.
2. Michael A. Weinstein, *The Wilderness and the City* (Amherst: University of Massachusetts Press, 1982), p. 1.

3. Weinstein, *The Polarity of Mexican Thought: Instrumentalism and Finalism* (University Park: Penn State University Press, 1976), p. 2.
4. Weinstein, *The Polarity of Mexican Thought*, pp. x, ix.
5. Weinstein, *The Wilderness and the City*, pp. vii–ix. He is citing Karl Jaspers, *Man in the Modern Age* (1957), p. 176.
6. Weinstein, *The Wilderness and the City*, p. vii.
7. Weinstein, *The Imaginative Prose of Oliver Wendell Holmes* (Columbia: University of Missouri Press, 2006), p. ix.
8. Weinstein, *The Wilderness and the City*, p. 73.
9. Weinstein, *The Wilderness and the City*, pp. 81, 73.
10. Weinstein, *The Wilderness and the City*, p. 9.
11. Weinstein, *The Polarity of Mexican Thought*, p. 8.
12. Weinstein, *The Wilderness and the City*, pp. vii, 23.
13. Weinstein, *Meaning and Appreciation: Time and Modern Political Life* (West Lafayette, IN: Purdue University Press, 1978), p. 5. Many thanks to Purdue University Press for granting permission to use this image on July 14, 2014.

12 Michael Weinstein and Félix Guattari
A Militancy of "Vivacious Despair"

Diane Rubenstein

> The relation between self -a reality that fluctuates between the poles
> of the purely observant ego and substantial mind, or psyche- and its
> internal and external environment is the only one to which the term
> 'belonging' properly applies, or at least applies in its fullest sense. . .
> The relation of self to its environs is not one of juxtaposition, but of
> comprehension.[1]
>
> *(Finite Perfection, 26–27)*

I read these sentences from *Finite Perfection* as effectively framing the motivational logic subtending Félix Guattari's analytical practice of institutional
psychotherapy at the La Borde clinic. For the affinity between Weinstein
and Guattari's respective *oeuvres*, as well as their similar philosophical trajectories from existentialism to more semiotic or deconstructive pursuits,
reposes upon the priority given to *singularization*: "a self-organizing process
involving the constitution of an assemblage of components (intrinsic references), relations with other assemblages, and the analysis of their effects on
subjectivity."[2] Whether parsed as "assemblage/arrangement/*agencement*"
(for Deleuze and Guattari) or as a "cluster,"[3] this process is constitutive of
both "finitude and authenticity"[4] (*DL* 67; *C* 193).

My comparison of Weinstein and Guattari is premised around the way
that certain thought *takes place* or has its place,[5] both philosophically and
pedagogically. What can it be about a singular place, the La Borde clinic
or "Mother Purdue" (Mike's[6] name for his university home), that makes
for a propitious site of transformative institutional practice, the artistic
creation of philosophic percepts ("rhizome" or the "civil savage"), or a
transformative undoing of the "repressive structure of militant subjectivity"?[7] I will argue that in Weinstein and Guattari's work with students and
inmates, collegial staff, and psychotics (I will leave the assignation of each
of these terms to the reader) at La Borde and Purdue, Sartre's "serialized"
life of the practico-inert was profoundly disrupted (*DL* 64; *C* 191). If
there is a lesson in this story of institutional practices, it will be in Guattari's understated phrasing: "It is surprising to realize that with the same

micro-sociological 'notes' one can compose a completely different score" (*DL* 66–7; *C* 193).

In his posthumous tribute, "*Pour Félix,*" Gilles Deleuze ranks the practice of institutional psychotherapy first in his appreciation of Guattari's specific contribution, as it formed the basis for his concept of transversality, which we will discuss in what follows.[8] As Guattari's background might not be as well known to readers of this volume as either Deleuze's or Weinstein's, I will note that he was at first a philosophy student (escaping from his pharmacy studies) when he came to the La Borde clinic in 1955 at the age of 25 upon Jean Oury's invitation. Guattari had been previously associated with Oury's brother, Fernand, as a militant in the international youth hostel movement (an *ajiste*) and had met Jean Oury when he was 15 years old (and Jean Oury was 21.) Fernand had been Félix's science teacher.[9] Jean Oury had already trained at Saint Alban with François Tosquelles, a survivor of the Spanish Civil War as well as a member of the extreme left Marxist workers' party (POUM: *Parti ouvrier d'unification marxiste*). Saint Alban was an emblem of pioneering programs in institutionalized psychiatry; it carried out its revolutionizing of technique at the same time as it struggled daily for survival under wartime conditions. During the war, Saint Alban provided hospitality for artists, militant doctors, and Résistants.

Two features stand out from Guattari's self-presentation of his arrival at La Borde, where he would live until his death at age 62. The first is its continuity with a dissident ethos that was congenial to him; the second was his total absence of formal training as a therapist as well as his ignorance concerning the illnesses that governed the lives of the residents. According to the account of Guattari (and its slightly different presentation by Marie Depussé[10]), he had little interest in madness and was ignorant about psychosis. His response before meeting inmates of Oury's clinic was an "esthetic" one, imagining them as a poetic inversion of the world, "strange, disquieting, fascinating." At La Borde, in contrast, the patients appeared under a different aspect: "familiar, friendly, human" (*DL* 61; *C* 188). What the psychotic offered was a hyperbolic picture of how a change of relation to the world corresponds to a readjustment of the components of personality. "The world and the 'other' no longer speak to him with the same voice" (*DL* 65; *C* 192).

Psychotics are in dialogue with a world that is not wholly imaginary and delirious but manifesting in banal, quotidian, social, and material practices of the type Weinstein, following Samuel Alexander, depicts in *Finite Perfection* as fundamental arts. These arts provide both the site and the stake of the psychotic's experience: art can only be understood for Weinstein within a "structure of temporal experience" (*FP* 88). Within this context, "art may be understood as an arrangement of the objective contents of experience according to a purpose. . . over a chain of momentary experiences" (*FP* 88). It does not matter if the purpose is a result or development of "the process of arrangement" or if it precedes it. Following Samuel Alexander, Weinstein sees art as a "mixing of 'mind and material'" and distinguishes between different arts according to the nature of the material as well as how the mind "arranges" it (*FP 89*). Although, for Alexander, these definitions were constructed to privilege the fine arts, Weinstein extends his insights in directions (such as in more practical arts) more conducive to Guattari's practice. Weinstein underscores that "fine art" works as a *"stopping point within the flux of life* that shows the finitude of momentary experience by forming an object that attracts attention *for its own sake*; not for its contribution to something else, including the desire and determination to preserve it" (*FP* 90, emphasis mine).

An example from Marie Depussé links the pertinence of this insight to the La Borde clinic. Guattari, Oury, and a group of monitors decided to disband a successful pottery workshop (*atelier*) comprising both clinical personnel and patients, as they were producing pots that were "too beautiful." These ceramics became their own purpose; the beautifully wrought pots, vessels of "finite perfection," cancelled out previous exchanges between *atelier* participants and established a superiority complex among the participants in relation to other workshops, further insulating them. There was thus no longer "institutional production," defined as the "production of subjectivities," only the making of "pots" (*DL 16*).

Referencing the work of trauma therapist and sculptor Gisela Pankow, Guattari notes that at La Borde, the modeling "plaster" is the *institutional material* engendered throughout the tangle of workshops and meetings, as well as the daily life in the dining rooms and bedrooms, in games, in sports, and in cultural life (*DL 66*; *C 193*). Weinstein would concur and add to the list with his own examples: mowing the lawn, repairing the lawn mower, and, in a class by itself, driving one's car. Neither Weinstein nor Guattari differentiates between these quotidian tasks and "exceptional" or "higher" forms of artistic expression. These daily mundane activities are "fundamental arts" testifying that improvisational possibilities are never given in advance: "speaking on the telephone, cooking, personal hygiene, driving a car, simple repair, and keeping an orderly account of and control over one's finances" (*FP 96*).

Two of these arts that Weinstein gives particularly loving attention to are cooking and driving. "Preparing a meal" links Weinstein philosophically with one of his interlocutors, Ortega's, sense of "occupation": surveying one's "ingredients" and deciding upon amending one's "initial plan" (*FP* 90). Moreover, cooking "attunes" us to our tastes and those we care for/cater to, and in this specific attention to nutritional matter and its sensuous arrangement, we are alerted to beauty. In *Culture/Flesh*, food similarly provides sustenance for the erotic life as a "simple pleasure" (to be distinguished from "subjective pleasures"): "Simple pleasures are the marvelous gifts of life, signaling both a substantial congruence of self and circumstance, and the contingency of that circumstance."[11] Among these pleasures of "being filled with the rhythm and melody of a song, witnessing a joyful smile" is "tasting a favorite food" (*C/F* 76).

As many contributors to this volume have noted, Weinstein's life-philosophy is situated in relation to an American context. So it should not be surprising that driving, "one of the fundamental arts of American civilization," is given a robust description in his writing (*FP* 97). Driving is first presented pragmatically, as a task whose art is "safely conducting a heavy machine at high speeds under a wide range of road conditions." Operating a vehicle opens one to climatic and road conditions of greater and lesser severity, commanding various levels of attentiveness and skill (traffic, snow, ice—we are near Chicago!) and under differing moods. This is what Weinstein wittily refers to as "the vicissitudes of the drive" (*FP* 98). One can never know the car's limits (or its capabilities) until one exceeds them; this adds to the necessary precarity and vulnerability of getting to know our "second body" and its delights (*C/F* 83–4).

> The artistry of driving demands the complete recognition that one's safety is entrusted to one's car, that one cannot stop at will, that a machine has become an extension of one's body, and that a car's parts can fail. Yet one must be close to one's car, feel it nearly as a part of one's body, make its movements responsive to one's discretion by getting to know those movements as well as those of one's arms and legs. Practicing the artistry of driving makes the activity a good for its own sake, because one becomes sufficiently self-controlled and skilled to fear neither the road nor oneself on the road. The destination no longer makes a difference nor do *the vicissitudes of the drive . . .*
>
> (*FP* 98, emphasis mine)

If we were to reinscribe driving under the national sign, it is fundamental in America precisely because it affords access to the "facilities for sustaining everyday life" with self-sufficiency. Anything that would overly facilitate "the drive"—cruise control, monitoring parking systems[12]—would be at the detriment of "one of the greatest supports of individuality in American society" (*FP* 99).

If we generalize these arts to other national imaginaries, they are "fundamental" because that make us aware of our vulnerability and finitude: our dependency upon extant technologies (not of our making), outside "reality" and our mortal bodies. Weinstein presciently notes (in 1985) how many of these tasks can be outsourced to burgeoning service industries (at the time of my writing this in New York, I witness the explosion of nail salons, blow-dry bars, home-delivered food; at this moment of neoliberalism, ordering meals over the phone, speaking on it, or even leaving voice mail seems quaint!). But he also notes that the psychic toll of losing contact with the mundane arts links the millionaire recluse Howard Hughes to the institutionalized or warehoused inmate.[13] For what one fears about institutionalization in a nursing home and no longer doing one's own cooking (or the autonomy renounced whenever one loses one's driver's license) is in fact the inability to reappropriate the meaning of one's existence through these daily rites and gestures.

Both Weinstein and Guattari continually demonstrate how "subjectivication" is "ethically" reappropriated (not "technocratically," as Heidegger would indicate) by foregrounding types of activities "founded on a re-singularization of the relation to work and more generally, personal existence" (*DL* 65; *C* 191). In the previous Weinsteinian examples of cooking and driving, "the vitality of the personal existent is the strength that is felt and produced in a controlled release of activity in which a task is successfully completed" (*FP* 97). Guattari's invention of the *grille* (or "grid") reposes upon this sense of a fundamental art; it rotated tasks among staff and patients, desegregating the spaces of each population, allowing for certain defensive structures of the staff to be abandoned as also affording unforeseen avenues of expression among some psychotic patients and staff. Life at La Borde comprised forty different activities for a population of one hundred resident patients (*pensionnaires*) and seventy staff members (*DL* 67; *C* 193).

This is quite an ambitious project for what Genosko describes in brilliantly understated terms as "literally the tabular representation upon which the evolving schedule of work rotation in which everyone participated was inscribed."[14] While the *grille* might just look like an elaborate technical gadget, an ur Excel spreadsheet, or "double book-keeping" system (*DL* 63; *C* 190), it was actually a quite subversive (cultural) revolutionary invention, attempting to "heighten and maximize an institution's 'therapeutic coefficient' by unfixing roles, thawing frozen hierarchies, opening hitherto closed blinkers and modifying the introjection of the local superegoisms and objects."[15]

Guattari realized that there would be resistances coming from people working at La Borde as gardeners, kitchen staff, maintenance personnel, and cleaning staff who did not necessarily share the militant motivations that directed therapists and nurses to the clinic. In the context of revolutionizing psychiatric practices in a more holistic way, how could one prevent a hierarchy between mental ("caregiving"/*soignant*) labor and the thankless material tasks of keeping the institution going? How to avoid the inevitable institutional creep toward favoritism or authoritarianism? The *grille* distributed tasks in such a manner that nurses accepted labor involving cleaning, maintenance, and cooking, whereas the household staff (somewhat more diffidently) collaborated with the medical staff in giving shots, putting in nighttime watch hours, and participating in collective activities such as group meetings and workshops.

Weinstein provides the rationale behind those material activities targeted by the *grille* at La Borde quite poetically:

> In the absence of the need for artistry in everyday tasks, the "me" is not tempered by the obduracy of rooted realities, the self control attendant upon artistry does not operate, love seems cheap, and there is little opportunity for the masterful unity with things to develop, the sense of power that supervenes upon detached deliverance.
>
> (*FP* 96–7)

Guattari's grid (*la grille*) acknowledges that one needs to forge new tools (or rededicate fundamental practices) for institutional as well as personal change. Both require taking on the Freudian "superego." Weinstein provides the best and most succinct definition I have ever encountered for the project of psychoanalysis: "a method for containing hatred for the evil proceeding directly from the self" (*FP* 74). His understanding of "hardcore" Freud elucidated in chapter 2 of *Finite Perfection* consists of *leaping* ahead, definitely *not* leaping (or leaning) in (62). It deploys a slightly different vocabulary for the aim of psychoanalysis: Weinstein terms "individualizing and personalizing" what Guattari would call "singularizing." This variant in phrasing should not deflect from the concord uniting them; both present a "personalized" or "singularized" version against Oedipal myth, viewed as a "fallacy of misplaced concreteness" (*FP* 68–69). As expressed by Weinstein: "(e)ach epic poem of the psyche will express a unique history." This is a militant acceptance of the self as a victory for the over-ego and not for the punishing superego. The over-ego is a benign overseer as the self becomes more tolerant of its own buried hatreds.

Guattari comes to these questions differently: How is the superego to be given access to something that doesn't trigger repression? Both Weinstein and Guattari state in their respective idioms that desire is not territorializable. For Weinstein, the beast will not go away. Guattari situated the superego as the key to Freud's topography: "It all boils down to these alternatives, either desire comes to desire repression and actively supports its aims, thus preserving itself as desire; or desire revolts against repression and loses itself as desire. Quite a clever mechanism!" (*C* 215).

The Guattarian concept of *transversality* might be best located here as "the capacity of an institution to remodel ways of access it offers the superego so that certain symptoms and inhibitions are removed[16]" (*C* 215). Both Guattari and Weinstein wager against the inevitability of *ressentiment* and the triumph of the reactive forces: a social formation *can* modify the "causality" that instigates the superego's activity; the topography can be transformed "so that repression/inhibition take on different meanings" (*C* 215). There can be a shift or change in an erotic focal point; for Guattari (and in Weinstein's pedagogical practice of the seminar, as I will later argue), a group eros can be created or there can be a takeover by a group subject.

Transversality is defined as:

> A dimension that strives to overcome two impasses: that of pure verticality and a simple horizontality. Transversality tends to be realized when maximum communication is brought about between different levels and above all in terms of different directions.[17]

The concept of transversality addresses the twin dead ends of public life obtaining in political groups as well as in psychiatric (or clinical) facilities: either remaining fixed in hierarchy ("verticality") or "accommodation" ("horizontality.") Vertical structures/relations of authority are predicated on a pyramid-structured division of labor and specialization of function. (We have already noted how the "grid" worked to check these tendencies.) Horizontality refers to the Hobbesian dynamic (in both the ward and academic department level) in which the most neurotic/psychotic/manic person prevails. For Guattari quite explicitly (and for Weinstein implicitly through his teaching), a group's goal is to maximize transversality, pursuing its desires and interests always with relation to an outside. This makes it a precarious and fragile entity. As described by Genosko, it is ambivalently alienated; the outside can "overwhelm" it; it can contract into its own form of madness or *huis clos*.[18] In the double-edged desire of expansion and contraction, groups struggle over their finitude in two directions: toward greater creativity and self-management or toward self-mutilation in the forms of despair or leader worship. Transversality effectively displaces a prior psychoanalytic concept of transference. It highlights what is specific to the psychoanalytic encounter (as in some pedagogical relationships) in which an asymmetrical yet reciprocal relationship obtains. Subject–subjugated distinctions (of personnel or knowledges) reconfigured via transversality can be now seen as two sides of the same institutional object.

Transversality, in attempting to establish a relation with the outside, would modify objects introjected by the superego, allowing both subjects and subjugated groups to use material in more productive or less toxic and recursive ways. As with the innovations afforded by the *grille*, new transferential potentialities (it is not as though transference goes away, it is just that it can be reimagined once its Oedipal residues are metabolized), affective bonds, and opportunities for analysis were invented. At La Borde, prior identifications with certain places shifted as other sites of fundamental arts—the kitchen and the laundry—become valorized. Weinstein reminds us that personal hygiene, comprising laundry as well as other aspects of grooming, "reveals the body in its concrete particularity and habituates one to attend to its signals closely, constituting a tight interpenetration of 'mind' and 'material' " (*FP* 97).

Transversality and the *grille* (grid) addressed what Weinstein denotes as the "structure of temporal experience" discussed earlier (*FP* 87). Thus, a most significant aspect of life at La Borde was in the way time itself changed its existential bearings. Time now mattered in *"how* it is beaten"[19](emphasis mine) once institutional life was organized toward the production of subjectivity and task rotation became less fixed and more nomadic. But one could see this presaged in the *grille*, which differs from Foucauldian "disciplinary" time/timetables. As Deleuze so astutely remarked about the "diagrammatic" nature of Foucauldian concepts,[20] the "grid" is an "abstract machine." It went through periods of high structuring and centralization (1958–66) as well as decentralization (1967–70) and a period combining strong centralization with decentralized elements (1970–3).[21] As most clearly formulated by Guattari in *La Révolution Moleculaire*,[22]

> Let's consider what we call at La Borde *la grille*. . .one can say that it involves the emergence of an abstract machine. The problem that faced us was how to conjoin temporal fluxes, work fluxes, duties and monetary fluxes, etc., in a way different than what is generally found in similar institutions and may be perhaps characterized by the existence of a relatively static functional organigramme. *La grille employs time—inscribed on paper; a machine for "rotating" duties—inscribed in a gestural semiology; the modification of hierarchical categories—inscribed in a juridical and social semiology.*
>
> (emphasis mine)

As elaborated by Genosko, as an abstract machine, the grid is an assemblage of diverse semiologies (gestural, social, juridical); it is a work in progress, untethered by an original referent and like art, unfinished, unpredictable, and open. One of its key aspects is the *roulement* (rotation) both of specific tasks as well as, more generally, in the disposition not to fetishize the grid itself: "The piece of paper is abstract in the sense that it is not fully formed. And it is a diagram since it needs to be worked out through a very long process that began in the late 1950s."[23]

The grid initiated a rotation of and restructured time; but transversality required a "mediating third object" which "exists outside of one-on-one contact, and upon which work is done cooperatively, and for which responsibility is collectively assumed through a series of obligatory exchanges."[24] Examples of such objects first derived from Freinet's Institutional Pedagogy movement included a school press and journal. Such objects erode previously noted oppositions between manual and mental labor as they also blur distinctions between onerous tasks ("work"/*travail*) and more ludic ones (creative play). What is at stake here is a collective creative endeavor (a collective "mind") that works upon the institutional "matter" in the mode suggested by Weinstein's discussion of art in *Finite Perfection*. I suggest that this third mediating object for Weinstein is the seminar itself.

In the concluding section of this chapter, I will look at Weinstein's pedagogy in the context of the seminar (a Barthesian space of love[25]) as an institutional subject group subtending a disruptive and transformative practice in America's heartland. I will also elaborate how the liberation of molecular flux and their intensities produced a different micropolitics of desire than did the Socratic model that Weinstein's teaching could be mistakenly assimilated to. However, to prolong the Guattarian parallels as well as to specify the effect of his practice (and, additionally, to further prepare for the pleasure of this attendant discussion,) I will precede this analysis with a brief case study.

SIMMEL/KAFKA/SIMMEL[26]

Attention to the artistry of the dreamwork aligns Guattari and Weinstein. A comparison of Deleuze and Guattari's *Kafka* (1975) with Deena and Michael Weinstein's *Postmodern(ized) Simmel* (1993) reveals methodological similarities. Texts are not read against critical or archetypical or ideological reductionisms *du jour* but positioned toward a multiplicity of openings and play. Both works are affirmative and experimental encounters with their respective author's writing. In the Simmel book, the Weinsteins experiment typographically, putting key words literally under erasure ("flaneur" to "bricoleur") and in the form of an imagined colloquy between Derrida and Simmel set within a Derridean dream. The persona of the "stalemater" is enacted in this staging (*PS* 88–98).

In the case of Deleuze and Guattari's *Kafka*, the authors refused to read him in light of a dominant Oedipal narrative that territorialized him through his letter to his father.[27] A comic, joyous *desiring* Kafka appears. In this revision, unterritorializable desire confronts three hateful (superegotic) repressive logics: Nazism, Stalinism, and what Weinstein calls liberal (American) fascism. Deleuze and Guattari's displaced reading is done through the emphasis on an *exteriorized* relation to the German language read through the "hybridity" of Kafka's status as a Czech-Jewish speaker of German. Kafka's "minor" literary status is not a duality in the sense of major versus minor literatures but attests (in a postcolonial fashion) to his external relation to language *within* that very language (like Joseph Conrad).[28] It is thus a third term, a peculiarity or strangeness, what is called an anomaly, neither normal nor pathological.[29]

Guattari's single-authored *Sixty-Five Dreams* (which also contains a film project)[30] echoes the "fictive stylization of the given," those "bio-fictions" (*PS* 6) at work in *Post-Modern(ized) Simmel*. The focus in the Weinsteins' book is on Simmel's "image" (*PS* 5); difference and plurality are affirmed and writing is allied with desire to understand (epistemophilia). As with Deleuze and Guattari's *Kafka*, there are no simple appraisals. Simmel is not presented within the familiar binary framings of an ethics of choice or contradiction against a neurasthetic decidaphobe; Simmel is neither undisciplined nor "supersane," nor is he "a scared" or scarred Jew (*PS* 7). For the Weinsteins, all of these binaries devolve into patterns of good and bad objects rather than into a greater appreciation of ambivalence and difference.

To translate this into the Guattarian terms that would best frame it, all of the familiar assertions concerning Simmel's character are recast into the following "molecularized" or "detotalized" affirmations: Simmel's name is a master form; this form is "rhizomatic"—it can not be reorganized (or reterritorialized) coherently into a logical system of forms; it forms itself after containing opposition within its own description. Its internal hybridity is constitutive of the "minor."

For Deleuze and Guattari, the "minor" has three characteristics: first, a high coefficient of deterritorialization affects its language. ("A minor literature doesn't come from a minor language; it is rather that which a minority constructs within a major language."[31]) The second feature is that everything within "the minor" is political (*K* 17). Last, "everything takes on a collective value." As explicated by Deleuze and Guattari, the literatures deemed "minor" do not suffer from an abundance of talent and overproduction of masterworks. Thus utterances are not traced back to a master enunciator; "scarcity of talent" proves a boon: "what each author says individually already constitutes a common action . . . even if others aren't in agreement" (*K* 17).

Post Modern(ized) Simmel in written in a "minor" mode; it works by "multiform clusters" (*PS* 48). The name (Simmel) adapts to specific contexts rather than imposing a regime of control; or a master name remains, but the boundaries shift (*PS* 46). One can read this book as an attempt to undo the Oedipal myth and as an affront to the symbolic register: "There is no disposition to settle some non-existent score between postmodernisms; instead there is an effort to hook Simmel into as many of them as possible" (*PS* 46). The Weinsteins self-consciously acknowledge a shift from existential phenomenology to a more "inclusivist" (*PS* 4) postmodernism, necessitating a new semiotic approach to the return of structuralism's repressed:[32] "We realized that Simmel's forms of philosophy were deconstructive in the sense that they did not allow any symbolic reconciliation of textual diversity even though they seemed to be ruled by master names such as 'Subject' or 'Life' " (*PS* 46–7).

Simmel also instantiates "the minor" in ways that Ramon Soto-Crespo has indicated, as he is a border theorist. The Weinsteins situate his philosophy as "bridging" the early twentieth-century vitalist philosophies and the interwar existentialist phenomenologies of thinkers such as Heidegger. Simmel's border is temporal and metaphysical: human existence resides "at the juncture between the infinite and the finite, . . . the unconditional and the conditional. . .No aspect of our existence can be defined unilaterally: By virtue of the fact that we *have* boundaries, everywhere and always, so accordingly, we *are* boundaries" (*PS* 103). However, the fact that "we are boundaries" does not solely confine; "every single determinate boundary can be stepped over." The boundary is unconditional (constituting "our given position in the world"), but the Derridean logic of the double bind/ boundary also underwrites the reading of Simmel: "*no* boundary is unconditional since every one on principle can be altered, reached over and gotten around—this pair of statements appears as the explication of the inner unity of vital action"[33] (*PS* 104).

CONCLUSION: TO THE SEMINAR

> An institution is treated in the utopian mode: I outline a space and call it *seminar* . . . One might put things differently: that the (real) seminar is for me the object of a (minor) delirium, and that my relations with this object are, literally, *amorous*.
>
> (*RL* 332)

I can find no better (meta) third mediating object to Weinstein's pedagogical practice and Guattari's conceptual innovation than Barthes's celebration of the seminar. Barthes figures the weekly seminar, an institutional practice, as a "hanging garden," a place for "peaceful speech" and notable for its suspended state: "a collectivity at peace in a world at war" (*RL* 341). It is a paradoxical site, at once "sustained by the world that surrounds it, but also resisting it." It achieves a "*partial* utopia": "the seminar says 'No' to the totality" (*RL* 341).

Before I discuss how this blessed state might be achieved—the requisites for the art of becoming seminarians, elsewhere described in Barthes's essay in ways wholly apposite to Weinstein's writings in *Finite Perfection* to those of self control (i.e., a "suspended relaxation of bodies," a "disarmed ascesis—connecting with an art of living. . .") (*RL* 331)—I will relate how I came to Weinstein's seminar. I was Michael Weinstein's colleague at the Purdue political science department from 1990 to 2000. The nineties in America might be likened to those "winter years" of the eighties in France that Guattari devoted many writings to, collected in an eponymous volume[34] tracking his disappointment with the rise of the new Right and with liberal forms of fascism during Mitterand's time in office. Julie Webber notes analogous preoccupations surrounding the crafting of *Culture/Flesh* as well as in his work produced with Kroker. By the time I decided to attend his weekly graduate seminar during a leave during which I remained in Lafayette, we had already worked in our subfield and served on PhD committees together. Several of those students were members of the seminar. My reasons for attending were various, including finding a weekly seminar both stimulating and a perfect support for sustaining long-term research projects. I also had a punctual review essay to write, and the seminar required the crafting of such an essay for its final requirement in lieu of a seminar paper. My presentation in this section will augment a theoretical or philosophical account of teaching with my personal reflections. I would not call my status "participant observation" as much as it was a full engagement. It did break down a hierarchical role of teacher–student, showing how both could be fluid; it also modified my "horizontal" or lateral relation with my theory colleague in unforeseen ways. I believe that it is precisely this type of transformative potential that is the goal of (Guattarian) transversality.

If the goal of Guattari's institutional practice was to produce subjectivities, the seminar's task is congenial with it, as its task is to produce "differences." Differences here do not signify those parodies of agonistic jousts or other stylized "conflicts" that popular media present as Socratic instruction; these usually occur at Harvard Law School (*Paper Chase, Legally Blonde*) or some other "questioning" practice in which forms of humiliation or "academic waterboarding" occur. "Difference," as the seminar's end purpose, is in making each relation "original." This is Barthes's term, but the ones for Weinstein and Guattari would be "individuated" or "singular," respectively. "Difference means what? That each relation, gradually (it takes time) is made original; discovers the originality of bodies one by one, breaks off the representation of roles" (*RL* 334). Given the devotion of Weinstein's students, one might have expected a caricature of Socrates, an absolute master (especially given Kaminski's reported example in this volume when his fellow student refers to him as a "walking encyclopedia"). Yet in contrast to the *interminable* encyclopedic or (Lacanian "university") discourse of the "Subject who is supposed to know," students in the seminar received only very short, phenomenologically bracketed "lecturettes" (Mike's word) of 15 minutes on a need-to-know basis to keep the discussion moving. The very set-off nature of these "lecturettes" further specified that Weinstein's job as a seminar teacher was not as a transmitter of his prior knowledge but a perfomative one, both creating new knowledge with and in front of the assembled participants and, in Barthes's words, to "set forth what I am doing" (*RL* 333).

The seminar may be the most condensed form of the teaching relation. It is small, Barthes reminds the reader not to preserve its "intimacy" but rather, its "complexity" (*RL* 332). The teacher is not a "professor" here as he may be in a lecture course but a "leader" or "facilitator": neither a " 'sacred' consecrated subject, nor a buddy—only a manager, an operator, a regulator" (*RL* 333). These are all roles that Guattari played at La Borde. He doesn't "lay down a law, but gives protocols. The seminar is a space of rules, not regulations" (*RL* 338). In this way, it also parallels the clinical practice at La Borde.

One of the particularities of a Weinstein seminar is that one is not permitted to arrive late; there is no allotted grace period of a few minutes. The door closes on the appointed time. Nor is there a set time for when it ends beyond the allotted three-hour period. I remember reflecting upon this in a more traditional Freudian psychoanalytical vein as such a powerful way to "jump-start transference." But it was actually in relation to this enabling structure that I was able to see how in fact this absolute limit desupposed

Weinstein's authority, allowing for the seminar to go off the rails as it is usually practiced (in political theory contexts) as highly Oedipalized. For what kind of teaching relation can there be without (founding) Fathers laying down a Law?

Barthes enunciates that the teaching relation is not what is commonly supposed as a transferential relation of the teacher to student "but the relation of those taught to each other." The role of the seminar teacher is to "clear the stage" to allow for those types of horizontal transferences between its members, not to reinforce a vertical bond between the student and master (*RL* 333). This liberated his seminar from the agonizing mimetic rivalry that is too often found in the seminar and allows for a mutuality that is rarely experienced in such an institutional setting. We must remember—and Weinstein never forgets as a good Althusserian—that this is a *partial* utopia, as the seminar takes place in an educational ideological state apparatus (ISA). This hospitality partakes of asymmetrical reciprocity between students who had attended prior seminars (Mike called them "veterans") and newcomers. As previously mentioned, it allowed someone as "vertically" situated as myself (a tenured faculty member) to invent and inhabit a different space for myself in the same dank basement classroom I taught in.

A successful seminar is one in which participants are bound to each other. As transference gives way to transversality in both psychoanalytic and pedagogical institutions, a group coherence/eros is formed. Creativity is heightened via self-control—the restrictions on coming late as well as the protracted sitting in what may well be a five-hour seminar. While this is not the same thing as Eastern practices of sitting, there is a type of "giddy listening" that such seminars provoke and that link its practice to the minor mode ("body over law, contract over code, speech over statement") and to minor euphorias found in "ideas generated by chance" (*RL* 340–341).

One of the things that puzzled me about Mike's name for his home institution was the gender-bending assignation of "Mother" to what was a very top-down bureaucratic (department heads, not chairs; only full professors decide on tenure, etc.) science and primarily *engineering school*. One does not commonly associate a "Boilermaker" with women and, indeed, he was named "Purdue Pete," complemented by the sequined "Golden Girl" drum majorette. Thinking about Michael's aberrant or, more accurately, transversal practice of teaching has led me to other theoretical conclusions. This is best contemplated by contrasting the common ways authority is mobilized in the teaching relation with his practice. A teacher may wield authority by virtue of his title (or prestige), as a technician who commands it by proficiency (a piano or language teacher), or in the exceptional body wisdom of a guru. However, these are only "occasions" of superiority, not relations of authority. The fact that Weinstein has produced the amount of published work in the myriad venues as well as receiving prestigious fellowships situates him (for Barthes) as "gratified" not as "authoritative" (*RL* 339). For what is truly interesting is how he eludes that very "mastery" which would reinstate the Law.

Let us look at another triad of gerunds: teaching, apprenticing, mothering. In teaching, a prior body of knowledge is transmitted verbally or by writing. In apprenticeship, a master imparts skills by having the novice watch him; he conveys this knowledge by parsimonious and deictic speech: "Here. . .I do *this* in order to avoid *that*." In "mothering," there is neither teaching nor demonstration. Barthes gives the example of walking. What the mother does is "support, encourage, calls (steps back and calls); she incites and surrounds: the child demands the mother and the mother desires the child's walking" (*RL* 336–337). For Barthes, this is what happens in seminar teaching, and it is what I believe Weinstein's practice does that achieves transversality.

> *To the seminar*: this expression must be understood as a locative, as an encomium (like the one the poet von Schober and the composer Schubert addressed "*An die Musik*"), and as a dedication.
>
> (*RL* 342)

For Michael Weinstein

NOTES

1. Michael A. Weinstein, *Finite Perfection: Reflection on Virtue*, Amherst: University of Massachusetts Press, 1985. All future references to this work in this chapter will be given as *FP*. Weinstein describes that this work was written in a determinate mood of "vivacious despair," where "despair is the substantive and vivacity the qualifier" (25).
2. Gary Genosko, *Félix Guattari: A Critical Introduction*, London: Pluto Press, 2009: 35. I remain theoretically indebted to Genosko's pellucid presentation of Guattari's concept of transversality and his innovation of the *grille* (grid) detailed in chapter 2, "Transversality and Politics," pages 48–68.
3. Deena Weinstein and Michael A. Weinstein, *Postmodern(ized) Simmel*, London: Routledge, 1993: 48 (future references to this work in this chapter will be given as *PS*).
4. Félix Guattari, *De Leros À La Borde*, Éditions Ligne/IMEC, 2012; an earlier version is published as "La Borde: a Clinic Unlike Any Other," in *Chaosophy*, Sylvere Lotringer, ed., New York: Semiotext(e), 1995. Further chapter references will be the *DL* (the French version) and *C* (the English semiotexte version).
5. Taking place as well as having a/one's own place is evoked in the French expression "*avoir lieu*." There is a juridical (as well as psychiatric) association with the negative form of this phrase: a "*non lieu*," when someone lacks the faculties to stand trial, such as Althusser after his wife's death.
6. When referring to a written work or practice (such as the seminar), I will be using "Weinstein"; this is in contrast to his spoken "idiolect," when I will refer to him as "Mike."
7. Franco "Bifo" Berardi, "An Interview with Bifo," *After the Future*, Gary Genosko and Nicholas Thoburn, ed., Oakland, CA: AK Press, 2011: 176. During this interview, there is a discussion of renewed interest in the figure of the militant in thinkers such as Badiou or Zizek without the concomitant

querying of the "repressive structure of militant subjectivity" that was a large part of post–68 critique. In his preface to *Anti-Oedipus: Capitalism and Schizophrenia* (Gilles Deleuze and Félix Guattari, Minneapolis: University of Minnesota Press, 1983), Michel Foucault describes one of the "adversaries" confronted by its authors as the "sad militant": "Bureaucrats of the revolution and civil servants of Truth" (xll).

8. Gilles Deleuze, "Pour Félix," *Deux Regimes de Fous*, Paris: Éditions de Minuit, 2003: 357.
9. For a cogent presentation of the hostel movement, the *IP* (Célestin Freinet's Institutional Pedagogy movement), as well as this time in Guattari's formation for future projects of transdisciplinary self experimentation, see Genosko, *op. cit.*, chapter 1: "The Formation of a Young Militant."
10. Depussé presents contrasting versions between that of Guattari and Jean Oury concerning Guattari's ending of his philosophy studies as she also underscores the affective uncanny that translated his first impressions. Marie Depussé, "*Présentation*," *De Leros*, 10 fn1. For an enchanting description of life at La Borde written by Guattari's daughter, see Emmanuelle Guattari, *La petite Borde (roman)*, Paris: Mercure de France, 2012.
11. Michael A. Weinstein, *Culture/Flesh: Exploration of Postcivilized Modernity*, Lanham, MD: Rowman and Littlefield, 1995: 76.
12. Delia Ephron, in "Less Sexy, Better for Sex," attacks the Google self-driving car. For Ephron, learning to drive is an exercise in self-control—it gives us something to master and take pride in (e.g., parallel parking) and the ability to get to and away from something on our own terms. The Google car, in contrast, "fosters passivity, nurtures infancy. It has no driver, only passengers," *The New York Times* July 6, 2014: SR2.
13. According to my friend, the theologian Cary Howie, neither the millionaire Hughes nor the nursing home resident "wipe their own ass"!
14. Genosko 29.
15. *Ibid.*
16. The discussion of transversality in the context of Freud is to be found in "The Best Capitalist Drug," also in *Chaosophy*. The French version can be found in *La Révolution Moleculaire*, Paris: Les Praires Ordinaires, 2012: 30; "La fin des fétichismes-a," 25–37.
17. Félix Guattari, "Transversalité," *Psychanalyse et transversalité*, Paris: Maspero/La Découverte, 1972/2003: 79–80; Genosko, *op. cit.* 51.
18. Genosko, *op. cit.* 52.
19. *Ibid.* 62.
20. Gilles Deleuze, *Foucault*, Sean Hand, trans., Minneapolis: University of Minnesota Press, 1988.
21. Genosko, *op. cit.* 60.
22. Félix Guattari, *La Révolution Moleculaire*, Paris: Les Prairies Ordinaires, 2012: 441–442. I am using Genosko's translation, *op. cit.* 57, that is based on the 1977 edition republished in 2002.
23. Genosko, *op. cit.* 59.
24. *Ibid.* 42.
25. Barthes eloquently writes about the teaching relation in two essays published in *The Rustle of Language*, Richard Howard, trans., New York: Hill and Wang, 1986: "Writers, Intellectuals, Teachers" and "To the Seminar." This will be cited as *RL* in the chapter.
26. This section could also be called D & M Weinstein/Deleuze & Guattari/D & M Weinstein. I am aware that this exception to the single-author format in both (M.) Weinstein and Guattari's case includes a work written in collaboration with an intimate collaborator.

27. For a quite different but equally militant reading of Kafka's letter, see Avital Ronell, *Loser Sons: Politics and Authority*, Urbana: University of Illinois Press, 2012.

28. This could also be read in relation to Jacques Derrida's *Monolingualism of the Other; or, The Prosthesis of Origin*, Patrick Mensah, trans., Stanford, CA: Stanford University Press, 1998.

29. François Dosse in *Gilles Deleuze et Félix Guattari: Biographie Croisée*, Paris: La Découverte, 2007 discusses the importance of *Kafka* as a transitional work between *Anti-Oedipus* (concept: desiring machine) and *Mille Plateaux* (concept: assemblage); Kafka is a "writing machine"; the "rhizome" is elaborated in a 1977 short text. (288–296) He also cites Georges Canguilhem's contribution to the concept of anomaly (292).

30. Félix Guattari, *Soixante-cinq Rêves de Franz Kafka*, Paris: Lignes, 2007.

31. Gilles Deleuze and Félix Guattari, *Kafka*, trans. Dana Polan, Minneapolis: University of Minnesota Press, 1986: 16.

32. Guattari's contribution to semiotics is detailed in section five of *La Révolution Moleculaire*, "Échafaudages Semiotiques."(*Échafaudages* signifies "scaffolding" as well as the erection of a new social order.)

33. These quotations are taken from Simmel's 1918 "*Lebesanschauung*" (which can be translated as a way of looking at life or an approach to life) discussed by the Weinsteins as his last major philosophical work. In their strong reading of this work, they situate Simmel as closer to "contemporary thinkers such as Derrida, Deleuze, Baudrillard, and Lyotard" than "any of the other classical sociologists" (e.g., Durkheim, Pareto, Weber, Tonnies). I would add the name of Félix Guattari to this list of contemporary philosophers. In *Postmodern(ized) Simmel*, there is an equivalence made between Derridean "wandering" (*errance*), Deleuzian (and Guatarrian) rhizomatic thinking, and Lyotardian "drifting" (170).

34. Félix Guattari, *Les Années D'Hiver 1980–1985*, Paris: Les Prairies ordinaires, 2009.

Epilogue

13 Performing Integral Consciousness
Simulation

Michael A. Weinstein

"They were doing something with each other. I was driving."[1]

Ideas are flying past me, as the landscape does when you kick the car up to 80 mph on a bare stretch of highway. Let's seize this moment when I am privy to the freshly minted images and thoughts thrown up into my consciousness by what Oliver Wendell Holmes called the "underground workshop" (a.k.a. Unconscious); nothing is yet thematized—it is William James's "blooming and buzzing confusion."

Thematization is only a position in "life grasped from the inside by a finite 'me-locus of reference.'" Holmes's "Bedlam of Ideals" is where all of us start (I presume), and then we find a content to work over intellectually, abstracted from all the others. That is what I am going to have to do if I want to do the present writing. Yet I have committed myself not to strategize this writing, to have no plan, just to let it be prompted by the underground workshop. I am no longer in Bedlam, I know the purpose of this writing, which will put the underground workshop to purposive work. Yet what is most insistent for it to express in this wonderful book, to which this writing will be a contribution?

LECTURETTE

I have no theme yet, but I do have the genre in which it will be expressed—the written simulation of the spoken genre of the lecturettes that I deliver in my classes when discussion reaches an impasse and we do some "knitting." Thank you, Diane, for your precise and generous description of the lecturette. It is always delivered off the cuff, at the spur of the moment, and I haven't planned what I am going to say. It is a particularized response to the promptings of a group of people—the "class"—at a particular place and time. The lecturette might turn out to be a posthuman rant like I did with Arthur in *Data Trash* (high cyberpunk), a systematic analysis of a philosophical conundrum, the performance of a relevant ideology, a (edifying) story, or the singing of a song that I find to be appropriate to the moment.

To whom am I to be delivering the lecturette? The answer is clear. My audience is myself, the part of which that has "always already" escaped me, what William James called the "social self," the ideas that others have of me.

What an unequivocal gift to me this book is—to be given my social self by reflective, sensitive, caring, intelligent, and insightful people who have mastered philosophy and who have known me face to face. What a privilege it is to be given one's philosophical social self so precisely and intensely. That kind of social self is to be treasured, and I do. Yet I still have no theme and no actual individual here to give me one. I just have a bunch of glorious texts.

I'm writing this at the lunch counter of the 7-Eleven (formerly the White Hen Pantry) where I wrote my last philosophy book, *The Imaginative Prose of Oliver Wendell Holmes*, that is still presided over and under the benevolent protection of its master of ceremonies, Bob Rinaldi. I'll walk outside and let the ideas fly by. It will be a more coherent experience now that I know what I have to do.

Before I leave the counter, I need to say that I completed the Holmes book with the judgment that "we don't know who we are." It's easy to see why I haven't written any of my "philosophical meditations" since then. I came to my "real assent," and it hasn't changed for a decade. Since then everything for me is ontic, so I keep up my photo criticism, practiced political analysis on Somalia, and now explore and teach about NASCAR. I am what Tim Yetman calls an "ontological nihilist." As one of my recent songs goes: "I'm a hardcore nihilist ontologically / But it's a different story ontically; / I play just to play / I won't fold my hand; / I want to be a player with the boys in the band." The last line is sung with heavy self-sarcasm. I play just to play. That is what Tim and I have come to call "positive nihilism." Another way of putting it goes back to *Data Trash*. After that book, I gave up on defending the flesh. I wished the coming androids well and decided to do deep play in the hospice where we are waiting for the androids to replace us. I am still at one with you, Arthur. The posthuman sucks, and it has arrived, but what is one supposed to do with organisms that "hate their condition in the world," as I sing in another song? I play some of their games my way, because I'm not ready to commit suicide or to renounce the world meditatively. I have no mission. Some more lyrics: "The pain will come and the pain will go / And I will be here 'til I die." That's the most I can say—I will be here 'til I die. I'm ready to leave the counter.

JOYRIDE: 7/5/14

I'm back at the counter and I know what to do—take a joyride through/with my philosophical social selves. Let's career, let's take the curves of a road course at breakneck speed. Let's go to the limit: BLACKOUT. Hardcore thrill seeking. We will court Blackout, the ultimate driving experience—you go so fast that you black out. It happens to the top-fuel dragsters who compete in the National Hot Rod Association races. It's an extreme sport—you can't get more Dionysian.

The Nietzsche of today (more than ever, Arthur—you describe me as I want to be) calls himself G-7. That's a play on G-6, the sixth-generation racing car in NASCAR that has lost its connection to a stock car, although there is still the pretension of a connection. It is a pseudo-stock car, yet another of the Baudrillardian simulacra, of which there is such a profusion. Well, I'm G-7, more advanced than the G-6, because I know the G-6 for the failed simulacrum that it is—a metonym for the posthuman culturescape—yet I still study NASCAR and watch races on TV with great pleasure, taking them for what they present themselves to be, events on the "sports-entertainment landscape," as it is called in the business.

G-7 is my "latest iteration" as the photographer Adam Holtzman has told me. As G-7, I contain all the personae that I have taken in the past—the renegade, the finite perfectionist, the civil savage, and Gamboole, not to mention the ones that come out in my lyrics, which are too many to mention. All of them are members of G-7's tribe and, as Joe would perceptively understand, G-7 is the God of this tribe of personae, all of which are now to be put to work in NASCAR Nation: "I'm coming out of NASCAR Nation / That is my home base. / I call myself G-7/ And I'm ready to restart the race."

Jon, I will always be indebted to you for the idea of privatism. I am a privatist, 100 percent. My intimate life and my solitary life when I take the position of ownness and commune with my home discourse and do a reflective review of my consciousness—take my life as radical reality—are my backstage. Public life always is front stage, always enacted through and mediated by personae, which I craft in my home discourse for my public engagements. Yet I am not "acting" when I perform those personae—when I am engaged in the heat of action, I become the persona that I am performing—I am not distant from it. Melba understands that—my breakdown in laughter, my expressions of professorial love. It is me at that moment. No alienation. I am indebted to Justin for understanding that all characterized presents are merely positions, even the seemingly privileged position of reflective review in home discourse. By this point I have an ample stock of positions and personae to go along with them. Joyride!

Thank you, Julie, for your great prescience in emphasizing integrality in my interpretation of life. The only philosophical "advance" that I have made since the Holmes book has been to understand better the meaning of integrality for me. I have reached the conclusion that the form of life grasped from the inside is what I call "integral consciousness."

I came to integral consciousness in the early hours of the morning in West Lafayette, alone, and I was seized with the idea of integrity, which was soon displaced by integrality. At that point, I went to my "trusty" 1938 *Oxford Universal English Dictionary*, where I found the following definition of "integral": "A whole consisting of component parts actually (not merely mentally) separable. Rare or Obsolete. 1588." You can imagine how excited I was—Deleuzian rhizomes and Lyotardian archipelagoes in the sixteenth century! A suppressed, a "minor" tradition. Just what I was and didn't know that I was looking for to cap off critical vitalism. Think back to the beginning of this writing—the point at which ideas are flying by. Then we picked one and abstracted it from the rest, but now we should remember the rest. They are different sectors or zones of consciousness that are ACTUALLY separable from one another . . . Yet they coexist in my conscious life and have all sorts of harmonious and oppositional relations with one another. Life as grasped from the inside is integral consciousness. We will/can experience the agonic conflicts that Robert deeply understands or the love of the individualist with which Jonathan cuts to my heart or the "creative engagement" from which both Kathy and I derive delight or—it just goes on. All of them coexist in multifarious relations and ruptures. It is dizzying. Blackout, overload, too much difference. Pour on more. Can you take it? That is integral consciousness. Take it into your intellect and let it penetrate your psyche and incite your body—a whole with parts that are actually separable from one another. Justin will see that it's just like Bergson's idea of "continuous change," a conceptual contradiction that is lived as a (dis)unity. You can only be a BORDER SAVAGE—thank you, Ramon. BLACKOUT

PHANTASMAGORIA, a word that is always lurking in my mind. It is a whirling phantasmagoria inside and outside. The human tragi-COMEDY. BLACKOUT

You can see that I've love-pirated Paul Virilio, his "dromology" and his doctrine of the inevitability of accident. He is the only serious philosopher who reflects on auto racing.

RESTART (WITH LYRICS)

"I'll run my race, I'll set my pace / Until the reaper comes for me. / The race is hard, the race is fun, / I'll never flee contingency." And then: "I'm living the NASCAR way. / I keep up my momentum, day by bleeping [this is a Weinstein seminar] day. / I'm living the NASCAR way. / I keep my edge, I always try, I always stay in play."

CAUTION

There's been a crash coming off turn two. (Sound familiar, Arthur?) We'll go at it again, another time. I'm exhausted.

JOYRIDE: 7/6/14

I went home after the crash. Why was it so taxing, even though it was the most pleasurable, most aleatory, writing that I have ever done? It seems to me that the effort came from driving the social selves given to me in this volume into myself, introjecting them. The crash happened—I can't say whether I was involved or whether, which is most likely, it was one or more of the social selves being introjected, which could only be done through this writing.

The underground workshop just answered the question. It was Arthur, it had to be Arthur. He's telling me, now that he is inside my mind, that I have done my-his work. I've thought in the *Data Trash* Super-Charged PM way and have come up with one of those polarities that Robert has identified (correctly) as a product/process of my form of thinking. In this case, it is the play between Blackout and Integral Consciousness, a relation that I have never made before, the kind of revelatory experience that happens some-times in seminars, new understandings, emergent categories being made at the moment.

I can say I'm sure (?) that I'm through with existentialism in this writing. Descartes said, "*Cogito ergo sum.*" I say that I will be around until I die, as whatever summed-up-self-in-process (gaining and losing memory) I happen to be. If you can feel that judgment with me, its stark simplicity, the sense I have of being bereft of any purposes beyond my finite life, where artistry and love can flourish unillusioned, then you understand what Whitehead called my "subjective response" to life. I am entirely bereft of ultra-vital meanings. I am desolate in the sense of being cut off from the continued functioning of the ideological state apparatus beyond the span of my life. And what I have left is my private life. This writing is done on the boundary of private and public life. It is a Border Savage essay written by a PRIVATIST who is allowed to call himself the Nietzsche of our times while he persists in loving (in this case professorial love) and ends up saying that all he can do is to try to KEEP HIS EDGE and committing to always staying in play: G-7. At that point, Arthur engineered the crash. He determined (he was already inside me as a social self) that the joyride had to end since nothing could be more thrilling than BLACKOUT followed by the explosion of personae, and, of course, he was correct. The god of my tribe is a limited god.

I have always rooted my thinking in some ultra-, hyper-, or abnormal experience that reorients my position. The clearest case is "expression" in Meaning and Appreciation. BLACKOUT plays a similar role in my thinking now—the ecstasy of the obliteration of experience momentarily and then its reappearance with everything whirling around as you try to regain control of a car that is careening uncommanded. And I have always found that core organizing experience spreading out and becoming a theme-in-relation-to-everything-else. It has had to be a fuller experience than simply having an idea. I have not written about what I have not lived. That is what Arthur means by "austere." I have "been there" in some way; I am not an idealist or a utopian, though I can and do perform their ideologies.

I have introjected all of you and know who made me crash. Now I'm going to leave the lunch counter and then come back and abandon the lecturette in favor of a kindred form, the colloquy with a student when we exchange ideas for as long as it takes, among the other members of the class, who can join in or will sometimes be dragged in by me.

RESTART

You're all in front of me, I see you all sitting around the seminar table, more vividly than I will ever see you again. I have devoted myself as completely as possible to you—my social selves in these texts—for more than a day. I will not be able to do that much longer as the pressures of practical life take over. Once the introjection is consummated, you will melt into my summed-up-self-in-process (home discourse).

I look at Robert and say: "Please be my comrade on a love-piracy expedition (joyride) through/with the social selves, including your own. You have given me the starting point through your insistence on the dialectical structure of my thinking.

"I have pushed through to my present dialectic, which is between extreme experience and (ultra-) (hyper-) reflexivity, the result of the latter of which is integral consciousness for the time being. The play of those two is now what structures my home discourse. I am the Border Savage, living between Dionysian ecstasy and Apollonian dispassion. As you can see, and Arthur and Ramon know, this is not an agonic dialectic. Indeed, it brings me back to where I started in my PhD dissertation, which tried to elucidate the ideas of liberty in Santayana's work, a typological phenomenology that boils down to the juxtaposition of vital liberty and spiritual freedom. I left Western Reserve University with the unhappy consciousness of trying to bring the two together. That's the basis of the dialectic, considered at its 'origins' and 'developmentally'"

I turn to Ramon and say: "So you can see how amazingly precise is your Border Savage persona. With the *zozobra* I came to myself as a philosopher. I have remained a Border Savage. Love-Piracy is what a Border Savage does. No text is excluded, whatever its provenance. The Mexicans, above all Uranga, gave me the permission to think out *The Tragic Sense of Political Life*. Uranga wore accidentality as a badge of honor and so could I. It is that accidentality, by the way, that has attracted me most to NASCAR racing. Each team works on its car obsessively to get the right setup for that particular track, and then the driven cars get out on the track to test their setups against the others. As they do so, they invariably get into each others' ways or they have mechanical failures or they have a bad pit stop or they inadvertently break a rule; and then the setup doesn't matter any more. Accidentality has changed everything. NASCAR is a form of speed competition that emphasizes accidentality. The enjoyment of watching a NASCAR race for the Border Savage is to follow its vicissitudes, which TV helps you to do. You get into the (ar)rhythmic flow and note how accidentality shifts the positions of the car drivers. It ends with one of them winning, but that has no interest for the Border Savage, who is not a 'fan' but an analyst enjoying a sport, '*pour le sport*' as my father used to say. One of the peak experiences of my childhood was when he would take me on 'adventure rides' to neighborhoods in Brooklyn, New York, that I had never seen. This book is bringing me way back. Since then I have been smitten by 'adventure rides.' NASCAR only brings adventuring back to its origins."

I turn to Kathy and say: "You can see how I wanted to cultivate 'creative innovation,' as an adventure. Each class is an adventure ride into the Bedlam of Ideals."

I draw back and say to the seminar: "Now I make the deepest cut."

I turn to Jonathan and say: "The BLACKOUT changed my life. I achieved it once and will never willfully experience it again. It gave me positive nothingness and displaced death with ecstasy. I should be saying this to Robert and Arthur—to Robert, so that I can report to him that I am altogether disburdened of agony; to Arthur to revel in letting me tie Nietzsche to BLACKOUT, showing me where I stand in 'philosophy'—; but I'm speaking to you, because between ecstasy and reflexivity is PRIVACY. We came to be by expressing one another to ourselves, but once we become our own, the zone of privacy opens up. We can become privatists who are unconcerned with allegiance to institutions and groups."

I turn to Justin and say: "And, of course, we have no obligations to those institutions or groups. We can take the position of ownness, which, of course, Stirner recognized was consistent with love; after all, he dedicated *The Ego and its Own* to 'My sweetheart, Marie Dahnhardt.'"

I turn to Joe and Julie and say: "I am, indeed, the 'God of my tribe' and the 'radical reality,' and I do practice the defensive life and I am sometimes the 'Son of Satan' who can mean it when he says, 'Don't tread on me or I'll stomp on you.' 'The Son of Satan wouldn't ever have been if it hadn't been for anti-Semitism' (being literally stomped on in high school). Both of you know that I don't lose sight of adversity and I am ready to be militant to protect my privacy and my intimacies. The seminar, of course, is within the erotic life, the site where it can be implanted in academia and where my privacy expands to include others; professorial love."

I turn to Diane and say: "Your intelligence is formidable and your will is so good. I remember one of the most important conversations in my philosophical life when we were talking about Althusser and you were joyously filled with the thought, 'He's a cracked foundationalist.' And so am I. The form of 'life' is integral consciousness, real separations that coexist in experience. And sometimes interpenetrate and sometimes are merely juxtaposed and sometimes are in conflict. Your analysis of the seminar has allowed me to take today's ride."

I turn to the seminar and say: "You have propelled me into a statement of my old-age philosophy that I thought I would never write and until today I had not articulated. I am the Border Savage/Privatist who exists between the ecstasy of BLACKOUT and the hyperreflexivity of a philosophically informed/(self-)critical home discourse. I express others to myself. I am the (limited) god of my tribe. I like to take intellectual joyrides with others. Between BLACKOUT and reflective review are all the engagements with the other-to-myself proceeding from different sectors and zones of integral consciousness.

Morgan Shepherd is in his seventies. Why does he get into Sprint Cup races that he knows that he won't be able to finish under any conditions? There are models in NASCAR.

It's time to leave the counter at 7-Eleven. There are hot-rod races on TV tonight for G-7 to enjoy and dinner to cook. I leave with the deepest gratitude.

JOYRIDE 3: 7/8/14

I thought I was done addressing you, but I had to take another joyride after I'd word processed this writing yesterday and got the new Nietzschean structure of critical vitalism straight. I now can state precisely the polarity that structures my thought about life at present, my new iteration: BLACK-OUT and hyperreflexive review with the "world" (Heidegger) in between them. This joyride will dive into the world at some point—it could be dangerous (for me). There's still a lot of the aleatory left.

What do we need for a new iteration? Again *Meaning and Appreciation* is paradigmatic. There is a core of experience ("expression," BLACKOUT) that is then juxtaposed and coordinated always by hyperreflective review. The latter has been the constant all my life, cultivating my home discourse by taking in what the world, including my psyche and body, throws at me, and then experiencing it to myself and analyzing it, allowing unexpected thoughts to emerge from the underground workshop or the outside other.

The core experience comes with a thirst to know the truth (a Nietzschean will to truth) that makes me go to the boundaries and trespass them, so that I know what there is to know about the "moveable mosaic" (remember that, Arthur? I think it all the time, and even more so since "integral consciousness") of experience. That will makes me an adventurer. I experience as much of life as I can, if not directly (preferable), then imaginatively. I push to get to a core experience without knowing what it might be, and then it sometimes befalls me. Blackout was unanticipated by and unknown to me before it happened, and then I heard a hot-rod driver talking about it on TV and I was immensely satisfied—he called it "the ultimate experience." I knew I had, indeed, trespassed a boundary of a wider experience than my own. I had become a member of that fraternity. I knew what people meant when they said certain things (in this case the thrill of speed), and that is what I have always wanted.

I know that there are many core experiences, and I cannot put any one of them at the center in a total reflection; instead, reflection on a particular core experience incites thoughts that eventually precipitate into a "structure of life." That structure will define a new iteration.

SPEED WRITING

Now let's speed through my philosophical iterations. I'm going to make my mind race without considering what I write, as G-7.

  1965–66: Santayana. Core experience: Read *Dominations and Powers*, and I found myself being able to anticipate the next sentence (almost verbatim). I decided to be a "chiropractor of philosophy," practicing philosophy in a political science department. I encountered unhappy consciousness—vital liberty (the problematic term) and spiritual freedom (hyperreflexivity, ever present).

  1966–72: Existential humanism with a New Left radical spin as an attempted synthesis of vital engagement and hyperreflexivity that culminates in *Philosophy, Theory, and Method in Contemporary Political Thought*. Arthur knows me during this period in Lafayette. We worked on inverting Talcott Parsons in a theory discussion group.

  1972–83: On sabbatical, I was hit by the collapse of the sixties and existential humanism crashed. I was walking alone in Lincoln Park in Chicago and was seized by the experience of "the beast" within me being loosed. A decade of early mid-life crisis followed with "hatred of existence," self-psychoanalysis, the *zozobra*, the agonic dialectic, panic fear, and then William James's "mortal leap" into the world (*Wilderness and City*) building to the nonagonic *Finite Perfection* (except for the account of "love," which I consider to be an original contribution that I have found nowhere else). Many personae in those years, most importantly the renegade who bites the hand that feeds it, and the finite perfectionist.

  1982–99: Postmodernization. "Restorations"—the first being Fernand Dumont (thanks, Arthur, as always). *(Post)Modernized Simmel*. *Data Trash*. Photography criticism based on Croce's "immanent criticism." Obviously the turn to the other; I was through with myself. But then erupts *Culture/Flesh*, which is the ultra-moral (objective hedonism) beyond virtue, BUT love hangs on. THE CIVIL SAVAGE. The article "East-West: Globalizing Civilization," in which I said my last word (for the time being, it has turned out?)—the subjective response to life of "indifferent devotion." That is, indifferent to success or failure.

1999–2012: Anti-Globalization Movement. 9/11. Holmes: "We don't know who we are." Living a "post"-humanist life in the hospice. Taking up political analysis after being unexpectedly aroused by Abu Ghraib. Somalia. Gamboole. Objective realist political analysis that all Somalis and external actors could accept as a baseline on which to spin around. Don't forget the anarchist punk band Vortis at the turn of the century, for which I was lyricist-TAKE THE SYSTEM DOWN. "Bleep, bleep, bleep the human race / We want androids in its place: / We hate our condition in the world."

2013–: I woke up one winter morning in Chicago, and when I got to the door to pick up the *Tribune*, I was seized by the idea that I have to open the sports section, something I hadn't done since puberty. Of course, I obeyed the underground workshop's prompting, and then I had the idea that I had to look at auto racing.

Screech to a halt. Were I to have reflected, there would have been much more—filled out. You have my "free associations." They stay there to be puzzled out. The core experiences are in my writings along with the attendant (provisional) structures resulting from hyperreflection.

POSTRACE

"So here I am locked in my skin, / Drinking it in, / Thinking of Sin." The last line was true when I wrote it some time between 1972 and 1983, but not now. I acknowledge good and evil, but they don't concern me. They are part of the PHANTASMAGORIA.

We are a "rope over the abyss" between boundary (transgressing) CORE EXPERIENCES (there are so many of them) and deeply, deeply, deeply private moments of hyperreflection. That "rope" is draped with the phantasmagoria, the human tragi-comedy, "ongoings" (Dewey), in medias res (Santayana), life grasped from the inside by a finite center of experience. It's all a game. It's play. It's dangerously close to the "veil of Maya." I'm hurtling into the idealism of the positive mystical tradition.

A Sufi story: A prophet came to the city and told the people that a deluge would come that would poison the water supply with madness. One man heeded the warning by taking jugs of pure water with him up a hill. The deluge came, the people became insane, and after a while the man smashed his jugs and joined Bedlam.

Why not? It's one game or another, given that "We're all gonna die and it doesn't matter, / Everything that is is gonna shatter; / The judgment of the world is a crock of bleep, / The only thing the world can do is give you a hit. / The world is nothing, I am nothing: / Absolute Zero, SHIVA HERO!"

The underground workshop tossed up those lyrics and the Shiva Hero persona, reveling in FINITE life. The "way through the world" that I have taken is a way through pleasure palaces and torture chambers, all of them ONLY intentionalities. The new Nietzsche is the early Husserl and the late Santayana. All of it is the "contemplation of essences" for the finite center of life grasped from within. AFTER BLACKOUT THE "WORLD" IS A PHAN-TASMAGORIA ("imaginary" as Diane uses the word). It was then, after I took the mortal leap and while reading for *Wilderness and City*, I had a core experience—my perception froze and I saw and otherwise sensed my back-yard in Lafayette on a hot and sunny July day—and then the picture was sur-rounded by a black border, frozen there that way with nothing beyond it. The American book grew out of that core experience. I was where I am now then; I just didn't draw the implications, I was still engaged. Blackout simply effaces the picture inside of life. The return has to be made with a smile. That's what ONTOLOGICAL NIHILISM does—it leaves the ontic FLOATING ALONE.

I'm leaving the lunch counter for my last break. Integral Consciousness is the form of the phantasmagoria.

RESTART

Let's go racing (again). I took a walk and came back with a fairly broad smile, my lips alternating between being open and closed, keeping contained a mirth about to burst out, that is expressed in the words: "It's all ridicu-lous." It burst out that day in class that Melba remembers. It has always been there. That's how I would come down the hill in the Sufi story. I felt that way as a teenager. The world was absurd to me and to my best friends. Only then I did not know how to love. I had too much fear. I needed support from the outside. Except for love, I play just to play, GROUNDLESSLY.

I experience no agony and only shrug with the real assent that everything is ridiculous and that I'm in love. G-7. ABSURD LOVE. The "effective real-ity." *Structure of Human Life*. Love makes the veil of Maya feel substantial. Integral consciousness/indifferent devotion.

POSTRACE

The last heat is over and these are the results—which of the social selves took me over and made me make admissions?

Jonathan finishes first—love has the last word. You understand me as I am. You show the transversal in action as I live it. You take what, as I said, I consider my original contribution to philosophy and elaborate it so precisely that I would have to smile at myself with Santayana's smile of self-mockery were I not to admit it as my bottom line. But you win only by a split second ahead of

Arthur. You exerted the counterforce. You infected me with the Data Trash mentality-sensibility. We are in a hospice waiting for the androids.

"Surplus bodies" are strewn around us. A searing contempt for the world. The (GRISLY) Phantasmagoria. Contempt as the substitute for hatred of existence.

Jonathan is the lead car driver of one drafting pack and Arthur is the lead car driver of the other drafting pact in this restrictor plate superspeedway philosophy race.

Jonathan could not have won without the bump-draft of Diane, who provided the power of her uniquely insightful psycho-structural analysis, which she applied with care to my theory and practice, making a most formidable case for the lover. Kathy was right behind her, providing the next push. Justin, of course, provided the last push. An amazingly powerful line, as it turns out.

But, wait, it was only a split-second win.

Arthur got an amazing bump draft from Ramon, even though he could just as well have been in the love line. And behind him in the draft was the team of Julie and Joe, and Robert who know doubt, agony, uncertainty, and suffering. They are in the agony line. They know hatred of existence.

I will not give the standings beyond one and two. There were two lines as is usual when drafting is the racing style. But where is Melba?

She could have started a third line had anyone followed her, but she remained alone as the only one between the two lines and, perhaps, by some miracle, she whizzed past them both. Melba insists on my moralism as a counterpoint to the *zozobra*, and she correctly places it as a virtue morality going back to Greek thought (despite all my protestations over the years that I've dispensed with morality). Melba grasps both sides and she knits them together through recourse to my reflection on Vasconcelos's use of analogy in his process/practice of coordination (vs. consensus).

That moralism, suppressed until now (in my self-assessment) has come clear in my turn to NASCAR. I used to despise competition—besting someone or being bested. I accept it now and can even embrace it in a sport. I have even had duels on the highway, but that no longer interests me. I'd rather not partake of it directly. Santayana's utopia was a rationally managed administrative apparatus and a powerless public in which hot heads confine their ideological conflicts to the arts. James advocated sports as the "moral equivalent to war," for the other hotheads who enjoy physical combat. I find competition to be ridiculous, but my sentiment won't wish it away.

I'm a lover, as Melba knows. Professorial love is not in the slightest agonized. When I express love for the class, I feel it fully—I am, at that moment, delighted and excited by the spirited exchange of ideas among the members of the class and by their insights and understandings. I never try to stage those moments. They are a result of "creative innovation."

Arthur disputes the result. When you transgress an experiential boundary, you are OUT OF CONTROL. Doesn't that have to beat anything ontic? Within the ontic, no. Across the ontic, yes—the onticological.

And so it will go in integral consciousness. It's not unhappy consciousness.

7/9 RACING COMMENTARY

IT'S A DEAD HEAT
What I called races (joyrides) were really practices and qualifying heats. Having proofread the text, I am no longer inside the seminar, inside the heat. I am in the position of reflective review. The introjection of the social selves is consummated.

I have lived integral consciousness in this inward adventure—one position after another in a dérive into/through the texts/social selves. I come out as I have been since adolescence, the reflective absurdist and the would-be lover. *Structure of Human Life* comes forward as the key text. The beloved other is the "effective reality," the world is the "absurd absolute."

The new wrinkle is BLACKOUT—ecstatic-death-in-life. The Dionysian brought to FINITE PERFECTION! An immense confidence follows from that core experience. Death isn't such a (bad) joke.

And now I will let my last thoughts straggle on to the page as they appear:
The above writing comes as close to the scrawls I make on the blackboard in a heated series of seminars as I can get. I owe it to you, Diane. You encouraged me to perform/write my text in the seminar.

It was a masterstroke to center the book on critical vitalism. Thank you, Robert.

I do unresolved probes. As deep as I can—and still unresolved. Integral and Unresolved. (Concrete and Incomplete)

We don't know who we are so
GO RACING
G-7 embodies the individual and the social through being the god of his tribe.

(we never get enough ego-strength to carry it off)

GO RACING! (ENVOI)

I'm going to email this out. The "digital" is great for the posthuman/human (too old to be fully posthuman). You have boxed me up, with my collaboration. But it's quite a pretty box, festooned with ribbons. You have made me become who I am as a philosopher.

I didn't realize that all my adult life I've been working on a problem bequeathed to me from my encounter with Santayana—the scission between spiritual freedom (constant) and vital liberty (variable), and I surely didn't realize that Santayana, as a follower of Aristotle, had "simply" given new words for the aporia of the contemplative and active lives. You've put me in the tradition. I have tried to knit together the contemplative and active lives by expressing others to myself. That mental activity/practice makes a link between the contemplative and active lives, but those lives are still really/actually separated, proceeding from/constituting different positions. That is integral consciousness at work. That has been my philosophical life('s) work. G7 = (Post-)modernized Aristotle. From now on, you'll know him as "philosopher," from a sector no more privileged than the others, but one that sees it whole and discovers/makes the links, and can be more personal than anything else. GO RACING!

NOTE

1. Kyle Busch said, after winning at Fontana (2013), breezing past Joey Logano and Denny Hamlin, who had gotten into a bumping match, in an elegant sweep on the outside line equal to ballet.

Appendix I

Weinstein's Intellectual Biography: A View from the Collective

Deena Weinstein and Michael A. Weinstein

Michael Weinstein is above all intellectually a philosopher of life. He began philosophizing in 1965, oriented by the question posed by his first and, in that sense, most important influence, George Santayana: "What does liberty bring to the free man?" "That is the great question of morals and politics," said Santayana. Santayana taught Weinstein how to philosophize and was his model for writing philosophy. From Santayana, Weinstein took the project—as he interpreted it—of clarifying conscious life. Weinstein was thrown into philosophy by Santayana through the experience of being able to anticipate what Santayana had written next as he read *Dominations and Powers*, often to the very words. He determined then to let Santayana be his guide and to read everything he could by and about him, resulting in his doctoral dissertation: "Santayana on Liberty, Interest, and Representation." In the spring of 1967, Weinstein was crossing Euclid Ave. in Cleveland, Ohio, and suddenly the thought came to him: "I'm not Santayana." Then the adventure began, and from then on Weinstein has been trying to define as precisely as possible the structure of (his) life. That has involved forays into many discourses, all with the aim of clarifying life-experience-strategy.

The following list comprises the writers who have helped Weinstein develop his project of clarifying the structure of life, divided into concentrations of reading. The categories are not exclusive, and there are a few writers who enter into nearly all of them. The list is not exhaustive, and the categories are not altogether coherent—they are regions of literature-themes.

Before presenting the list of writers who span categories and then the lists within categories, let us begin with the books that encapsulated Weinstein's philosophy before discovering Santayana—as Alfred Adler might put it, Weinstein's proto-philosophy.

In 1960, a high-school senior, Weinstein read George Lundberg's *Can Science Save Us?* to which Lundberg, a purist positivist, gave a resounding, "Yes!" Weinstein adopted Lundberg's views whole and thought he would become an international lawyer with expertise in mathematical economics. Such is adolescence. That conceit was blown away in Weinstein's freshman year in college when he discovered the nineteenth-century French Romantics, jumping to subjectivism to the point of carrying Baudelaire's *Fleurs de Mal* in his pocket on drinking excursions and gigs with his rock 'n roll band. Among the Romantics, Benjamin Constant's *Adolphe* made the greatest impression. In the 1950s, rock 'n roll lyrics also played their part—black rockin' blues, white rockabilly, and black doo-wop.

When Weinstein set off for graduate school in 1964, his center of intellectual gravity had shifted to political science. The break came in the summer of 1965 when Weinstein received his M.A. and felt an emptiness. He had the idea that he should look at philosophy, and through reading Morris Cohen's history of American philosophy, he found Santayana, to whom he had already been exposed in a course taught by Sidney Hook at New York University. With that, the period of proto-philosophy ends and the lists can begin.

THE COMPREHENSIVE INFLUENCES

George Santayana (dominations and powers)
Samuel Alexander (wandering cause)
Georg Simmel (central idea)
Miguel de Unamuno (tragic sense of life, invasive charity, mutual imposition)
José Vasconcelos (consciousness as the coordination of the heterogeneous)
John Dewey (instrumental, consummatory)
William James (radical empiricism)
Josiah Royce (viciously acquired naiveté)
William Ernest Hocking (self, its body, and freedom)
Alfred North Whitehead (actual occasion)
Edmund Husserl (intentionality)

All of these figures articulated vitalistic ontologies and, in so doing, covered all the major sectors of human experience. Weinstein philosophizes as he takes it that they did but without the aim of creating an ontology, which he calls a "symbolic substitute for life"; he is an ontological nihilist.

METHOD/STRUCTURE

José Vasconcelos (organic logic)
James K. Feibleman (connotative inference)
Elijah Jordan (analogical identity)
Michael Polanyi (pattern recognition)
Charles Sanders Peirce (tychism)
William James (pluralistic universe)
Georg Simmel (form)
Carlos Vaz Ferreira (fermentative thinking)
José Ortega y Gasset (transmigration)
Jacques Derrida (deconstruction, empirical wandering)
Guy Debord (derive)

Claude Levi-Strauss (bricolage)
Jean-Franççois Lyotard (drifting)
John Dewey and Arthur Bentley (experimental naming)
Arthur Bentley (socio-analysis)
Michel Foucault (discourse, archeology of knowledge)
Gilles Deleuze (nomad, rhizomatic thinking)
Louis Althusser (relative autonomy)
Emilio Uranga (accidentality, the cynical gesture)
Benedetto Croce (immanent criticism)
Gore Vidal (style model—kindred appreciator of Santayana)
Karl Barth (kerygmatic and apologetic theology)
Jean Baudrillard (third-order simulacrum)

All of these writers defined ways of thinking consciousness as nonsystematic integrality. Weinstein's method in appropriating their concepts (and many more hints about method/form) is what he calls "love-piracy"—taking the experiential component from the text and throwing away the ontology.

THE SELF/*EXISTENZ*/PSYCHE

J. V. Bateman ("me-locus of reference")
Justus Buchler (summed-up-self-in-process)
Max Stirner (ownness)
José Ortega y Gasset ("My life is the radical reality")
Henri Bergson (fundamental self and conventional ego)
George Herbert Mead (*The Philosophy of the Present*)
Henry David Thoreau (moss trooper)
Alejandro Korn (creative liberty)
Miguel de Unamuno (agony)
Jean-Paul Sartre (*en soi—pour soi*)
Albert Camus (quantitative experience)
Martin Heidegger (being-toward-death)
Karl Jaspers (life-order)
Gabriel Marcel (secondary reflection)
David Swenson (objective insecurity)
John Henry Newman (real assents)
Sigmund Freud (compromise formation)
Georg Groddeck ("It")
Wilhelm Stekel (perversion)
Alfred Adler (proto-personality)
Samuel Ramos (inferiority complex)
Carl Gustav Jung (personal mythology)
Friedrich Nietzsche (ressentiment)
Oliver Wendell Holmes (underground workshop)
Mohamed Iqbal (radical Sufism—"I am the creative truth")
Feodor Dostoevsky ("The Adolescent")

For Weinstein, as for Santayana, the self arises within a wider experience as a function within it, yet, in contradistinction to Santayana, Weinstein does not diminish the ego—indeed, he radicalizes it and makes it the center of his reflections, all the way from its momentary hegemony in the position of ownness to its most abject dependency and frailty. Weinstein philosophizes from the position of "My life is the radical reality." Yet self-determination for him, as for Holmes, can be likened to a little drop of water inside a crystal. That position leads to the hardcore experience that constitutes philosophizing for Weinstein.

HOME DISCOURSE

Irving Babbitt (interior monologue)
Miguel de Unamuno (autodialogue)
E. Cioran (intellectual autobiography)

Weinstein can be said, in one sense, to have spent his life learning to speak with himself according to the standards of how he has construed philosophical discourse.

SOCIOLOGY OF KNOWLEDGE

Karl Mannheim (interest)
Karl Marx (German ideology)
Louis Althusser (interpellation)
Max Scheler (axiology)
Georges Sorel (utopia and myth)
Talcott Parsons (institutionalized individualism)
Fernand Dumont (emplacement)
Chantal Mouffe and Ernesto Laclau (dislocation)
Wyndham Lewis, Ezra Pound (vorticism)
Leopoldo Zea (positivism in Mexico)

Beyond the self are all the ways in which the content of the self is socially conditioned. Sociology of knowledge is at the interface of self and society. Ideology is, for Weinstein, "street philosophy."

SOCIOLOGICAL THEORY

Karl Marx (class conflict)
Lucien Goldmann (total social fact)
Max Weber (bureaucracy)
Émile Durkheim (social fact)
Stuart Hall (conjuncture)

George Grant (intimations of deprival)
Paul Virilio (dromology)
Arthur Kroker (technological dependency, surplus bodies)
Friedrich Baerwald (object and project orientations)
McQuilkin De Grange (the ellipse)
Paul Hanley Furfey (positivistic, noetic, and pistic societies)
Deena Weinstein (transaction)

This list is just a small sampling to give an idea of the way in which Weinstein has approached sociology, which is through a structural analysis that tends to objectify social as opposed to personal phenomena. Whereas his interpretation of the self is highly subjectivized (philosophy here is an "invitation" to experience with him), his interpretation of the social/public world attempts to be clinically observational and structural, relying on pattern recognition and experimental naming to characterize particular conjunctures.

POLITICAL THEORY/ANALYSIS

Francisco José Moreno (*Basic Principles of Politics*, divergent and convergent political communities). Moreno was Weinstein's mentor in political science, his maestro, and in Weinstein's judgment was the greatest political scientist of his generation.

Arthur Bentley (interest group)
Gaetano Mosca (ruling class, social type, political formula)
Roberto Michels (proletarian culture at a higher level)
Michael Ostrogorske (pluto-democracy)
David Easton (political system: supports and demands)
E.H. Carr (utopianism and realism)
Arnold Toynbee (challenge and response)
Harold Lasswell (garrison state, displacement of private affect on public objects)
Ahmed Egal (fission and fusion)
Howard Smith (public interest distortion)

Again, this list is only a small sampling. As in the case of sociology, the influences are from the realist tradition and stress objectivity and nonpartisanship. The writers listed gave Weinstein his formula of interest-power-strategy for defining the parameters of political analysis.

PREMODERNIST/POSTMODERNIST WESTERN THOUGHT

Plato (philosophy as a preparation for death)
Aristotle (active and contemplative lives)
Epictetus (formulation of what Dewey called the "arts of acceptance")
René Descartes (the *cogito*)

Blaise Pascal (spirits of logic and finesse)
George Berkeley (critique of abstraction)
David Hume (moral sense)
Immanuel Kant (critical rationalism)
Johann Gottlieb Fichte (the ego)
George Wilhelm Friedrich Hegel (phenomenology of mind, dialectic)

Weinstein has studied the entire Western canon and many thinkers who have been marginalized by it. These are the thinkers who have stayed with him in his "home discourse" over the years.

NON-WESTERN PREMODERNIST/POSTMODERNIST THOUGHT

Kama Sutra ("Passion begets passion")
Bhagavad Gita (Karma Yoga)
Quran ("Fretful when evil befalleth him and when good befalleth him grudging")
Lao-Tzu ("Do Nothingness")
Zen Momentalism
Bible (story of Jonah—the abused prophet)
Christian Gospels ("take the beam out of your own eye . . . "; "gain yourself by losing yourself")

These writings represent the key non-Western texts for Weinstein. Far wider than this selection, his readings have reinforced the insights contained in the listed texts.

Appendix II

Michael A. Weinstein's Publications and Creative Activity

PUBLICATIONS

Books

Identity, Power and Change (Glenview: Scott, Foresman, 1970).

Systematic Political Theory (Columbus: Charles E. Merrill, 1971). Japanese Translation Published by Tokai University Press, 1973.

Philosophy, Theory and Method in Contemporary Political Thought (Glenview: Scott, Foresman, 1971).

The Clash of Perspectives (Hinsdale: The Dryden Press, 1972), with D. Weinstein.

The Political Experience (New York: St. Martin's Press, 1972).

The Roles of Man (Hinsdale: The Dryden Press, 1972), with D. Weinstein.

The Ideologies of Violence (Columbus: Charles E. Merrill, 1974), with K. Grundy.

Living Sociology (New York: David Mckay, 1974), with D. Weinstein.

Choosing Sociology (New York: David Mckay, 1976), with D. Weinstein.

The Polarity of Mexican Thought: Instrumentalism and Finalism (University Park: The Pennsylvania State University Press, 1976).

The Tragic Sense of Political Life (Columbia: University of South Carolina Press, 1977).

Meaning and Appreciation: Time and Modern Political Life (W. Lafayette: Purdue University Press, 1978).

The Structure of Human Life: A Vitalist Ontology (New York: New York University Press, 1979).

The Wilderness and the City: American Classical Philosophy as a Moral Quest (Amherst: University of Massachusetts Press, 1982).

Unity and Variety in the Philosophy of Samuel Alexander (West Lafayette: Purdue University Press, 1984).

Culture Critique: Fernand Dumont and New Quebec Sociology (Montreal: New World Perspectives, 1985) American Edition, St. Martin's Press, 1985.

Finite Perfection: Reflections on Virtue (Amherst: University of Massachusetts Press, 1985).

Schopenhauer and Nietzsche, by Georg Simmel; Translated With Introduction by D. Weinstein, H. Loiskandl, and M. Weinstein (Amherst: University of Massachusetts Press 1986) Paperback Reprint by the University of Illinois Press, 1991.

Postmodern(Ized) Simmel (London: Routledge, 1993), with D. Weinstein. Reprinted in Routledge Revivals series, 2011.

Culture/Flesh: Explorations of Postcivilized Modernity (Lanham, MD: Rowman and Littlefield, 1995).

Data Trash: The Theory of the Virtual Class (Montreal: New World Perspectives, 1994) American Edition St. Martin's Press, 1994, with Arthur Kroker. Italian Translation Published by Libri Urra, 1996.

The Imaginative Prose of Oliver Wendell Holmes (Columbia: University of Missouri Press, 2006).

Monograph

"Some Problems in the Theory of Political Coalitions," Virginia Polytechnic Institute Monographs in Political Science, 1, 1969, with J. Bernd

Catalogue Essays

"Robert Stiegler: Compounding Abstraction," in *Robert Stiegler: Retrospective* (Chicago: University of Illinois at Chicago, Gallery 400, 1992), 4ff.

"Arthur Bell's Photographic Concerns: Abstract Representation," in *Arthur Bell: Abstract Representation* (Chicago: Northern Illinois University Art Museum Gallery in Chicago, 1994), 3ff.

"Popularly Yours: Art Beyond Limits," brochure and wall text for the exhibit "Popularly Yours," DePaul University Art Gallery, September 16–November 19, 1996, with D. Weinstein.

"Introduction," in *Together: Barbara Crane and John Miller* (Chicago: Flatfile Gallery, 2002), 2–3.

"Perceptual Adventures," in *Urban Anomalies: Chicago: Barbara Crane* (Santa Fe: Center for American Places, 2002), 3ff.

"The Deadliest Sin of All," wall text for the exhibit "Axis of Evil: The Secret History of Sin," Glass Curtain Gallery (Chicago), April 6–May 11, 2005.

"Introduction," in *Thomas Masters: Paradise Lost and Found* (Chicago, 2005), 2–3.

"Portraits of the Architectural Landscape," in *Paul Lurie: New Landscapes* (Chicago, 2005), 5–7.

"Beyond the Binaries: Crossing the Boundaries of Identity Politics," in *Barbara Degenevieve: Objectifying the Abject* (Chicago: University of Illinois at Chicago, 2006).

"Claude Andreini/Susan Aurinko," Molini Gallery (Venice, Italy, 2006).

"Studies in Self-Reference: Ted Preuss's 'Simple Beauty' Series," *Large Format Camera* (Summer 2006), 5 pp.

"The Annunciation Reconceived," in *Luis Gonzalez Palma: Hierarchies of Intimacy* (Chicago: Schneider Gallery, 2008), 6–7.

"Paper," in *Paper* (Chicago: PolPress, 2010), 1.

"Art Shay," in *Re: Chicago* (Chicago: DePaul University Art Museum, 2011), 76.

"Introduction," in Charles A. Swedlund, *The Whole Show* (Chicago: 2054 Press, 2012), 5.

"Portrait of an Art Critic—Michael Weinstein," in Jane Fulton Alt, *On Life, Love, and the Creative Process*, online, May 28, 2013, 2 pp. http://janefultonalt. blogspot.com/2013/05/portrait-of-art-critic-michael-weinstein.html

Book Chapters

"Sartre and the Humanist Tradition in Sociology," in Mary Warnock (ed.), *Sartre* (New York: Anchor Books, 1971), 357–386, with D. Weinstein.

"The Uses of Privacy in the Good Life," in J. Roland Pennock and John Chapman (eds.), *Privacy: Nomos XIII* (New York: Atherton Press, 1971), 87–103.

Republished in Tom D. Campbell (ed.), *The International Library of Essays in Law and Legal Theory* (London: Dartmouth Publishing Company, 1993).

"Coercion, Space and the Modes of Human Domination," in J. Roland Pennock and John Chapman (eds.), *Coercion: Nomos XIV* (New York: Aldine-Atherton, 1972), 63–80.

"A Fourth Branch of Government: For Whom?" in Michael A. Weinstein (ed.), *The Political Experience* (New York: St. Martin's Press, 1972), 325–336.

"Socialism and Humanism," in Jeffrey Orenstein and Louis Patsouras (eds.), *The Politics of Community: New Aspects of Socialist Theory and Practice* (Dubuque: Kendall-Hunt, 1973), 13–40.

"A Binary Theory of the Limits of Law," in J. Roland Pennock and John Chapman (eds.), *The Limits of Law: Nomos XV* (New York: Lieber-Atherton, 1974), 102–114.

"Foreword" to Frederic D. Homer, *Guns and Garlic: Myths and Realities of Organized Crime* (W. Lafayette: Purdue University Press, 1974), xi–xiii.

"C. B. Macpherson: The Roots of Democracy and Liberalism," in Anthony de Crespigny and Kenneth Minogue (eds.), *Contemporary Political Philosophers* (New York: Dodd, Mead, 1975), 252–271.

"Introduction" to Francisco J. Moreno, *Between Reason and Faith: An Approach to Individual and Social Psychology* (New York: New York University Press, 1977), ix–xiii.

"A Critique of Policy Research: Auguste Comte Lives!" in Michael McGrath (ed.), *Liberalism and the Modern Polity* (New York: Marcel Dekker, 1978), 229–250, with D. Weinstein.

"The Sociology of Nonknowledge: A Paradigm," in Robert Alun Jones (ed.), *Research in Sociology of Knowledge, Sciences and Art: An Annual Compilation of Research, Vol. 1* (Greenwich: JAI Press, 1978), 151–166, with D. Weinstein.

"Dostoevsky and Unamuno: The Anti-Modern Personality," in Benjamin R. Barber and Michael J. Gargas McGrath, *The Artist and Political Vision* (New Brunswick: Transaction Books, 1982), 67–86.

"Unamuno y las Normas de la Imaginacion," in Angel G. Loureiro (ed.), *Estelas, Laberintos, Nuevas Sendas: Unamuno, Valle Inclan, Garcia Lorca. La Guerra Civil* (Barcelona: Anthropos, 1988), 81–94.

"Panic Ads," in Arthur Kroker *et al.* (eds.), *Panic Encyclopedia: The Definitive Guide to the Postmodern Scene* (New York: St. Martin's Press, 1989), 53–56, with D. Weinstein.

"Dimensions of Conflict: Georg Simmel on Modern Life," in Michael Kaern *et al.* (eds.), *Georg Simmel and Contemporary Sociology* (Boston: Kluwer Academic Publishers, 1990), 341–355, with D. Weinstein.

"Simmel and the Theory of Postmodern Society," in Bryan S. Turner (ed.), *Theories of Modernity and Post-Modernity* (London: Sage Publications, 1990), 75–87, with D. Weinstein.

"Singularity and Transcendence in Unamuno's Political Thought," in Nora de Marval-McNair (ed.), *Selected Proceedings of the Singularidad y Transcendencia Conference* (Boulder: Society of Spanish and Spanish-American Studies, 1990), 61–69.

"Martin Heidegger," in Robert Benewick and Philip Green (eds.), *The Routledge Dictionary of Twentieth Century Political Thinkers* (London: Routledge, 1992), 94–96.

"The Postmodern Discourse of Metatheory," in George Ritzer (ed.), *Metatheorizing* (Newbury Park, CA: Sage, 1992), 135–150, with D. Weinstein.

"The Liberation of Religiosity from Religion: Simmel on the Religious Impulse in Postmodernity," in Felicitas Dorr-Backes/Ludwig Nieder (eds.), *Georg Simmel Between Modernity and Postmodernity* (Wurzburg: Konigshausen & Neumann, 1995), 129–141, with D. Weinstein.

"Georg Simmel," chapter for the Craig Calhoun/George Ritzer Primis database series *Perspectives* (New York: McGraw-Hill, 1997), 20 pp, with D. Weinstein.

"NetGame Cameo," in Arthur and Marilouise Kroker (eds.), *Digital Delirium* (New York: St. Martin's Press, 1997), 159–164, with D. Weinstein. Reprinted in David Bell and Barbara Kennedy (eds.), *Cyberculture Reader* (London: Routledge, 2000), 210–215.

"Anti-Positivism," in *The Routledge Encyclopedia of Philosophy* (London: Routledge, 1998), 14 pp. typescript.

"Data Trash Update," in Nettime (ed.), *Readme! ASCII Culture and the Revenge of Knowledge* (Brooklyn, NY: Autonomedia, 1999), 478–481.

"Ideology," in David Gabbard (ed.), *Education in the Global Economy: The Rhetoric of Reform* (Mahwah: Lawrence Erlbaum Associates, 1999), 95–101.

"McDonaldization Enframed," in Barry Smart (ed.), *Resisting McDonaldization* (London: Sage, 1999), 57–69, with D. Weinstein.

"Preface" to Lee Rademacher, *Structuralism vs. Humanism in the Formation of the Political Self* (Lewiston: Edwin Mellen Press, 2002), i–iv.

"Introduction" to Francisco J. Moreno, *Principios Basicos De Politica* (Miami: Ceratex International, 2004), xi–xiv.

John Laird, "Alexander, Samuel (1859–1938)," rev. Michael A. Weinstein, *Oxford Dictionary of National Biography* (Oxford: Oxford University Press, 2004), article #30372.

"Daniel Hernandez-Salazar: Postmodern Humanist," in Oscar Maldonado (ed.), *So That All Shall Know: Photographs by Daniel Hernandez-Salazar* (Austin: University of Texas Press, 2007), 39–52.

"Individual and Society in Twentieth and Twenty-First Century Views of Life," in Cecile Roi and Christian Papilloud (eds.), *Soziologie Als Moglichkeit 100. Jahre Georg Simmels Untersuchungen Uber Die Formen Der Vergesellschaftung* (VS-Verlag, 2008), with D. Weinstein.

"The Emotive Document," in Jane Fulton Alt, *Look and Leave: Photographs and Stories From New Orleans's Lower Ninth Ward* (Chicago: The Center for American Places, 2009), 3–5.

"Oliver Wendell Holmes's Depth Psychology: A Reconstruction," in Scott H. Podolsky and Charles S. Bryan (eds.), *Oliver Wendell Holmes: Physician and Man of Letters* (Sagamore Beach: Science History Publications, 2009), 93–103.

"Indian Sensibility," in Susan Aurinko, *Still Point India* (Chicago: Shakti Books, 2013), viii–ix.

"Sublime Fire," in Jane Fulton Alt, *The Burn* (Heidelberg, Germany: Kehrer, 2013), 83–85.

Translation

Antonio Caso, "The Concept of Universal History," *Canadian Journal of Political and Social Theory* IV, 3 (1980), 51–68 (from Spanish).

Articles

"The Political Uses of Imagination," *Transition* (Kampala), 30 (1967), 20–24, with K. Grundy.

"Hocking's Existential Sociology," *Sociology and Social Research* 52, 4 (July 1968), 406–415.

"Seduction of the Social Sciences," *National Review*, (August 27, 1968), 851.

"Santayana: Conservative or Philosopher of Reason?" *Modern Age* 13, 1 (Winter 1968–1969), 52–61.

"Sociological Jurisprudence: Crime Prevention or Control?" *Prospectus: A Journal of Law Reform* 2, 2 (April 1969), 431–449, with L. Massotti.

"Ontology and Social Science," *International Review of History and Political Science* VI, 3 (August 1969), 30–42.

"The R and D Contract and Democratic Theory," *Policy Sciences* 1, 1 (1970), 113–121, with D. Kash.

"Politics and Moral Consciousness," *Midwest Journal of Political Science* XIV, 2 (May 1970), 183–215.

"The Paradox of Representation: Criticism," *The Journal of Value Inquiry* IV, 2 (Summer 1970), 119–125.

"Synthesis of Two Natural Law Positions," *The New Scholasticism* XLIV, 4 (Autumn 1970), 574–584.

"A Critique of Contemporary Democratic Theories," *Western Political Quarterly* XXIV, 1 (March 1971), 41–44.

"Basic Political Rights," *The Southern Journal of Philosophy* 9, 1 (Spring 1971), 75–84, comment by W. T. Blackstone, 85–89.

"Life and Politics as Plural: James and Bentley on the Twentieth Century Problem," *Journal of Value Inquiry* V, 4 (Winter 1971), 282–291.

"The Revival of Liberalism," *Journal of Social Philosophy* III, 2 (April 1972), 6–8.

"Towards a New Role for Sociologists: Morris Ginsberg on Sociology and Social Philosophy," *Sociological Focus* 5, 3 (Spring 1972), 40–53, with D. Weinstein.

"Blau's Dialectical Sociology," *Sociological Inquiry* 42, 2 (Spring 1972), 173–182, with D. Weinstein, comment by Peter M. Blau, 182–188, rejoinder by authors, 188–189.

"The Political Morality of Talcott Parsons," *Social Science* 47, 3 (Summer 1972), 153–157.

"Political Education and the Social Scientist," *Indiana Academy of Social Sciences Proceedings*, Third Series, VII (1972), 118–126.

"New Ways and Old to Talk About Politics," *The Review of Politics* 35, 1 (January 1973), 41–60.

"The Inclusive Polity," *Polity* V, 3 (Spring 1973), 363–373.

"The Sociology of Public Morality: Talcott Parsons and Phenomenology," *Sociological Focus* 6, 2 (Spring 1973), 10–31.

"The Structure of Human Freedom," *Serbian Democratic Forum* 2 (April 1973), 17–18. Reprinted as "Historical Essay on Human Freedom," *The Diocesan Observer* (Libertyville, IL) 9, 409 (December 19, 1973), 1–2.

"Politics and Historical Consciousness," *Towson State Journal of International Affairs* VII, 1 (Fall 1973), 23–40.

"The Mutation of Dialectics," *Serbian Democratic Forum* 4 (January 1974), 33–34. Reprinted in THE DIOCESAN OBSERVER (Libertyville, IL) 9, 418 (March 13, 1974), 1, 4.

"Utopian Pluralism: A Review Essay on Recent Contributions," *Journal of Voluntary Action Research* 3, 2 (April 1974), 27–35.

"Philosophical Mentality and the Public Situation," *Review of Social Theory* 2, 2 (May 1974), 134–142.

"Josiah Royce's Idealist Sociology of Knowledge," *Social Science* 49, 4 (Autumn 1974), 213–219, with D. Weinstein.

"Creativity and the Cybernetic Hierarchy: Two Models of the Human Condition," *Social Science* 49, 1 (Winter 1974), 11–18.

"Alternative Political Perspectives: The Problem of Minorities," *Agora* III, 1 & 2 (1975), 45–48, with F. Homer.

"The Structure of Anti-Positivist Philosophy in Latin America," *Humanitas* (Monterrey) 16 (1975), 165–183.

"Mass Society and the Crisis of Public Responsibility," *The Midwest Quarterly* XVII, 1 (Autumn 1975), 39–57.

"The Problem of Relativism: A Reinterpretation," *The Human Context* VII, 3 (Autumn 1975), 422–425.

"Unamuno and the Agonies of Modernization," *Review of Politics* 38, 1 (January 1976), 40–56.

"Vasconcelos on Analogy and the Appreciation of World Views," *Journal of Value Inquiry* X, 2 (Summer 1976), 132–136.

"The Political Defense of Human Rights," *Serbian Aurora* 1 (April 15, 1977), 1, 3. Reprinted in THE DIOCESAN OBSERVER (Libertyville, IL) 12, 563 (June 8, 1977), 2.

"Self, Society, and Social Control," *Humanity and Society* 1, 1 (Summer 1977), 104–115, with D. Weinstein.

"Anarchy and History: An Existentialist View," *Minus One* 39 (1977), 1–2.

"Political Philosophy and the Public Situation," *Canadian Journal of Political and Social Theory* I, 1 (Winter 1977), 35–48.

"An Existential Approach to Society: Active Transcendence," *Human Studies* 1, 1 (1978), 1–10, with D. Weinstein.

"Sociologies of Knowledge as Rhetorical Strategies," *Free Inquiry* 16, 1 (May 1978), 1–14, with D. Weinstein.

"The Role of Ideas in Freud's Theory of Civilization," *Canadian Journal of Political and Social Theory* 3, 2 (Spring–Summer 1979), 31–44, with D. Weinstein.

"Creativity, Law and Human Value," *Proceedings of the Sixth Conference on Value Inquiry*, James B. Wilbur (ed.), State University of New York, College at Geneseo, 1979, 251–262.

"Freud et le probleme de l'ordre social ou le retour a Hobbes," *Diogene* 108 (Octobre–Decembre 1979), 47–67, with D. Weinstein.

"Jewish Ethics: The Tension Between Particularism and Universalism," *Listening* 14, 1 (Winter 1979), 6–12, with D. Weinstein.

"Morris Ginsberg on the Unity of Reason: Reflections on the Possibility of a Rational Sociology," in P. Abrahms and P. Lewthwaite (eds.), *Development and Diversity: British Sociology* 1950–1980 (Transactions of the British Sociological Association Annual Conference, 1980), 18 pp.

"The Ethics of Charity: Antonio Caso's Defense of Civilization," *Canadian Journal of Political and Social Theory* IV, 3 (1981), 69–82, with D. Weinstein.

"Intellectual Transcendence: Karl Mannheim's defense of the Sociological Attitude," *History of European Ideas* 2, 2 (1981), 97–114, with D. Weinstein.

"Introduction to Antonio Caso's 'The Concept of Universal History,'" *Canadian Journal of Political and Social Theory* IV, 3 (1981), 48–50.

"The Problematic of Marginality in Mexican Philosophy," *Canadian Journal of Political and Social Theory* IV, 3 (1981), 21–25, with D. Weinstein.

"Freud's Encounter with Religion: A Study in Bad Faith," *Thought* 56, 223 (December 1981), 463–476, with D. Weinstein.

"Lament and Utopia: Responses to American Empire in George Grant and Leopoldo Zea," *Canadian Journal of Political and Social Theory* 3 (Fall 1981), 44–55. Republished as "Lamento y Utopia: Respeustas al Imperio Norteamericano en George Grant y Leopoldo Zea," *Nuestra America* III, 8 (Mayo–Agosto 1983), 145–164. (Translation of "Lament and Utopia," 1981).

"On the Possibility of Society: Classical Sociological Thought," *Human Studies* 5, 1 (January–March 1982), 1–12, with D. Weinstein.

"The Problem of Individuality in Karl Mannheim's Sociology," *Sociological Inquiry* 52, 4 (Fall 1982), 335–348, with D. Weinstein.

"Twentieth-Century Realism and the Autonomy of the Human Sciences: The Case of George Santayana," *Analecta Husserliana* XV (1983), 119–130.

"On the Visual Constitution of Society: The Contributions of Georg Simmel and Jean-Paul Sartre," *History of European Ideas* 5, 4 (1984), 349–362, with D.

Weinstein. Republished in Larry Ray (ed.), *Formal Sociology: The Work of Georg Simmel* (Brookfield, VT: Edward Elgar, 1991), 168–191.

"Liberalism Goes Postmodern: Rorty's Pragmatism," *Canadian Journal of Political and Social Theory* X, 1–2 (1986), 10–19.

"Perspective on America: Politics," *Purdue Alumnus* (Summer 1986), 14–15.

"George Grant y Leopoldo Zea: Conciencia de Marginalidad," *Cuadernos Americanos: Nueva Epoca* 3 (Mayo–Junio 1987), 70–85. (Translation of "Lament and Utopia," 1981).

"The Dark Night of the Liberal Spirit and the Dawn of the Savage," *Canadian Journal of Political and Social Theory* XII, 1–2 (1988), 165–179. Republished in Arthur and Marilouise Kroker (eds.), *Ideology and Power in the Age of Lenin in Ruins* (New York: St. Martin's Press, 1991), 210–224. Simultaneously republished in *Canadian Journal of Political and Social Theory* XV, 1, 2, 3 (1991), 210–224. (Fifteenth Anniversary Retrospective Vol.).

"Intellectuals: Public and Proletarian," *Canadian Journal of Political and Social Theory* XII, 3 (1988), 37–47.

"Simmel and the Dialectic of the Double Boundary: The Case of 'The Metropolis and Mental Life,'" *Sociological Inquiry* 59, 1 (Winter 1989), 48–59, with D. Weinstein.

"Deconstruction as Cultural History/The Cultural History of Deconstruction," *Canadian Journal of Political and Social Theory* XIV, 1–2, 3 (1990), 11–20, with D. Weinstein.

"La Deconstruction: Un Jeu Symbolique. Simmel/Derrida," *Diogene* 150 (Avril–Juin 1990), 121–144, with D. Weinstein. Reprinted in *Chinese Anthology of Diogenes* 1 (1992), 98–117.

"Georg Simmel: Sociological Flâneur Bricoleur," *Theory, Culture & Society* 8, 3 (1991), 151–168, with D. Weinstein.

"Photographic Realism as a Moral Practice," *Journal of Value Inquiry* 26 (1992), 175–188.

"Thinking the Death Camps with Heidegger," *Modern Age* 34, 3 (Spring 1992), 214–221.

"Irving Babbitt and Postmodernity: Amplitude and Intensity," *Humanitas* 6, 1 (Fall 1992–Winter 1993), 42–48.

"Concentric Imagination: An Alternative to Philosophical Reason" *Humanitas* VI, 2 (1993), 91–99.

"Postmodernizing (Macro)sociology," *Sociological Inquiry* 63, 2 (May 1993), 224–238, with D. Weinstein.

"George Grant y Leopoldo Zea: Conciencia de Marginalidad," in Leopoldo Zea (ed.), *Filosofar a La Altura Del Hombre: Discrepar Para Comprender* (*Cuadernos De Cuadernos* #4) (Mexico: Universidad Nacional Autonoma de Mexico, 1994), 329–344.

"The Political Economy of Virtual Reality" *Canadian Journal of Political and Social Theory* 17, 1–2 (1994), 1–31, with A. Kroker.

"A Contribution to a Dialogue on Political Commitment and Teaching Modern Philosophy," in "On Teaching Modern Philosophy and Making Political Commitments: A Dialogue between Michael A. Weinstein and Paul Gottfried," in *Theologies and Moral Concern* (*Religion and Public Life*) 29 (1995), 70–80.

"Dignity in Old Age: The Poetical Meditations of Peter Viereck," *Humanitas* VIII, 2 (1995), 52–67.

"Civic Liberalism and Educational Reform," *Educational Theory* 47, 3 (Summer 1997), 411–424.

"Peter Viereck: Reconciliation and Beyond," *Humanitas* X, 2 (1997), 22–40.

"Is Postmodern Organization Theory Sceptical?" *Journal of Management History* 4, 4 (1998), 350–362, with D. Weinstein.

"Simmel-Eco vs. Simmel-Marx: Ironized Alienation," *Current Perspectives in Social Theory* XVIII (1998), 63–77, with D. Weinstein.

"Falling Through Time with Cioran," *Romanian Journal of Liberal Arts* I, 1 (1999), 26–37.

"L'operationalisme, l'interpretation et l'imaginaire collectif: re-actualiser l'anthropologie Dumontienne," *Carrefour* XXI, 1 (1999), 61–74.

"Data Crash: Apocalypse and Global Economic Crisis," *Angelaki* 4, 2 (September 1999), 91–94.

"What Today's Undergraduates Need: Realism," *Thresholds in Education* XXV, 2 & 3 (May/August 1999), 47.

"East/West: Globalizing Civilization," *Romanian Journal of Liberal Arts* I, 2 (Spring 2000), 5–17.

"Virtual Bataille," *Parallax* 7, 1 (2001), 76–80.

"Hail to the Shrub: Mediating the Presidency," *American Behavioral Scientist* 46, 4 (December 2002), 566–80, with D. Weinstein.

"Celebrity Worship as Weak Religion," *Word & World* 23, 3 (Summer 2003), 294–302, with D. Weinstein.

"The Power of Silence and the Limits of Discourse at Oliver Wendell Holmes's Breakfast Table," *The Review of Politics* 67, 1 (Winter 2005), 575–595.

"The Status of Conflict in the Southern and Central Regions of Somalia," *CTC Sentinel* 2, 7 (July 2009), 12–15.

Electronic Articles

From 1993 to 2013, Michael Weinstein published more than 230 electronic articles, typically on matters of topical interest, with subjects ranging from Abu Ghraib, Iraq, and the Middle East more generally to Central Europe, Central and South America, and especially the Horn of Africa, with a particular emphasis on the problems Somalia presents. These articles have found a variety of outlets for dissemination, the principal ones being *Power and Interest News Report* and *Garowe Online*.

Columns and Art Features

From 1992 to 2013, Michael Weinstein published more than 1,900 columns and art features, including photography reviews in various publications, including *Free Fest*, *Dialogue*, *New Art Examiner*, *NewCity*, etc.

EPISODES OF TELEVISION SHOWS

(Critiques of photography shows and interviews filmed at openings)

Photo Encounters

Morris Engel, recorded at Stephen Daiter Gallery, first aired 7/25/00, CAN TV (Chicago).

Laura Letinsky, recorded at Carol Ehlers Gallery, first aired 11/9/00, CAN TV (Chicago).

Zen Meditative Images (Group Show), recorded at Flatfile Gallery, first aired 11/16/00, CAN TV (Chicago).

Art Shay, recorded at Carol Ehlers Gallery, first aired 3/1/01, CAN TV (Chicago).

DISCOGRAPHY

Vortis

(Lyricist and Singer)
"Ball of Contusions," *All in the Family*: Hatekord Records Compilation, 2002.
    (Cover of "Ball of Confusion" with new lyrics by M. Weinstein).
Take The System Down, Chicago: Thick Records, 2002. 12 songs.
"We Hate Our Condition," "When the Rap Begins to Roll," *Love&Rebellion*:
    Thick Records Label Sampler, 2002.
"Christmas in Kabul," *Sex&Subversion*: Thick Records Label Sampler, 2003.
God Won't Bless America, Chicago: Thick Records, 2003. 12 songs.
"Word Song," *Let's Try It Another Way*: The Laughing Madcaps Salute Syd Barrett,
    Laughing Madcaps, 2003. (Cover with new lyrics by M. Weinstein).

MUSICAL PERFORMANCES

Vortis

(Lyricist and Singer)
Empty Bottle, Chicago, 12/8/00 (35 min. set, 9 songs).
Hideout, Chicago, 1/27/01 (90 min. set, 13 songs).
Artists of the Wall Festival, Chicago, 6/17/01 (50 min. set, 10 songs).
Underground Lounge, Chicago, 6/27/01 (50 min. set, 9 songs).
Nevin's Live, Evanston, IL, 6/30/01 (50 min. set, 9 songs).
Sputnik Coffee House, Homewood, IL, 7/5/01 (50 min. set, 9 songs).
Delilah's, Chicago, 10/27/01 (30 min. set, 6 songs).
Nevin's Live, Evanston, IL, 11/24/01 (50 min. set, 9 songs).
Empty Bottle, Chicago, 12/15/01 (15 min. set, 3 songs).
Hideout, Chicago, 12/21/01 (70 min. set, 12 songs).
Blue Note, Chicago, 3/8/02 (50 min. set, 9 songs).
Fireside Bowl, Chicago, 3/30/02 (30 min. set, 7 songs).
Nevin's Live, Evanston, IL, 5/17/02 (50 min. set, 11 songs).
Fireside Bowl, Chicago, 5/24/02 (35 min. set, 8 songs).
Hideout, Chicago, 8/2/02 (90 min. set, 17 songs).
Nevin's Live, Evanston, IL, 9/21/02 (40 min. set, 8 songs).
Cactus Club, Milwaukee, WI, 11/1/02 (40 min. set, 9 songs).
Nevin's Live, Evanston, IL, 2/1/03 (50 min. set, 11 songs).
Gunther Murphy's, Chicago, 4/4/03 (45 min. set, 9 songs).
TV appearance, Chic-a-go-go, 5/7,8/03, CAN TV (Chicago), "God Won't Bless
    America Again."
Nevin's Live, Evanston, IL, 5/24/03 (50 min. set, 10 songs).
Gunther Murphy's, Chicago, 7/18/03 (50 min. set, 10 songs), with lyceum lecture
    "Renaming the National Animal."
Grog Shop, Cleveland, OH, 8/8/03 (40 min. set, 11 songs).
Lager House, Detroit, MI, 8/13/03 (40 min. set, 11 songs).
Elbow Room, Ypsilanti, MI, 8/14/03 (40 min. set, 11 songs).
Founder's, Grand Rapids, MI, 8/15/03 (40 min. set, 11 songs).
Mac's Bar, E. Lansing, MI, 8/16/03 (40 min. set, 11 songs).
Gabe's, Iowa City, IA, 8/22/03 (40 min. set, 11 songs).
Seventh Street Entry, Minneapolis, MN, 8/23/03 (40 min. set, 11 songs).

The Abbey, Chicago, 9/7/03 (40 min. set, 11 songs).
Fireside Bowl, Chicago, 11/8/03 (30 min. set, 8 songs).
No Exit, Chicago, 12/12/03 (40 min. set, 9 songs; Amnesty International Benefit).
Bottom Lounge, Chicago, 12/26/03 (40 min. set, 9 songs).
Lyon's Den, Chicago, 2/27/04 (40 min. set, 11 songs).
Lyon's Den, Chicago, 6/18/04 (40 min. set, 12 songs).
Double Door, Chicago, 7/21/04 (35 min. set, 12 songs).
The Abbey, Chicago, 8/19/04 (40 min. set, 13 songs).
The Abbey, Chicago, 10/7/04 (35 min. set, 12 songs).
The Cell Block, Chicago, 2/25/05 (30 min. set, 10 songs).
The Note, Chicago, 6/17/05 (40 min. set, 13 songs).
Empty Bottle, Chicago, 8/19/05 (40 min. set, 13 songs).
Studio, Chicago, 10/15/05 (40 min. set, 13 songs).
Studio, Chicago, 11/26/05 (40 min. set, 12 songs).
Nite Cap, Chicago, 1/27/06 (40 min. set, 13 songs).
Nite Cap, Chicago, 4/28/06 (30 min. set, 11 songs).
Memories, Chicago, 8/25/06 (30 min. set, 11 songs).

Rap Performances

"Rap-Song Responses to Bryant Johnston's Photographic Series 'Songs of Desire,'" Enid Okla Homa Gallery, Chicago, IL, February 4 and 18, 1994.
"Rap-Song Responses to Mike Linz's Exhibit of Paintings 'Living Bodies, Tribal Dark,'" Enid Okla Homa Gallery, Chicago, IL, March 4 and 25, 1994.
"Rap-Song Responses to Kirby Briske's Exhibit of Paintings 'Earth and Spirit,'" Enid Okla Homa Gallery, Chicago, IL, March 31, 1994.
"Rap-Song Responses to Luis Gonzalez Palma's Exhibit of Photo-works," Schneider Gallery, Chicago, IL, April 29, 1994.
"Rap-Song Performance at 'Sooner Salon,'" Enid Okla Homa Gallery, Chicago, IL, May 6, 1994.
"Rap-Song Responses to Andy Kane's Exhibit of Paintings and Prints," Enid Okla Homa Gallery, Chicago, IL, July 8, 1994.
"Rap-Song Performance on Militia Movement," Enid Okla Homa Gallery, Chicago, IL, July 21, 1995.
"Rap-Song Response to Celeste Sotola's Exhibit of Paintings," Enid Okla Homa Gallery, Chicago, IL, September 8, 1995.
"The Civil Savage Performance," Lecture Performance on *Culture\Flesh*, Enid Okla Homa Gallery, Chicago, IL, June 7, 1996.
"Unabomber Performance," Lecture Performance on UNABOMBER MANIFESTO, Enid Okla Homa Gallery, Chicago, IL, July 5, 1996.
"Future of Technology," Lecture Performance, Enid Okla Homa Gallery, Chicago, IL, August 2, 1996.
"Unabomber Performance" (Mike Kaczynski), Leftist Student Network, Purdue University, October 29, 1996.
"Unabomber Performance" (Ted Weinstein), Phyllis' Musical Inn, 1579 N Milwaukee Avenue, Chicago, IL, March 7, 1997.
"Timothy McVeigh Performance," Phyllis' Musical Inn, 1579 N Milwaukee Avenue, Chicago, IL, July 3, 1997.
"Saddam Hussein Performance," Gallery 203, 1579 N Milwaukee Avenue, Chicago, IL, March 6, 1998.
"Slobodon Milosevic Performance," Gallery 203, 1579 N Milwaukee Avenue, Chicago, IL, July 2, 1999.

Photography

"Barbara Crane as Zen Photographer," Gallery 954 (Art Institute Program), Chicago, IL, September 16, 1994.

Panelist on Discussion of "Popularly Yours," DePaul Art Gallery, Chicago, IL, October 3, 1996.

"The Theory and Practice of Photographic Criticism," Flatfile Gallery, Chicago, IL, July 18, 2000.

"The Purpose of Criticism," Carol Ehlers Gallery (Art 2000 Series), Chicago, IL, August 15, 2000.

"The Types of Political Art," Flatfile Gallery, Chicago, IL, October 8, 2002.

"Introduction to 'Within the Garden,'" Merwin & Wakeley Galleries (Illinois Wesleyan University), Chicago, IL, October 3, 2004.

"Claude Andreini, Jan Saudek and Kimiko Yoshida," Flatfile Gallery (Vision Ten), Chicago, IL, July 20, 2005.

"Veronica Riedel's Imaginative Anthropology of the Mestiza," Aldo Castillo Gallery, Chicago, IL, February 25, 2006.

"Beyond Photography," Flatfile Gallery, Chicago, IL, October 19, 2006.

"Sebastian Lemm," David Weinberg Collection, Chicago, IL, March 1, 2008. Recorded and Archived by Chicago Public Radio.

"10 Years of Contemporary Cuban Photography," ArteAhora (Aldo Castillo Gallery), Chicago, IL, April 27, 2008.

"How to be an Art Critic," 826CHI Workshop for K–6 Students, Chicago, IL, July 12, 2008.

MEDIA INTERVIEWS

Interview on Unabomber, WASK, Lafayette, IN, 6/25/96.

Interview on Unabomber, *Indianapolis Star*, 6/26/96.

Interview on Unabomber, KAKD, Eureka, CA ("In the Spirit of Tom Paine" Show—One Hour Segment with Sheldon Wolin), 8/25/96.

Interview on Suicide Skyjacking, WNUR, Chicago, IL, 9/15/01.

Interview on Abu Ghraib Scandal, "Criminal Justice Forum" (Florida Radio Show), 6/16/04.

Interview on Kyrgyzstan, WBEZ, Chicago, IL, ("Worldview" Show), 3/24/05.

Interview on Hugo Chavez, South Florida Public Radio, ("Sasha's Show"), 4/8/05.

Interview on Somalia, EthiopiaFirst, 4/24/07.

Interview on Somalia, SBS Radio (Australia), 10/19/07.

Interview on Somalia, Press TV (Iran), 8/16/09.

Appearance as Somalia Expert on Fox News Channel hour-long documentary, "Pirates of the Twenty-first Century," aired during 11/09.

Notes on Contributors

Kathy E. Ferguson is Professor of Political Science and Women's Studies at the University of Hawai'i, specializing in political theory, feminist theory, and militarism. Her most recent book is *Emma Goldman: Political Thinking in the Streets* (Rowman and Littlefield, 2011). With coauthor Phyllis Turnbull, she wrote *Oh, Say, Can You See? The Semiotics of the Military in Hawai'i* (University of Minnesota Press, 1999). Her website "Emma Goldman's Women" (www.politicalscience.hawaii.edu/lists/emma-goldman/index.html) documents the participation of women in the classical anarchist movement. She is currently writing two books: *Anarchist Women of the First Wave* and *Anarchist Printers*.

Melba Hoffer is Assistant Professor of Communication Studies at Grand Valley State University. Born and raised in Caguas, Puerto Rico, Dr. Hoffer researches communication ethics and environmental communication in the United States and the Caribbean. Her work examines the ways in which the long-term success of conservation efforts depends upon fundamental shifts in cultural values, in aesthetic and moral communication, and in shared understandings of how the individual fits into social and ecological communities. In addition, she has researched and published in the era of Latin-American/Caribbean/Latina-o philosophy and intellectual history.

Joseph J. Kaminski (Ph.D. Political Science, Purdue University, 2014) specializes in the areas of political philosophy, international affairs, and public policy and administration. He is the author of two peer reviewed articles: "Bureaucracy and Modernity: A Comparative Qualitative Analysis of Bureaucratic Development in the US and OIC States," (2013, *Politics, Bureaucracy and Justice*), and "The Importance of Historical Understanding: Evaluating the Strengths and Weaknesses of the Current Counter Narcotics Policy in Afghanistan," (2012, *Review of International Law and Politics*). Originally from the south suburbs of Chicago, Dr. Kaminski has taught, conducted research, and presented academic papers in Chicago, New York, Indianapolis, San Diego, and Boston, and

Beirut, Lebanon among other cities. In his free time, he enjoys watching American football and baseball, practicing Arabic, and mastering his culinary skills in the kitchen. He is currently an Assistant Professor at the International University of Sarajevo.

Arthur Kroker is Canada Research Chair in Technology, Culture and Theory, Professor of Political Science, and the Director of the Pacific Centre for Technology and Culture (PACTAC) at the University of Victoria. He is the editor with Marilouise Kroker of the internationally acclaimed scholarly, peer-reviewed journal *CTheory and Critical Digital Studies: A Reader* (University of Toronto Press). His recent publications include *The Will to Technology and the Culture of Nihilism: Heidegger, Nietzsche, and Marx* (University of Toronto Press, 2004) and *Born Again Ideology: Religion, Technology and Terrorism* (CTheory Books, 2007). Dr. Kroker's current research focuses on the new area of critical digital studies and the politics of the body in contemporary techno-culture.

Jonathan McKenzie is an Assistant Professor in the Political Science Department at Northern Kentucky University. He recently completed a book on Henry David Thoreau's privatism. He has published work on Heidegger, Goldman, William James, Nietzsche, Thoreau, and Freud and is currently at work on a book on Nathaniel Hawthorne's political theory. Jonathan was a PhD student under Michael Weinstein from 2003 to 2009.

Justin Mueller is the last of Michael Weinstein's PhD students in the Department of Political Science at Purdue University. His dissertation is titled *Times That Bind: Theories of Obligation Considered Through Bergson's and Deleuze's Philosophies of Time*. He is at present preparing a book manuscript based on the dissertation as well as two working papers, "Consent and Horizontal Time-Binding" and "Max Stirner's Critical Presentism." He received his PhD in August 2014.

Robert L. Oprisko is a Research Associate at Indiana University's Center for the Study of Global Change. He is also the senior editor of International Theory for *E-International Relations* and a contributing author for *The Chronicle for Higher Education*. His research focuses on contemporary political philosophy, international relations theory, and critical university studies. He has published *Honor: A Phenomenology* (Routledge, 2012) and is currently writing two books: *Existential Theory of International Politics* and *The United States' Nobility: American Exceptionalism at Home and Abroad*. He earned his PhD in political science from Purdue University in 2011, where he studied under Michael Weinstein.

Diane Rubenstein is a Professor of Government and American Studies at Cornell University, where she teaches in the fields of French Studies,

Comparative Literature, and Visual Studies. She is the author of *What's Left? The Ecole Norale Supérieure and the Right* (Wisconsin, 1991) and *This Is Not a President: Sense and Nonsense in the American Political Imaginary* (NYU, 2008). Her articles have appeared in *Political Theory, theory and event, umbr(A)*, and *Cultural Politics* as well as edited volumes such as the *Hysterical Male* and *The Final Foucault*.

Ramón E. Soto-Crespo is an Associate Professor of Transnational Studies, American Studies, and Comparative Literature at the State University of New York at Buffalo. His essays have appeared in *American Literary History, Modern Language Notes, Modern Fiction Studies, Contemporary Literature, Atlantic Studies*, and *Textual Practice*. He is the author of *Mainland Passage: The Cultural Anomaly of Puerto Rico* (University of Minnesota Press, 2009), which won honorable mention at the 2009 Modern Language Association Prize in United States Latina and Latino and Chicana and Chicano Literary and Cultural Studies. His essay is related to his book in progress, *Hemispheric Trash: Despised Forms in the Cultural History of the Americas*.

Julie Webber is Professor of Politics and Government at Illinois State University. She is the author of *Failure to Hold: The Politics of School Violence* and *The Cultural Set Up of Comedy*, among others.

Deena Weinstein is a professor of sociology at DePaul University. Her research focus is on popular culture, and she is well known for her research on George Simmel and heavy metal. She earned her PhD from Purdue University and is the beloved colleague of Michael A. Weinstein.

Michael Weinstein is interested in general political science and the analysis of ideology. Professor Weinstein's scholarship ranges over political thought in the United States, the political ideas of the Hispanic world, Canadian thought, philosophical sociology, psychoanalytic theory, existential phenomenology, the sociology of knowledge, philosophy of photography, and structuralism and poststructuralism. His recent published work includes studies in deconstruction, metatheory, and culture critique, among them the books *Postmodern(ized) Simmel* (Routledge, 1993) *and Data Trash* (CTheory Books, 1994).

Index

For Product Safety Concerns and Information please contact our EU
representative GPSR@taylorandfrancis.com
Taylor & Francis Verlag GmbH, Kaufingerstraße 24, 80331 München, Germany